PETER NALDRETT

AROUND THE COAST IN 80 DAYS

YOUR GUIDE TO
BRITAIN'S BEST
COASTAL TOWNS
BEACHES
CLIFFS & HEADLANDS

C✺NWAY
LONDON · OXFORD · NEW YORK · NEW DELHI · SYDNEY

CONWAY
Bloomsbury Publishing Plc
50 Bedford Square, London, WC1B 3DP, UK

BLOOMSBURY, CONWAY and the Conway logo
are trademarks of Bloomsbury Publishing Plc

First published in Great Britain, 2020

A catalogue record for this book is available from the British Library

Library of Congress Cataloguing-in-Publication data has been applied for

ISBN: PB: 978-1-8448-6559-8; ePub: 978-1-8448-6558-1; ePDF: 978-1-8448-6560-4

2 4 6 8 10 9 7 5 3 1

Typeset in Adobe Garamond by carrdesignstudio.com
Printed and bound in India by Replika Press Pvt. Ltd

To find out more about our authors and books visit www.bloomsbury.com
and sign up for our newsletters

ACKNOWLEDGEMENTS

I would like to thank my wife, Nicola, for not complaining while being dragged around the coast. Not complaining too much, anyway. My children, Toby and Willow, have been an inspiration and passionate believers in this project, not least because they munched their way through dozens of portions of fish and chips. Several people have provided their expertise about different areas of the coast. Thanks to The Thurtles, who are unofficial ambassadors for Grimsby and Cleethorpes, Allan Perkins who knows the east coast of Scotland like the back of his hand, and Kevin Lowes, who was almost able to explain about the north-east without the use of an interpreter. Thanks also to Mandy Middleton-Lund for going on a virtual coastal trip by proofreading.

PHOTO CREDITS

CONTENTS

ACKNOWLEDGEMENTS   iii

PHOTO CREDITS   iii

FOREWORD by Ian McMillan   viii

INTRODUCTION   1

NORTH-WEST

1. LIVERPOOL – P.S. I Love You   6
2. CROSBY – More Than Just *Another Place*   9
3. BLACKPOOL – Towering Above the Competition   11
4. MORECAMBE BAY – Bringing You Sunshine!   15
5. GRANGE-OVER-SANDS – Walk This Bay   18
6. RAVENGLASS – Full Steam Ahead!   21
7. ST BEES – Coast-to-Coast Adventures   24
8. SILLOTH – Like Toy Soldiers   27

WEST SCOTLAND

9. MULL OF GALLOWAY – Plenty to Mull Over   32
10. TROON – Finding Some Fresh Ayr   35
11. GLASGOW – Scotland's Biggest City   38
12. MULL OF KINTYRE – My Desire is Always to Be Here   41
13. OBAN – A Town Fuelled by Whisky   44
14. FORT WILLIAM – All Aboard for Mallaig!   46
15. KYLE OF LOCHALSH – Star of the Screen   49
16. ULLAPOOL – A Fishing Town of Beauty on the NC500   51
17. CAPE WRATH – At World's End   53
18. BALNAKEIL – A Crafty Bit of Coastline   56

EAST SCOTLAND

19. JOHN O'GROATS – To the End of the Earth   60
20. CROMARTY – Wildlife and the Ghosts of Industry   63
21. SPEY BAY – A Dolphin's Tale   66
22. PETERHEAD – The Bloo Toon!   68
23. STONEHAVEN – Great Balls of Fire!   70

24 **DUNDEE** — Discover a Proud Industrial Heritage   **73**

25 **ST ANDREWS** — Time for a High Tee   **76**

26 **FALKIRK KELPIES** — Spirits of the Water   **79**

27 **SOUTH QUEENSFERRY** — Building Bridges   **81**

NORTH-EAST

28 **HOLY ISLAND** — Watch the Tides!   **86**

29 **BAMBURGH** — A View to Inspire   **89**

30 **CRASTER** — Of Crabs and Castles   **92**

31 **NEWBIGGIN-BY-THE-SEA** — A Lovely Couple   **94**

32 **WHITLEY BAY** — Girl, It Looks So Pretty to Me...   **97**

33 **REDCAR** — The Windy City   **100**

34 **STAITHES** — Cache of Coastal Creations   **102**

35 **WHITBY** — Full of Gothic Charm   **105**

EAST COAST

36 **SCARBOROUGH** — A Tale of Two Bays   **110**

37 **BEMPTON CLIFFS** — City of Birds   **113**

38 **THE HOLDERNESS COAST** — Life on the Edge   **116**

39 **HULL** — Chip Spice and a Dead Bod   **119**

40 **CLEETHORPES** — Where Size Matters   **123**

41 **SKEGNESS** — Welcome to Fabulous Skegvegas!   **126**

42 **THE WASH** — England's Biggest Bay   **129**

43 **NORTH NORFOLK** — The Incredible Shrinking Coast   **131**

SOUTH-EAST

44 **LOWESTOFT** — My Sweet Broad   **136**

45 **FELIXSTOWE** — The Port of Britain   **139**

46 **CLACTON-ON-SEA** — Pier to Fraternity   **141**

47 **SOUTHEND-ON-SEA** — Rethink Your Idea of a Pier   **144**

48 **LONDON** — Space to Breathe in the Big Smoke   **146**

49 Down to **MARGATE!**   **149**

50 **DOVER** — At the Heart of the Battle   **152**

51 **FOLKESTONE** — More than Just a Hole in the Ground   **155**

52 **DUNGENESS** — On the Right Tracks   **158**

SOUTH COAST

53 **BEACHY HEAD** – Beacon of the South Coast   164

54 **BRIGHTON** – Your Day!   167

55 **PORTSMOUTH** – Harbouring Treasures   170

56 **SOUTHAMPTON** – Cruising to Success   172

57 **SANDBANKS** – Wonderful Beaches, Naturally   174

58 **THE JURASSIC COAST** – Become a Fossil Hunter!   177

SOUTH-WEST

59 **DAWLISH WARREN** – Amusement by Nature   182

60 **PLYMOUTH** – A Port with a Beating Heart of History   185

61 **ST AUSTELL BAY** – Boats, Biomes and Beer   188

62 **THE LIZARD** – Adventures at England's Most Southerly Point   191

63 **PORTHCURNO** – A Real Cliffhanger!   194

64 **CAPE CORNWALL** – Beans on Coast!   196

65 **ST IVES** – A Haven for Foodies and Artists   199

66 **NEWQUAY** – Days of Surf and Parties   201

67 **PADSTOW** – Cornwall's Foodie Heaven   204

68 **TINTAGEL** – A Place of Legends   206

69 Beautiful **BUDE!**   209

70 **CLOVELLY** – Where Deliveries Arrive by Sledge   211

71 **THE TARKA TRAIL** – A Journey Along the River Taw   214

72 **WESTON-SUPER-MARE** – Sand of Hope and Glory   216

WALES

73 **CARDIFF** – Capital of a Proud Nation   220

74 **RHOSSILI** – Our Finest Gower   223

75 **SAINT GOVAN'S HEAD** – Peace Among the Missiles   227

76 **ST DAVIDS** – A Pembrokeshire Pilgrimage   230

77 **ABERYSTWYTH** – A Place to Study and Play   233

78 **PORTMEIRION** – Taking No Prisoners   236

79 **LLŶN PENINSULA** – Into Hell's Mouth   239

80 **LLANDUDNO** – Great Days Beneath Great Orme   241

INDEX   244

INVERNESS

ABERDEEN

DUNDEE

GLASGOW

EDINBURGH

NEWCASTLE

BLACKPOOL

LEEDS

MANCHESTER

LIVERPOOL

SHEFFIELD

NORWICH

BIRMINGHAM

LONDON

CARDIFF

SOUTHAMPTON

BRIGHTON

PORTSMOUTH

PLYMOUTH

FOREWORD
BY IAN McMILLAN

Smell that? It's sea air, filling the view and enlivening the day. Feel that, ruffling your hair like one of your aunties used to? It's a sea breeze dancing in the space between the harbour and the beach. Hear that, rolling into your ears like the tide? It's the sound of sandcastles being built, being decorated with shells and then demolished to the noise of laughter. Taste that? Fish and chips, edible artworks of batter and potato, eaten with the fingers as you dodge the seagulls. See that, bobbing towards the horizon and getting smaller as the clouds fold into themselves? It's a boat going to a tiny island that's only a little bit bigger in real life than it is on a map.

Yes, this is the sensuous coastline of this country, explored, annotated and celebrated in this remarkable book. The thing about the coast is that it's two things at once; there's the real coast, the one that tumbles or glides into the sea and that you will always come to if you just walk far enough and there's the Coast of the Mind, which hangs around at the back of your head and just pops in and reminds you of the time you wandered by the water's shifting edge just before the sun rose, or the time you ran into the sea and then ran out again as fast as you could because the water was colder than a fridge, or the time you climbed a long hill for what seemed like forever and then suddenly, behind a hedge that looked like it had been dragged through itself backwards, you saw the sea.

This book is a guide, an almanac, a history lesson and a box of delights; it should be used to take you to new corners of the places you already think you know really well, and it should be used as a pathfinder to lead you into Unexplored Territory.

I have two favourite strips of coastline; the first one is the festival of mud and sand and childhood laughter that is Cleethorpes, the place that used to be a kind of Barnsley-on-Sea where my mother and father in law had a caravan next to their next door neighbours at home, and where my wife went as a child and our children went as children and now my grandchildren go as, well, grandchildren. The cliché about Cleethorpes is that the tide is always so far out that it may as well be sitting in a bar in Holland, but to me this strand of sea and sand and sky has a Rothko feel to it, layers of half colour

resting gently on top of each other. My mother in law, on her own for many years, still spends the summer in the same caravan and when we go and visit her we go for a walk on the tops and feel the wind slapping our faces and my mother in law says 'It would be lovely if only that bit of wind would drop' and I recall my late father in law saying 'That air, Ian lad; it's like wine' and so it is.

My other favourite place to meet the sea meeting the earth is the only western facing harbour on the East Coast; that's right, Beadnell in Northumberland just below Seahouses. The harbour is like a toy harbour built from an ancient kit and in the shadow of the old limekilns you can walk along the walls and almost touch the sea. I was there once in a fierce March gale and it felt to me that the harbour was about to lift itself out of the water and stagger inland.

And maybe, because we're never really all that far from the coast, memories are what this book is about. Memories that splash over us when we're sitting on a broken down train a long way from anywhere, or memories-in-the-making occasioned by following in this book's footsteps.

I'll see you in the places where the damp meets the dry.

COAST

This country's bracelet,
This land's necklace
Washed every morning,
Cleaned each night.

Place of sunsets, sunrises,
Architecture of deckchairs,
A harbour enclosing
All but the gull's cry.

This country's myth-hoard
This land's songsheet
Sung every morning,
Told each night.

We are all islands
When we come here;
Buckets of memories
Filling with sand.

This country's breath-space
This land's welcome
Waves every morning
Waves each night.

INTRODUCTION

It was a November evening, with clouds drifting in front of a bright moon and fireworks shooting into the sky, exploding with a flurry of colour and prompting gasps from the crowded promenade. Standing within sight of our coastline's most iconic building, the lights on the tower changed shade and the neon displays in the street below gently swayed in the wind.

It's the end of the season at Blackpool, the last weekend when the famous illuminations – some elegant, some gaudy – stretch the summer months into autumn. To mark Bonfire Night, the Pleasure Beach has an enviable display of rockets to keep people enthralled well after closing time. Earlier in the day, my family had been on the huge roller coaster that dominates Blackpool's skyline and got a soaking in a heavenly ride called Valhalla. We'd scoffed a generous portion of fish and chips, put a small fortune of 2ps into the amusements and marvelled at the hen parties stumbling past with 'Kiss Me Quick' hats on. Packed with stereotypes, full of life and ingrained with memories, this was a day out at the coast none of us would ever forget. Don't get me wrong, there are aspects of Blackpool I am happy to leave on Lancashire's coastline and I couldn't go through that 24 hours every week. But there's something alluring about British coastal days out that keep pulling us back, and it comes down to them being a very enjoyable playground where you don't have to bring your workaday, inland troubles. No matter what kind of a day out we want to have beside the seaside, we do like to be beside the sea. It has everything we need to entertain and keep us happy. Romance. Adventure. Energy. History. Mystery. Isolation. Friendship. Nature. Regeneration. You can find it all along Britain's coast.

I used to live just a few hundred metres from the sea, and I loved it. The cheesy Sunday market selling boxes of broken biscuits, the wafting smell of unhealthy doughnuts cooking on a mobile kiosk, the air of quiet despair when the summer season ended, the glorious well-being of an early-morning walk on the promenade. Like many seaside resorts, Morecambe has had its ups and downs and it was in a bit of a trough when I was there in the 1990s. But even among the disused shops, there was a homely feel. Whether the sun shone bright on to the glistening sea or waves crashed over the sea wall during a storm, it was always a friendly, alluring place. Returning to Morecambe and visiting many more of the country's coastal gems has been an absolute treat. Here I've collected 80 places on the edge of our nation that should be on your list to head to. Factor in the places nearby to this collection of choice destinations and you have hundreds of activities to do along the coast – enough to keep you busy for many years. Each one of the 80 locations will make a fantastic day trip if you

△ Millions of pounds have been spent managing Britain's coastline.

find yourself within driving distance, while a weekend or even longer will help you truly to get the most out of these very special places.

My journey around the coast of Britain didn't start with a paddle in the sea or the building of an extravagant sandcastle. The significance of a day out at the coast hit me in the most unlikely of places. With a few trips for my seaside adventure in the planning stages, I coincidentally found myself passing through a lovely village in deepest Derbyshire. Coton in the Elms is typical of many places in the county; it's a picturesque village with a nice church, a pub and a sleepy feel. But Coton has an unusual claim to fame in that it's the settlement in Britain located furthest from the coast. Those living here face the lengthiest route to the beach of all the people in the country – it's 113km (70 miles) away from Fosdyke Wash in Lincolnshire and, in the opposite direction, Flint in North Wales. Church Flatts Farm, to the south of Coton, is the actual point where the sea is furthest away when the tide is out.

And yet even here, at this geographical novelty, a day trip to the seaside is entirely possible. You can be standing on Welsh sand after a drive of around two hours. Other countries have a 'pole of inaccessibility' that's far more extreme and would have children weeping into their plastic buckets and looking forlornly at pictures of people having fun bodyboarding. Those living in Moscow have nearly a 650km (400-mile) journey to see waves lap on the shore. Kids going to school in South Dakota's Pine Ridge Reservation in the USA will have to travel just over 1,600km (1,000 miles) to feel a sea breeze. And spare a thought for those near China's border with Kazakhstan, who are an incredible 2,500km (1,560 miles) away from the ebb and flow of the tide. These momentous distances make Coton in the Elms look like a coastal community and brings home just how lucky we are to be an island nation with the sea on our doorstep.

Spending time at the seaside is beneficial in so many ways. Victorians would head to the coast for the health benefits of taking in the 'sea air' and, although they had a few odd ideas about medicines, it seems they were right on this one. The air at the coast is full of negative ions, which improve our ability to absorb oxygen, make us feel more alert and can reduce the impact of troublesome particles that cause us to cough and sneeze. Being next to a large body of water and walking barefoot on sand also has a calming effect that can reduce stress. And let's not forget the benefits to our work-life balance that can come from seeing a show, letting your hair down on a night out, enjoying white-knuckle rides and spending time in the arcades with your kids. Visiting the seaside is good for our well-being.

Fortunately, Britain is blessed with thousands of miles of beautiful coastline. And the variety of places to visit and things to do means there literally is something for everyone. If partying all night is your thing, head to Brighton or Blackpool. Those wanting physical exertion should try coasteering in Cornwall or tackling the clifftop paths of Pembrokeshire. If you enjoy views or want to take cool photos, spend time with the incredible landforms of the Jurassic Coast. Those needing peace and solitude can find

△ Many places have ways of improving access to the bottom of cliffs.

KEY TO SYMBOLS

 Telephone

NORTH-WEST

The north-west coast may be the wettest in England, but even rainy days can be packed with fun on this lively stretch of seaside. Liverpool has reinvented itself as a city in the last couple of decades and is now one of the most fashionable tourist destinations in Europe, pulling in thousands from abroad to explore the city's colourful history of music and the darker shadow cast upon it by the slave trade.

A little up the coast, Antony Gormley's life-size sculptures stand in and around the sea to create a hypnotic beach at Crosby. Travel the whole of the British coastline and you won't find anything that truly compares to Blackpool. Packed with family fun and with an 'illuminations' light show that stretches out the peak season, this north-west city is on the rise once more after decades of seeing its primary market favour package holidays to Spain.

Don't miss

- ✓ Checking out the story of the Beatles in Liverpool
- ✓ Antony Gormley's sculptures dotted on the beach at Crosby
- ✓ A visit to the top of the Blackpool Tower
- ✓ The chance to take a guided walk

If the sun is shining, everything you need is here. Thousands of hotel rooms, a plethora of bars, top indoor attractions for the kids, fabulous rides and a lovely beach are among the reasons why families, hen parties and stag nights keep flocking back. All the action takes place, of course, under the iconic tower. Once you see it rising into the horizon, there's nowhere else in the country you could possibly be. Fun in the north-west doesn't stop at Blackpool, though. At Arnside, you can join hundreds of others rolling up their trouser legs to cross Morecambe Bay on a specially organised walk led by the Queen's Guide to the Sands. Head into Morecambe afterwards for fish and chips and a picture next to Eric Morecambe's statue.

Across the bay, Edwardian splendour and a day at the races await in and around Grange. From here, the train can take you up the coast to enjoy outstanding views of the Lake District at Ravenglass, where one of the most scenic heritage railways in the country leaves the seaside and heads for the fells. The often overlooked Cumbrian coast has many highlights moving north, including the town of St Bees which is the start of the famous Coast to Coast walk. The quiet town of Silloth is the perfect place for coastal walks, a belting hot chocolate and has one of the quaintest museums in the country – you'll never think of toy soldiers in the same way again!

LIVERPOOL
P.S. I LOVE YOU

1

Why visit?

★ Get down to the sounds of Liverpool's most famous bands at various Beatles attractions

★ Explore the unsavoury history of the slave trade at an honest and informative museum

★ Save room for a traditional dinner of scouse – an 18th-century sailors' stew

Roll up for the Mystery Tour!

A day tripper to Liverpool would be missing out if they didn't indulge themselves in some Beatles nostalgia. A walk along the water's edge of this great city gives a fascinating insight into The Fab Four. Start opposite the Royal Liver Building with a compulsory photograph next to Andrew Edwards' brilliant Beatles statue. Souvenirs celebrating Beatlemania are available in shops on the way to the city's top attraction about the band, The Beatles Story (☏ 0151 709 1963 www.beatlesstory.com ♥ L3 4AD). Beginning with the tale of how Lennon and McCartney met and progressing through the band's studio albums and post-Beatles achievements, the self-guided audio tour is engaging, entertaining and informative as it takes you to recreated venues, huge recreations of album covers and, of course, a yellow submarine. There's so much to take in, everybody will leave The Beatles Story with a different stand-out moment, be it seeing John Lennon's round glasses, reading the poster that inspired 'Being for the Benefit of Mr Kite' or sitting in an aircraft seat learning about the band's trip to America.

Setting off from the Albert Dock, there's a two-hour Magical Mystery Tour experience that takes you to significant Beatles sites in the city, including Penny Lane and Strawberry Fields (☏ 0151 703 9100 www.cavernclub.org ♥ L2 6RE). When the magical bus brings you back, you can experience live music in the legendary Cavern Club; this one is a new version close to the original. Elsewhere in the city, you'll find plenty of Beatles-related souvenirs. And be sure to visit the confectioners in Albert Dock to see a fantastic jelly-bean mosaic of Liverpool's most famous band.

Fill up on scouse!

The distinctive Liverpudlian accent known as Scouse is named after a meat stew popular among sailors here in the 18th and 19th century. You can still get hold of good-quality scouse and it's the most traditional dish of the city. Head for the Baltic Fleet Pub, on Wapping (☏ 0151 709 3116 www.balticfleet.co.uk ♥ L1 8DQ), to get a taste of scouse in a historic pub with secret tunnels leading to the docklands and rumours of a ghost or two.

△ Sgt Pepper outfits at The Beatles Story.

A bleak history

Much of Liverpool's wealth in the 18th century came on the back of the slave trade. The port was one of the most important sites in the 'slave triangle' that linked Europe with Africa and North America. The town and its population at the time benefited from the trade in people, with nearly 100 ships a year leaving here for West Africa in the 1770s. Goods were taken to Africa and exchanged for people, who were loaded on to the ships against their will. They were taken across the Atlantic and put to work in North America as slaves. The ships then returned to Liverpool and other ports, carrying the products of slave labour, including cotton, tobacco, sugar and coffee. The disturbing story about the city's past is effectively told in the International Slavery Museum at the Albert Dock (☎ 0151 478 4499 www.liverpoolmuseums.org.uk/ism ♥ L3 4AQ).

Getting here

Take junction 21A off the M6 and follow the M62 to reach Liverpool city centre. There are excellent train links with other parts of the country, the main station being Liverpool Lime Street.

▽ No trip to Liverpool is complete without a visit to the famous Cavern Club.

Ferry cross the Mersey

The ten-minute journey across the River Mersey is so much more than a way of commuting to and from Wallasey. It's an opportunity to enjoy an iconic trip, embedded in the city's history thanks to Gerry and the Pacemakers' classic anthem. Take a little longer and enjoy a cruise or venture out on the colourful Beatles-esque Dazzle Ferry. Contact Mersey Ferries for more information (☎ 0151 330 1003 www.merseyferries.co.uk Pier Head Terminal ◆ L3 1DP).

Stay a while

🛏 **The Barn,** Ramsbrook Lane, Hale, Liverpool, L24 5RP. ☎ **0151 425 2781** www.barnbandb.com

🛍 **Crowne Plaza,** Princes Dock, Liverpool, L3 1QW. ☎ **0151 243 8000** www.cpliverpool.com

⛺ **Hidden Corner Campsite,** Millbank Lane, Liverpool, L31 9AT. ☎ **0151 531 0688**

△ The colourful Beatles-esque Dazzle Ferry.

The Albert Dock

One of the nicest ways to spend your time in Liverpool is to wander around the Albert Dock and gaze at buildings that date back to the 1840s. These wonderful warehouses were designed to store imported and exported goods, but by the 1920s a decline in their use had begun, which eventually led to their abandonment. Industrial decline had a devastating impact on Liverpool and, as in many other northern cities, a redevelopment programme was kick-started in the 1980s. The Albert Dock was reopened in 1988 with a fanfare of new initiatives. A northern

Tate gallery was launched, Richard and Judy hosted *This Morning* from here and The Beatles Story opened soon after, putting the area well and truly on the map for tourists. Today, a stroll around the dock – now part of a UNESCO World Heritage Site – is a joyful saunter by restaurants and cafes. The Tate Liverpool (☎ 0151 702 7400 www. tate.org.uk/visit/tate-liverpool ◆ L3 4BB) is a delightful place to spend a couple of hours, and simply walking on the riverside by the thousands of love locks can breathe new life into people more used to inland viewpoints.

△ The Albert Dock was reopened in 1988 with a fanfare of new initiatives.

② CROSBY
MORE THAN JUST
ANOTHER PLACE

Why visit?

★ Pose for pictures next to Antony Gormley's magnificent coastal installation, *Another Place*

★ Be the coolest tourists by checking out the unusual lawnmower and model railway museums

★ Catch the north-west wind and fly a kite on the beach

Bare Naked Men

Some are up to their necks in salty water; others are knee-deep in mud. A few have been half buried in sand, while some of their brothers are festooned with barnacles. All one hundred of Antony Gormley's cast-iron, life-size figures that comprise *Another Place* are identical, gazing out towards the same spot on the horizon of the Irish Sea. The mesmerising figures weigh 650kg (1,433 pounds) each and were made from casts of the famous sculptor's own body. As soon as you arrive at this stretch of the English coast, you'll see the jaw-dropping scale of this work as it mixes human achievement with natural surroundings. The naked figures are framed by an offshore wind farm and the huge docks further down the coast at Liverpool, but they stand here exposed to the elements and their appearance changes as a result. Visit *Another Place* a few months later and there will be subtle changes brought about by the tides, which erode sand in some areas and deposit it in others. These shifting sands are terribly muddy in places, so visiting all of Gormley's iron men is not feasible; official guidance suggests visitors stay within 50 metres (55 yards) of the promenade and wander around the figures on the sandy beach. From here, look out on to the spectacular figures that stand as far as 1km (over half a mile) out to sea. With every step the angle of your view slightly changes, and so does the perspective you have of this piecemeal installation. Antony Gormley is well known for his *Angel of the North* statue. That piece of work has become a symbol of Gateshead, welcoming home all folk returning to the north-east. *Another Place* is a

more thoughtful, profound and morose artwork, with the hundred figures being consumed and revealed by the sea twice a day.

▽△ **With every step the angle of your view slightly changes.**

9

Fancy a chippy?

For some of the finest fish and chips on this stretch of coast, head to Formby to visit The Good Catch. You'll find hearty portions and a range of freshly cooked treats on offer, including cod and scampi (☎ 01704 878111 thegoodcatch.co.uk ♥ L37 5EB).

Where's the sea?

Renowned for low tides when the sea is barely visible, Southport has one of the few piers that often stands entirely above sand. It's a lengthy construction as well, with a small train taking day trippers to the end. There's plenty of cheesy seaside pizzazz to make Southport a popular destination, even without the sea, including the usual smattering of amusements and ice-cream sellers. Two of the more quirky places that deserve your attention are the immaculately presented Model Railway Village at Kings Gardens (☎ 01704 538001, www.southportmodelrailwayvillage. co.uk, ♥ PR8 1QX) and the bizarrely intriguing British Lawnmower Museum on Shakespeare Street (☎ 01704 501336, www.lawnmowerworld. co.uk ♥ PR8 5AJ).

Let's go fly a kite

Although sprawling Southport beach has plenty of space for playing games and stretching your legs, it can get crowded at times and many prefer the shoreline a little further south at Ainsdale.

△ People with a passion for horse riding enjoy galloping along the sand.

This stretch has been awarded Blue Flag status several times and is one of the most popular places in the country for extreme kiting. Zones on the beach are set aside for kite buggies and kite surfing, while this is also a top location for permit holders to fly power kites. People with a passion for horse riding enjoy galloping along the sand and splashing in the sea on this multipurpose beach, which is large enough to cater for a wide range of activities. Parking is available on the beach, though there may be a queue to get on during sunny weekends.

Nature along the coast

The wetlands to the north of Southport are a popular spot for twitchers to look out for avocets and lapwings in the summer, while the winter brings in scores of pink-footed geese. Marshside RSPB reserve has circular routes to enjoy a walk and a hide that's open every day between 8.30am and 5pm (www.rspb.org.uk, ♥ PR9 9PJ). The Sefton Coast between Southport and Crosby is a Site of Special Scientific Interest and is the home of wild orchids, rare butterflies and sand lizards. It's also one of the only places in England where natterjack toads breed.

 ## Stay a while

♥ Vale House, 16 Talbot Street, Southport, PR8 1HP. ☎ 07532 024352 www.valehousesouthport.co.uk

🧳 The Leicester, 24 Leicester Street, Southport, PR9 0EZ. ☎ 01704 530049 www.theleicester.com

⛺ Century House Campsite, 100 Turning Lane, Scarisbrick, PR8 5HZ. ☎ 01704 535164 www.centuryhousecampsite.co.uk

3

BLACKPOOL
TOWERING ABOVE THE COMPETITION

Why visit?

* Ride to the top of the Blackpool Tower, perhaps the most iconic of all coastal structures
* Experience the white-knuckle rush of speeding along The Big One
* Chuckle at lines on the Comedy Carpet before strolling along the promenade and down one of the three piers

Blackpool Tower

Arguably the most iconic symbol of all our nation's seaside towns, the Blackpool Tower was a typically ambitious Victorian engineering project. Containing 2,493 tons of steel, 93 tons of cast iron and 5 million bricks, it's one of the most recognisable landmarks in the country and dominates the north-west coast for miles around. For visitors to the town, the tower's Big Ticket is one of the most sought-after ways to spend the day and allows entry to a wide range of top attractions. After enjoying an immersive 4D cinema experience with music provided by Kylie, the pass gets you to the top of the tower in one of the two lifts that travel 3,500 miles up and down each year. The sights up at the viewing platform are stunning, both north and south along the

△ Fans of TV's *Strictly Come Dancing* need no introduction to the Tower's famous ballroom.

coast and straight down to the streets below through the glass walkway. Back on the ground, public access is allowed into the Tower Ballroom, known to millions for its appearances on *Strictly Come Dancing* and a favourite haunt of dancers from all over the country. At the same time as the tower opened, the circus also sprang to life and has not missed a season since. Situated at the base of the tower directly between its four legs, the circus ring can flood with 42,000 gallons of water, allowing unique water-based acts to take place. Tickets to the popular circus can sell out, so make sure you book your time slot at the same time you buy your ticket. Entrance to the nearby Sealife Centre, Madame Tussauds and Blackpool Dungeon is also included with the Big Ticket available at the Blackpool Tower ticket office (☎ 01253 622242 www.theblackpooltower.com ♥ FY1 4BJ).

TOWER FACTS

* Opened in May 1894, it was inspired by the Eiffel Tower in Paris and stands 158m (518 feet) tall
* Giving the tower a full coat of paint takes seven years
* Reginald Dixon was the organist in the Tower Ballroom between 1930 and 1969, earning him the nickname 'Mr Blackpool'
* The tower acts as a transmitter for local radio stations
* It became a Grade I list building in 1973

There is perhaps no coastline in Britain more iconic than Blackpool.

Albert and the Lion

The well-known Lancashire dialect poem about a lion called Wallace scoffing a young lad called Albert at the menagerie in Blackpool Tower has been loved by many generations of children. Famously read by Stanley Holloway, it's a chuckle from start to finish. Kids arriving at the Blackpool Zoo's lion enclosure are often surprised to learn that one of them is actually called Wallace and he frequently adopts a somnolent pose. The excellent elephant enclosure and the extended gorilla zone are other highlights of the 13ha (32-acre) Blackpool Zoo that make it worth straying away from the beach to the town's suburbs (☎ 01253 830830 www.blackpoolzoo. org.uk ♥ FY3 8PP). Parents worried about the fate of 'our Albert' needn't lose sleep over it. A follow-up poem some years later revealed the lion spat him out, allowing Albert to appear in other poetic adventures. The poem is honoured at the pub called The Albert and The Lion, which occupies pride of place near Blackpool Tower on the seafront (☎ 01253 743690 www. jdwetherspoon.com ♥ FY1 4RU).

△ The huge rollercoaster on Blackpool's seafront will take your breath away.

Blackpool Pleasure Beach — king of the thrill

What Blackpool Pleasure Beach lacks in space compared with other theme parks, it makes up in ingenuity. The roller coasters are spectacularly designed to make the best use of limited urban space, twisting tightly over the same ground so thrill seekers on different rides see each other as they whizz past. Dating back to 1896, the Pleasure Beach (☎ 0871 222 1234 www. blackpoolpleasurebeach.com ♦ FY4 1EZ) has been owned by the same family since its inception and manages to keep its rich history at the heart of modern visits. From the art deco ticket hall to the brilliantly preserved wooden

PIER FACTS

- 💡 **North Pier: opened 1863,** length 430m/1,410 feet (now 402m/1,318 feet)

- 💡 **Central Pier: opened 1868,** length 463m/1,518 feet (now 341m/1,118 feet)

- 💡 **South Pier: opened 1893,** length 150m/492 feet

PIER REVIEW

The Victorians loved their wooden piers and Blackpool went further than any other coastal resort by having three of them jut out into the Irish Sea. All of them survive today and still attract plenty of visitors, thanks to their dazzling display of amusements, shows and rides. The first of Blackpool's three piers was the North Pier, making a name for itself from 1863 with gentile orchestral performances, dances and comedians. Five years later, the Central Pier opened and had a bigger emphasis on family fun thanks to its boat trips and dancing facilities, with roller skating and fairground rides joining in the 20th century. The last of the trio, the South Pier, opened in 1893 and is now home to dodgems, fairground rides and a bar hosting live entertainment. Admission charges are now a thing of the past, meaning all three of Blackpool's piers are free to wander along.

roller coasters like the Grand National, there's a definite sense of being part of something iconic. One of the most famous rides is The Big Dipper, dating back to 1923 and designated a Grade II listed building in 2017. The fact that this and other wooden roller coasters are still here, and still popular, shows Blackpool day trippers want more than just the latest technology – they want to take their children on rides they enjoyed when they themselves were young. Plenty of experiences lie in wait, but the coaster that really stands out is The Big One, which opened in 1994 as the tallest in the world. The initial climb up the incline, taking the cars to 72m (235 feet) above sea level, seems to last an age. After the initial 62m (203-foot) drop, the rest of the three-minute ride takes place at breakneck speeds up to 85mph (137kph). Award-winning water ride Valhalla is another experience not to be missed. Riders emerge both drenched and in good spirits from this indoor journey to the Viking afterlife, which features fire and splashes – plenty of the latter. The Pleasure Beach was recently voted top theme park in the UK and earned a treasured place in Europe's top ten. It stands head and shoulders above roller-coaster experiences elsewhere on the coast.

△ Enjoy sweeping views of the north-west coast from the top of the tower.

Just for laughs!

Visible from the top of the tower, the huge Comedy Carpet is one of the more inventive of Blackpool's recent innovations. There's plenty here for a nostalgic chuckle as comedic catchphrases from down the decades are placed at various angles, in a range of different fonts and sizes. The comedians quoted are named around the edge and cross many genres, from Morecambe and Wise to Julian Clary. Strolling across the carpet can be an addictive experience; once you've stopped and read a couple of jokes, you want to see more snapshots of genius from these comedy legends.

△ Blackpool boasts a huge range of wet weather attractions, including an aquarium.

Fish and chips

Blackpool is awash with fast food eateries, many of them offering fish and chips. Among the finest is Bentleys on Bond Street, near the Pleasure Beach (☎ 01253 346085 📍 FY4 1HG). Closer to the tower, try out The Sea on Foxhall Road near the Promenade (☎ 01253 752131 www.thesearestaurant.co.uk 📍 FY1 5AE).

MORECAMBE
BRINGING YOU SUNSHINE!

4

Why visit?

★ Explore the regenerated seafront that has breathed new life into Morecambe

★ Take afternoon tea looking out to the Lake District at the art deco Midland Hotel

★ Spend an afternoon walking along the coast from Silverdale

Morecambe – on the rise

After decades in the doldrums, investment in Morecambe is paying off. This famous seaside destination, which overlooks the Lake District and glistening Morecambe Bay, is unrecognisable from the town it was 25 years ago. Redesigned public spaces and newly introduced street art make the seafront an intriguing place to wander along – and more regeneration is planned. At the centre of it all is the statue of Eric Morecambe. The legendary comedian – born in the town as John Eric Bartholomew in 1926 – adopted Morecambe as a stage name and is captured mid-dance, surrounded by some of his best-remembered lines. Look out for the binoculars

△ The town is rightly proud of its comedic history.

△ Gazing out from Heysham over magical Morecambe Bay.

around his neck – Eric Morecambe was a keen birdwatcher and the RSPB named a local hide after him. Nearby, the town's stone jetty, built as part of a coastal management scheme, is covered with bird-inspired designs and features a huge compass, while an innovative metal display points out the Cumbrian peaks seen across the water. Take a stroll down Victoria Street, where street art has been at the heart of redevelopment, and wander along the Flock of Words, a 300m (985-foot) celebration of literature that connects the train station with the promenade. The muddy beach is not really one to lounge around on, but cycle lanes, parks and cafés encourage plenty of activity along the promenade. The town has also developed a healthy reputation as a festival destination. Whether it's for the 'Vintage by the Sea' festival, a crime-writing convention or the winter lantern celebration, Morecambe's hotels and guest houses are making the most of a seaside town on the way back.

△ A beacon of Morecambe's revival is the Midland Hotel.

Art deco on the coast

A beacon of Morecambe's revival is the Midland Hotel, built in 1933 by the London, Midland and Scottish Railway. It's on a site across the road from the town's original train station. Now a Grade II Listed Building, the famous white hotel is an important example of art deco and once more a thriving place to stay after a restoration that started in 2006. Notable features of the Midland include the curving design of the building, the circular tower at the entrance, the remarkable spiral staircase in the lobby and a rounded café at the north side of the building. Look out for the distinctive art deco seahorses that adorn the top of the building. A luxury place to stay with outstanding views, it was once used in an episode of *Poirot*, capturing the style of the times perfectly. Experience your own trip back to the 1930s by enjoying afternoon tea overlooking the bay (01524 424000 www.englishlakes. co.uk/the-midland LA4 4BU).

Getting here

New road developments mean there's quick access to Morecambe from the M6 at junction 34. The town's train station is centrally located. Silverdale is reached by leaving the M6 at junction 35, with the train station being close to Leighton Moss nature reserve.

△ Morecambe's seafront is on the rise again after serious investment.

△ Morecambe Bay, framed by Lakeland fells, is an important source for fishermen.

MORECAMBE BAY

- 💡 Largest estuary in north-west England
- 💡 Contains UK's second largest gas field
- 💡 Has rich cockle beds, fished for many generations
- 💡 Over 300,000 people live on this coastline
- 💡 Notorious for dangerous quicksand and fast-moving tides

 Fish and chips

Tuck in at Atkinsons on Lancaster Road, where you can just turn up or order in advance online. (☎ 01524 411632 www.atkinsons-fishandchips.co.uk ♥ LA4 5TJ)

Heysham

A decent stroll along the coast from Morecambe, the village of Heysham has two sides to it. One is a live-wire industrial centre, with a nuclear power station and busy ferry terminal where boats leave for the Isle of Man. By contrast, the other side to Heysham is quaint and charming, with cottages on narrow streets and an historic church commanding extraordinary views. From St Peter's Church (♥ LA3 2RN), the view across Morecambe Bay is fabulous and makes the churchyard a very serene, spiritual place to visit. A little further up the hill, St Patrick's Chapel dates back to the eighth century and is home to remarkable stone-cut graves. Originally covered over with slabs, these were a burial site for Anglo-Saxon Christians. Some believe this may have been the final resting place of St Patrick himself. Choose a warm, sunny evening and park yourself on a bench to see the sun set over Barrow-in-Furness.

Silverdale – a haven for birders

The calm, peaceful environment of Leighton Moss RSPB nature reserve is a fabulous place to unwind and recharge your batteries (☎ 01524 701601 www.rspb.org.uk ♥ LA5 0SW). Sit in a hide with a pair of binoculars, take your time and look out for black-tailed godwits, bitterns, little egrets, green sandpipers and a wide range of other birds that settle here. Head into Silverdale village to enjoy a cuppa at the Wolf House Café (☎ 01524 702024 ♥ LA5 0TX) and follow the signs to take a walk along the coast towards Jenny Brown's Point. It's a perfect excursion from Morecambe if you have more time to spare.

🛎 *Stay a while*

🛏 The Gateway, 19 Marine Drive, Hest Bank, LA2 6DY. ☎ 01524 823762 www.thegatewayathestbank.co.uk

🧳 The Midland, Marine Road West, Morecambe, LA4 4BU. ☎ 01524 424000 www.englishlakes.co.uk/the-midland

⛺ Regent Bay Holiday Park, Westgate, Morecambe, LA3 3DF. ☎ 0330 123 4980 www.parkdeanresorts.co.uk

5

GRANGE-OVER-SANDS
WALK THIS BAY

Although often overshadowed by the beauty of the Southern Lakes, a weekend in Grange-over-Sands can include delicious food, an unusual cross-bay walk and a day at the races!

Grange-over-Sands

The name is a little deceptive. There are no sands at Grange where you can take a walk or enjoy a picnic. You won't be going for a paddle in the sea here, but you can enjoy a lovely stroll along a promenade that has the most delightful views of Morecambe Bay and the Lake District. Grange-over-Sands is a lovely, quiet retreat. It's a wonderful place to relax and watch the world go by. Stepping off the train at Grange's renowned Victorian station is like drifting back in time. The slow pace is infectious, the tea rooms so tempting, and the Edwardian architecture is typically elegant. If you're not sure when to visit Grange-over-Sands, look up the date of the Edwardian Festival in early June for a special historical trip.

△ Grange-over-Sands has plenty of Edwardian elegance and splendour.

Off to the races

There's only one racecourse where winners take home a coveted portion of sticky toffee pudding – and that is, of course, at Cartmel. Just a couple of miles from Grange-over-Sands, in the middle of the peninsula sticking out into Morecambe Bay, the small village of Cartmel has made a name for itself as the maker of fine Lakeland desserts and the organiser of great race meetings. Only a handful of race days take place at Cartmel each year, so you'll have to plan your visit. But when they happen, thousands of people converge near the coast to enjoy a day at the races. Each Cartmel race meeting takes place over three days with a rest day in the middle so organisers can

Getting here

From the M6 at junction 36, take the A590, which loops around the southern edge of the Lake District. Grange-over-Sands is signed off down the B5277. A regular train service brings passengers in from Carnforth and Lancaster.

△ One of the best walks in the nation is a guided trip across Morecambe Bay.

get tidied up and visitors can enjoy some time visiting the coast and Lake District fells. The national hunt events you can see at Cartmel are well known because of the unusual layout of the course; jockeys negotiate the longest home straight in the country, which covers 4 furlongs. Whether your horse comes in or not, make sure you allow time to sample the village speciality. Cartmel Village Shop (☎ 01539 536280 www.cartmelvillageshop.co.uk ♥ LA11 6QB) came up with the delicious recipe in the 1990s and now prides itself as being the home of sticky toffee pudding. The distinctive packages are sold from the shop as well as being available across the region.

Fish and chips

At Grange-over-Sands, check out Fish over Chips. The quirkily, locally named shop is on Kents Bank Road (☎ 015395 32277 ♥ LA11 7EY).

A guided walk on shifting sands

There has been a royally appointed guide helping people across Morecambe Bay since the 1500s. These experts got to know how the fast-moving tides interacted with the bay's quicksands and – hopefully – which places were safe to cross. The passage did not always end well; many lives have been lost in Morecambe Bay over the centuries. Since the arrival in 1857 of the railway and time-saving viaducts that slashed the journey time between Grange-over-Sands and Lancaster, there's been no need for people to risk their lives crossing the notoriously dangerous sands. But in the summer, charity walks give folk the chance to roll up their trousers and get knee-deep in sea water on the unusual walk. Fundraisers collecting cash for a range of good causes take the 14.5km (9-mile) stroll across Morecambe Bay under the careful guidance of the current royal guide. Still a potentially hazardous trip

that could get called off if tidal conditions are not safe, it's a journey that should only be taken on with the official guide. You'll need to register with a charity before taking the plunge. Once you sort out the logistics and get signed up, you can look forward to what will be an incredible experience. Carefully following the direction of the guide, you'll wade through the river, trudge through sinking sand and have the group spread out in a long line through some of the wetter sections. Most of the walks start off from Arnside on the east side of the bay, finishing up a few hours later in Kents Bank, where you can get a train back to the starting point. Check out www.guideoversands.co.uk for the latest news about cross-bay walks.

🛎 Stay a while

🛏 Corner Beech House, Methven Terrace, Grange-over-Sands, LA11 7DP.
🕿 015395 33088
www.cornerbeech.co.uk

🏨 The Grange Boutique Hotel, Kents Bank Road, Grange-over-Sands, LA11 7EY.
🕿 015395 33076
www.grangeboutiquehotel.com

⛺ High Fellgate Caravan Park, Cartmel Road, Grange-over-Sands, LA11 7QA.
🕿 015395 36231
www.highfellgate.co.uk

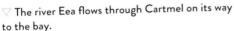

▽ The river Eea flows through Cartmel on its way to the bay.

6

RAVENGLASS
FULL STEAM AHEAD!

Why visit?

★ Chug from the seaside to the mountains on a delightful steam train destined for the Lake District

★ Explore Roman ruins in what was one of the most northerly outposts of the Empire

★ Get away from it all with an afternoon on quiet Silecroft beach

△ A beautiful ride aboard a steam train into the Lake District awaits.

All aboard La'al Ratty!

The guard blows his whistle, the engine gives a toot and the open-top carriages start chugging away. Steam plumes into the sky, while the nostalgic aroma of burning coal drifts by. Catching the heritage railway from Ravenglass to Dalegarth leaves the coastal flats behind and takes you 11km (7 miles) into the Lake District National Park, which was designated a UNESCO World Heritage Site in 2017. The line at Ravenglass and Eskdale Railway (📞 01229 717171 www.ravenglass-railway.co.uk Postcode for Ravenglass Station: CA18 1SW) is affectionally known as La'al Ratty, which means Little Railway in the old Cumbrian dialect. It's a charming route that has an industrial background; the narrow-gauge railway was opened in 1875 to transport iron ore to the main line down by the sea. Instead of raw materials,

△ The open-air carriages are a must on sunny summer days.

it's now the surrounding natural splendour that encourages many folk to travel on the line, with plenty of opportunities to alight at the small stations and enjoy a peaceful stroll. At the Dalegarth terminal, a short walk along the road and up a path takes you to an impressive waterfall, Stanley Ghyll. There's a café at the station to enjoy a cuppa before the return journey takes you away from the peaked landscape and back to the salty air.

Silecroft

South of Ravenglass, one of the best stretches of beach on the entire Cumbrian coastline is found at remote Silecroft. There's hardly anything at Silecroft, and yet this enchanting stretch of Cumbrian coast has everything you need for some quality beach time. Close to the free car park, there's a basic toilet block and the small Silecroft Beach Café (☎ 07907 431202) selling drinks, snacks and ice creams. You can even pick up a bucket and spade there. The main attraction that pulls people to this hidden gem is the beach, and there's plenty of it. Below a pebble-strewn upper shore, the tide draws out to reveal an extensive golden, sandy playground. You won't have to walk far to have an area all to yourself because this seaside haven is rarely busy. And all this against a backdrop of prominent Lake District fells. Sublime! Set your satnav for LA18 4NY or catch the train down the coast to Silecroft Station.

Roman history

Remains of a fort have been found in Ravenglass, dating back to Roman times and evidently built to defend what would have been a working port. The most significant part of the ruins is the Roman Bath House, which is a short stroll from the railway station and now under the care of English Heritage (☎ 0370 333 1181 www. english-heritage.org.uk ♥ CA18 1SR). The site contains the highest surviving Roman walls in

▽ **An atmospheric walk along a deserted beach is good for the soul.**

northern England, with many original features still visible. Visitors can see the doorways, windows and a niche that was made for a bust. The bath house contained two underfloor heating systems and was a hub for socialising, exercise and bathing.

Getting here

Follow the A595 on the western edge of the Lake District towards Ravenglass, which is sandwiched between Gosforth and Bootle. Ravenglass is also accessible by train, using the line that connects Carlisle with Lancaster and runs along the majority of the Cumbrian coast.

Muncaster Castle

Just outside Ravenglass, one of the Lake District's most treasured castles occupies an important place near to the coast. Muncaster Castle is home to the Pennington family line and there is evidence to show they have been around this site since 1026 (☎ 01229 717614 www.muncaster. co.uk ♥ CA18 1RD). Changes to the castle over the centuries have rendered it one of the most charming and architecturally delightful in the region, something visitors appreciate as soon as they step into the Great Hall. The audio tour takes you around the family's rooms in around 40 minutes, while the 31ha (77 acres) of magnificent gardens deserve more of your time.

Stretch your legs

Silecroft is positioned directly on the Cumbria Coastal Way, so there's plenty of opportunities to stride out along this route, both to the north and south. The path is not too strenuous, and you can take a there-and-back route to match your spare time. For those feeling more energetic, take

△ Children of all ages love time to play in the sand – and there's plenty of it.

the track up to the top of Black Combe. This is one of the outlying southern fells of the Lake District and on a fine day will provide you with fine views of the coast and the fells deeper into the National Park.

Pub grub

In Silecroft, the Miners Arms (☎ 01229 772325 ♥ LA18 5LP) is less than a mile from the beach on the road to the train station. In Ravenglass, enjoy a pint at the Ratty Arms (☎ 01229 717676 ♥ CA18 1SN) as you watch passengers from the steam train come and go.

Stay a while

🛏 The Bay Horse, Main Street, Ravenglass, CA18 1SD. ☎ 01229 717015 www.bayhorseravenglass.co.uk

🧳 The Pennington, Main Street, Ravenglass, CA18 1SQ. ☎ 01229 717222 www.penningtonhotel.co.uk

⛺ Ravenglass Camping and Caravanning Club Site, Ravenglass, CA18 1SR. ☎ 01229 717250 www.campingandcaravanningclub.co.uk

7

ST BEES
COAST-TO-COAST
ADVENTURES

Walker's paradise

Few long-distance walks have the romance and intrigue of the Coast to Coast path devised by Lakeland legend Alfred Wainwright. The man who wrote the famous guides to the Lake District fells was the one who came up with the idea of a cross-country route leaving from the sea at St Bees and meandering over the hills to Robin Hood's Bay on the east coast. Wainwright wrote the first guide to accompany those taking on the challenge and it remains a good asset for the walk, which usually takes around 16 days to complete. Before setting out on the 294km (183-mile) hike, it's tradition for those taking part to dip their toe in the sea at St Bees and look forward to a paddle in the North Sea a little over two weeks later. If setting out on the 'C2C' route is not for you, there are plenty of shorter circuits to enjoy around St Bees, including an amble up to the lighthouse on the clifftop.

A special cliff

The headland at St Bees gives this Cumbrian coastline a glorious backdrop but is of significance for more than its natural beauty. Incredible though it seems, this is the only cliff to peak above the British coastline between Anglesey and the Scottish border. The rest of this stretch of English seaside is fairly flat. The striking cliffs at St Bees, rising swiftly up to 91 meters (300 feet), are made up of red sandstone and on a clear day you can walk up the path for a far-reaching view to the Isle of Man and southern Scotland. The beach here has also been

△ A man at work in Whitehaven harbour at sunset.

 Fish and chips

Get involved with the food at Fraser's, near Whitehaven's harbour, for great fish and chips (☎ 01946 62622 ♦ CA28 7UZ).

△ Whitehaven is a lovely place to enjoy fish and chips by the boats.

recognised as important. This Site of Special Scientific Interest has a significant number of gemstones washed on to it, as well as being home to many crabs and mussels.

Whitehaven – built for shipping and mining

Although both the industries Whitehaven was created to support have long since declined, this town to the north of St Bees remains a busy place worthy of spending a sunny evening. The harbour is a delightful place to hang out when the sun is shining and many visitors head for The Rum Story to discover the pivotal role Whitehaven played in the UK's booze trade (📞 01946 592933 www.rumstory.co.uk 📍 CA28 7DN). Aside from being at the centre of the spirit business, this north-west town has several other reasons to celebrate its influence upon the rest of the world. When originally planned, Whitehaven was unusual as it was designed on a grid system, which can still be recognised today. Several historians believe it was Whitehaven's

blocks that led to planners in New York developing a much larger version of it. The link with the United States doesn't stop there. Local girl Mildred Warner Gale went on to become grandmother to the first American President, George Washington. And Whitehaven was, curiously, the last British place to be attacked by American naval forces. During the American War of Independence, the naval commander John Paul Jones arrived with a plan to destroy the British fleet, but the scheme was soon detected and he was quickly sent back.

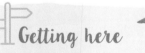

Getting here

The centrally located train stations at St Bees and Whitehaven have regular links along the Cumbrian coast towards Lancaster and Carlisle. Follow the A595 along the north-west's coast to reach both St Bees and Whitehaven.

△ There are few cliffs on this coastline, but St Bees atones for the absence.

Cycle C2C

While St Bees is the Coast to Coast starting point for walkers, cyclists head to Whitehaven to begin their challenge. The tough 221km (137-mile) cycle route is not for the faint-hearted; spare a thought for anyone having pictures taken by the marker in the harbour before or after the journey.

Shipwreck tales

There are many stories told about shipwrecks around the coast of St Bees, perhaps none more tragic than that of the *Luigi Olivari*, which killed 11 Italian sailors and a Cornish deep-sea pilot in 1879. On a night of poor visibility and wintry weather, one local boy thought he saw a ship in trouble, but nobody else could make it out. The sight that greeted townsfolk in the morning, however, was shocking as bodies were washed up on to the shore. A service was held for them at the local church, where a large monument still stands today. The plinth of it is decorated with old seashells, while the remains of the 12 seafarers are buried in the layers beneath it. Although the Cornishman was identified as Henry Legg because of papers he was carrying, to this day it remains unclear who the Italian mariners were.

△ Coastal art celebrates the importance of the fishing industry.

SILLOTH
LIKE TOY SOLDIERS

Why visit?

★ Stay late on a summer's evening to enjoy a beautiful sunset
★ Indulge your inner child by spending an afternoon among thousands of toy soldiers
★ Stroll along lengthy, windswept beaches on the edge of Cumbria

See a Silloth sunset

There are more than a few surprises in store for people making their way to Silloth. In a remote part of Cumbria with few settlements of notable size, Silloth's 3,000-strong population is rightly proud of its quaint and tidy town. Silloth was developed by Carlisle businessmen who wanted to make use of the port, a transport link that played an important role in establishing Silloth. Among the many materials imported was the Irish grey granite used to build the eye-catching church that gives Silloth the true feel of a border town. In front of the church, the huge green space known as The Green is well utilised by tourists in the summer. It's a great place to enjoy a picnic, make use of the pop-up café and spend some time in the deckchairs. On warm, sunny days, make sure you hang around for the sunsets. With its west-facing seafront and views over the water to hills in southern Scotland, this is one of the best spots in the country to see the sun go down, an opinion shared by Turner, who came here to paint the scene. A sky blazing with many different colours provides the ultimate end to a day on this part of our coast.

▽ There are huge stretches of beach to explore at Allonby.

△ See old and new battles recreated at Silloth's fun toy soldier display.

He had 10,000 men...

It's not just the grand old Duke of York who had an army of marching men. A toy soldier collector in Silloth has amassed a private collection of 10,000 toy soldiers, guns and vehicles in what has become one of the greatest collections of its kind. Wanting to share his passion for the little fighting men, he dedicated his miniature army and the building that houses them to the town, and it pulls in plenty of enthusiasts. Adults are charmed by the breadth of the collection, while children have their imagination fired by the scale of the displays. Run by local volunteers, Soldiers in Silloth (☎ 016973 31246 www.soldiersinsilloth. co.uk ♀ CA7 4BZ) has metal and plastic toy figures from around the world. And the themes on display span the ages, starting with battling Roman centurions and leading right the way up to the tiny green guys from the Second World War featuring in *Toy Story*. This is a lovely little museum that does a good job of keeping the focus as local as possible. Nearby Hadrian's Wall and the local Second World War airfield both feature, alongside battles at Agincourt, Waterloo and Rorke's Drift.

Dine with fairies

If you like your food with generous helpings of unicorns and make-believe, there's a café in Silloth that's going to charm your socks off. Expect fluffy marshmallows on your hot chocolate at the Fairydust Emporium (☎ 016973 31787 ♥ CA7 4AD), a carefully decorated and delightfully run café serving up sweet and savoury dishes for sprites of all ages.

Getting here

On the north-west of the Cumbrian coast, within view of Scotland across the Solway Firth, approach Silloth on the A596 before taking either the B5301 or B5302 to the town centre.

△ The curving seafront at the often overlooked seaside town of Silloth.

Fish and chips

You can tuck into fish and chips at Silloth Café, which you'll find on Station Road (☎ 016973 31319 ♥ CA7 4AE).

Allonby beach

The long stretch of sand at Allonby, 14.5km (9 miles) south of Silloth, is a stunning space to spend an afternoon. Part of an Area of Outstanding Natural Beauty, the scenery is amazing, sandwiched as it is between the hills of Scotland and the Lake District. Many come here for the sporting activities that are available on such a great expanse of often windy shoreline. Kite surfing and wind surfing are popular pastimes and there is a great section of coastal path ideal for walkers and cyclists. This is also a birdwatcher's paradise, with oystercatchers, curlews, teals and grebes all regular visitors. The buildings in Allonby tell a story themselves, many dating back to the days when herring fishing was a major local employer and Quakers helped to develop the settlement.

Stay a while

🛏 Green View Guesthouse, Criffel Street, Silloth, CA7 4DQ. ☎ 07763 881737

🏨 Golf Hotel, Criffel Street, Silloth, CA7 4AB. ☎ 016973 31438 www.golfhotelsilloth.co.uk

⛺ Stanwix Park, Greenrow Meadows, Silloth, CA7 4HH. ☎ 016973 32666 www.stanwix.com

Time for a round?

Silloth Golf Club (☎ 01697 331304 www.sillothgolfclub.co.uk ♥ CA7 4BL) is a lovely place to enjoy 18 holes. It's also historically significant in the development of the women's game. Cecilia Leitch was a local golfer who dominated the scene around the First World War. The strong link with the women's game has led to several major female tournaments being held in Silloth over the years.

WEST SCOTLAND

Our first port of call as we reach Scotland is Galloway, a place which offers a feeling of wild Scotland without venturing too far north. Enjoy coastal walks and a sublime feeling of peace on the Mull of Galloway before continuing your journey further north to Troon. This is a golfer's dream, with top quality links sitting next to family fun on the beach. Scotland's biggest city needs no introduction, and Glasgow is thriving on its modern reputation as a tourist destination. The banks of the Clyde offer many ways to explore the industrial, shipbuilding heartland north of the border.

Moving up the coast, away from the urban charm of Glasgow, our next destination is the Mull of Kintyre. It's a priceless peninsula offering a wonderful opportunity to get away from it all. After spending time here, you'll see why this coastal setting appealed so much to Paul McCartney in his post-Beatles days. You may even see a mist rolling in from the sea. If there's one place to enjoy a wee dram on Scottish coast, it's Oban. The western town was pretty much developed around the golden drink and distillery tours remain a popular attraction today. At Fort William, attention moves from indoor

Don't miss

✓ Enjoying the solitude and tranquillity of the Mull of Kintyre

✓ Gazing out of a steam train along one of the planet's most scenic rail lines – to Mallaig

✓ Taking a road trip along the world-famous NC500

✓ Standing on the edge of the nation at the most remote part of the coast – Cape Wrath

✓ Enjoying the wonderful craft village and a steaming hot chocolate at Balnakeil

to outdoor as the range of adventurous challenges increases. From walking by the Caledonian Canal to climbing Ben Nevis and taking a breath-taking train journey to beautiful Mallaig, there's plenty to get the blood pumping here. The quaint village of Plockton has been star of several TV shows and it's not difficult to see why directors are drawn to this spot, close to the Kyle of Lochalsh. Continue north along the coast and you'll come to a brand-new road trip route that has got many people talking. A marketing dream for the north and western coasts of Scotland, the North Coast 500 – or NC500 – has provided a massive boost to the region's economy and opened up parts of the shoreline to tourists from all over the world. The pretty town of Ullapool, flanked by mountains and an atmospheric

loch, has seen an upturn in its fortunes because it's a must-stop destination. The NC500 doesn't go near the most isolated place on Scotland's north coast – the wonderful Cape Wrath. And that's for good reason, because a journey to this remote shoreline is something that takes some planning. A ferry and minibus are needed to reach the most northerly lighthouse on the mainland, but it's well worth making the effort. You can't see Iceland as you gaze out across the sea, but somehow the whole experience of looking to the northern horizon feels more barren, more adventurous. Drive along the Scotland's north road to Balnakeil and round off your north-western coastal adventure by exploring home-made crafts in a village designed to detect dangers in the Cold War.

Epic sand dunes on Balnakeil Beach give the north coast of Scotland a Tatooine-style landscape.

9

MULL OF GALLOWAY

PLENTY TO MULL OVER

Why visit?

★ Spend a sunny evening on a lovely walk around Scotland's most southerly lighthouse

★ Take a bite of the local smoked fish, a delicacy in Dumfries and Galloway

★ Flick through the pages of Wigtown's many second-hand bookshops and grab yourself a good read

The Mull of Galloway

Standing on Scotland's most southerly spot on a clear day provides an exciting opportunity. Even without binoculars, you'll be able to feast your eyes on Northern Ireland, the Isle of Man and the coast of Cumbria as you look out to sea. Douglas is just 60km (37 miles) away and Belfast lies 68km (42 miles) off the mull. The immediate landscape is dominated by the lighthouse, which

△ Outstanding walks around the Mull of Galloway peak at the lighthouse.

has provided a life-saving beacon for ships since 1830. It was built by prolific lighthouse designer Robert Stevenson, the grandfather of *Treasure Island* writer Robert Louis Stevenson. Standing 26 metres (85 feet) tall, it's one of 200 lighthouses dotted along the Scottish coast, the others all being further north. Until the Mull of Galloway Lighthouse was automated in 1988, the lighthouse keeper and two assistants lived on site with their families. It was a lonely existence, especially back in the 19th century, when they would grow their own vegetables and keep chickens in order to provide for themselves. They also kept a horse to transport much-needed supplies from the nearby boat landing. Follow the path around the back of the lighthouse to see the foghorn. It has recently been refurbished and is only sounded on special occasions. It's the only operational foghorn on mainland Scotland.

This is a very significant place for both flora and fauna; there are ground-nesting birds and coastal wildflowers. Follow the advice of local signs that ask for dogs to be kept on leads and walkers to keep on the paths. Since 2013 this Site of Special Scientific Interest has been owned by a community initiative, the Mull of Galloway Trust, and is leased and managed by the RSPB. A well-marked and rewarding circular walk around the lighthouse provides the chance to calmly reflect. It really is a spiritual and engaging place to spend a lovely evening.

Try some smokin' fish

The guys who run Galloway Smokehouse certainly know their fish. They're fishermen themselves and head out into Wigtown Bay in search of sea bass and grey mullet. The menu at the smokehouse's Fisherman Café (☏ 01671 820350 www.gallowaysmokehouse.co.uk ♀ DG8 7DN) is packed with different seafood treats, cakes and breakfast rolls. The fish is caught using sustainable methods and excess catch is returned to the sea. Ask a staff member if you want to take a look at the smokers and find out about the methods used in the smokehouse.

Getting here

The A75 runs from Gretna Green towards the Galloway coast. Turn off on the A714 for Wigtown, while the B7084, A716 and B7041 will take you to the Mull of Galloway. Rail services feed into the port at Stranraer.

Paradise in Galloway

A walk through Logan Botanic Garden, just north of the Mull of Galloway (☏ 01776 860231 www.rbge.org.uk ♀ DG9 9ND), allows an exploration of exotic species of plants not commonly found in the UK. Because it's warmed by the Gulf Stream, species from Australia, New Zealand and Central America thrive. Expect to see palm trees, tree ferns and giant gunnera.

▽ A formidable landscape in a remote corner of Scotland.

Book your place at Wigtown

Any self-respecting bibliophile will try their best to set aside a week in September and explore the latest releases at the Wigtown Book Festival (www.wigtownbookfestival.com). An hour's drive east along the coast from the Mull of Galloway, the town has a literary significance that belies its size. Even when the book festival is not on, there are over a dozen bookshops competing for your reading time. The range of titles they have to offer is extraordinary. Anybody with even a slight interest in browsing through different tomes will be able to lose themselves among the pages in Wigtown. Although not going to win any prizes for inventive names, The Bookshop (☎ 01988 402499 www.the-bookshop.com 📍 DG8 9HL) is one of the largest second-hand book stores in the country, with an extensive range of local, regional and Scottish publications. If you need a drink or something to eat while choosing what to buy, there's a popular café at

ReadingLasses Bookshop (☎ 01988 403266 📍 DG8 9EH). As this clever name suggests, you're welcome to bring your reading glasses to browse through the large selection of books by and about women.

🔔 Stay a while

🛏 Hillcrest House, Maidland Place, Station Road, Wigtown, DG8 9EU. ☎ 01988 402018 www.hillcrest-wigtown.co.uk

💼 The Crown Hotel, 102 Queen Street, Newton Stewart, DG8 6JW. ☎ 01671 402727 www.the-crown-hotel.com

⛺ Drumroamin Farm Camping and Caravan Site, South Balfern, Kirkinner, Newton Stewart, DG8 9DB. ☎ 01988 840613 www.drumroamin.co.uk

△ Clear skies allow views across to Northern Ireland and north England.

10

TROON
FINDING SOME FRESH AYR

△ Wide open spaces on the beach meet the busy town at Troon.

Royal Troon

The coastal town of Troon is dominated by the Royal Troon golf course. It's impossible to visit and not be amazed by the extensive site of the famous links course stretching out next to the sea with a mountain backdrop that's enough to distract the keenest amateur golfers. Out and about around the town, you'll come across visitors and locals talking about golf, eyeing the weather to see if it will affect their game. Royal Troon is up there with the finest golf courses in the world. If you're lucky enough to book a round, you'll tee off with a tingling in your spine and a feeling of being among golf royalty. The Open Championship first came to Royal Troon in 1923 and became a regular venue, going on to hold the famous event nine times. The Old Course it's played on adopted the current design in 1888. Players follow a traditional 'out and back' route, tackling the first nine holes moving away from the club house before turning and returning via holes 10 through to 18. The opening holes and the later ones that finish off the course are thought to be easy going, leaving a difficult middle section that has seen the plan of many pros fall apart. When you add a fierce sea wind to the mix, Royal Troon's Old Course can be one of the toughest in the world (☏ 01292 311555 www.royaltroon.co.uk ⚲ KA10 6EP).

△ Explore the incredible legacy of Burns' 18th-century poetry.

IN THE FOOTSTEPS OF THE BARD

- In Twa Brigs, old and new bridges in Ayr argue with each other. The auld brig north of the church in Ayr was built in 1491.

- Find the Auld Kirk on Blackfriars Walk, Ayr, where Robert Burns was baptised.

- Get a view of Brig o' Doon from the Burns Monument in Alloway.

- The ruins of the old church in Alloway were the setting for the Burns classic 'Tam o' Shanter'.

Take a Cup of Kindness

Poetic genius Robert Burns hailed from these parts and a visit to Ayr is not complete without calling at his birthplace museum (☏ 01292 443700 burnsmuseum.org.uk ⚲ KA7 4PQ). The literary legend is celebrated with whisky toasts and poetry on 25 January to mark the day in 1759 that he was born in an Alloway cottage on the outskirts of Ayr. Growing up in and around Alloway, Burns wrote his first song here – 'O Once I Lov'd (a Bonnie Lass)' – when he was 16. A string of poetic classics came from his pen over the next two decades, including 'Auld Lang Syne', 'To a Mouse', 'Tam o' Shanter', 'Holy Willie's

Getting here

Ayr and its surroundings are well connected thanks in part to the proximity of Glasgow Prestwick Airport. The A77 and A78 run parallel to the coast, while Ayr and Troon have their own train stations.

Prayer' and 'Cock Up Your Beaver'. He died at the young age of 37. Today, the importance of Robert Burns cannot be understated. Once voted the 'Greatest Ever Scot', he is a global Scottish brand that is important to many Scots living at home and abroad. When Burns penned the song 'A Man's a Man for a' That', he could not have dreamed it would be used to open the Scottish Parliament in 1999.

All shook up

Just to the north of Ayr, the airport at Prestwick sees holidaymakers taking off over the Firth of Clyde. This is famously the only place where Elvis Presley stood on British soil. The King of Rock 'n' Roll never played a gig here but stopped off for a two-hour transfer after completing his national service. The departure lounge makes the most of this with a bar and information wall honouring the event.

Ayr Beach

The long sandy beach has made Ayr a very popular holiday destination for well over 100 years. The fall in demand for British seaside breaks has had an impact here just like everywhere else, but the pull of Robert Burns has been a boost for the area. The superb Ayrshire Coastal Path (www.ayrshirecoastalpath.org) offers walkers 160km (100 miles) of coastal trails with delightful views.

The Varyag

A little further down the coast from Ayr, an eye-catching memorial marks the spot where a famous Russian cruiser ran aground in 1920. The *Varyag* came to an end on rocks near the village of Lendalfoot in the Firth of Clyde while being towed to Germany. She was left in situ and scrapped in the years that followed. In a rare British tribute to Russian naval bravery, the memorial plaque was unveiled in 2006 and a bronze cross added to the site the following year. Although the final resting place of the *Varyag* is here off the Scottish coast, the vessel is better known for the resolute crew at the start of the Russo-Japanese War of 1904–5. The battle of Chemulpo Bay saw the *Varyag* surrounded by Japanese ships demanding its surrender. Rather than give in, the Russian sailors scuttled the *Varyag* and were taken aboard boats from other countries. The crew returned to Russia as heroes, while the Japanese eventually salvaged the *Varyag* and repaired it.

Stay a while

🛏 The Beechwood 37 Prestwick Road, Ayr, KA8 8LE. ☎ 01292 262093
www.ayrguesthouse.com

💼 Western House Hotel, Craigie Road, Ayr, KA8 0HA. ☎ 01292 294990
www.westernhousehotel.co.uk

⛺ Culzean Castle Camping and Caravanning Club Site, Culzean, Maybole, KA19 8JX. ☎ 01655 760627
www.campingandcaravanningclub.co.uk

GLASGOW
SCOTLAND'S BIGGEST CITY

Why visit?

★ Sitting on the banks of the Clyde, Glasgow has a rich history of shipbuilding

★ World-class attractions that are brilliant for families have opened up on the riverside

★ Take a trip on one of the world's last seagoing paddle steamers

Glasgow Science Centre

Inspiring children and adults alike to investigate the world of science, this innovative attraction on the Clyde's waterfront is somewhere you could easily lose yourself for the day (☎ 0141 420 5000 www.glasgowsciencecentre.org ♥ G51 1EA). Plenty of hands-on, interactive displays cover a wide range of scientific themes, with rolling exhibitions ensuring there's new material for returning visitors. An IMAX cinema shows many jaw-dropping films, including documentaries about the universe and life under the sea. A thought-provoking section of the museum deals with the challenges of producing enough energy for future generations. The stand-out experience is a trip up Glasgow Tower, a building that rockets up in the sky next to the Clyde and provides unrivalled views of Scotland's biggest city. It's the only structure on Earth that can rotate 360° into the prevailing wind and holds the record for the tallest rotating structure in the world. The top of the tower stands 127 metres (417 feet) above the water, making it the tallest free-standing building in Scotland.

△ The waterfront at Glasgow has been revitalised in recent decades, now including the Science Centre.

△ It's called The Titan for a reason – the crane on the Clyde is enormous.

Mass of the Titan

Dominating the banks of the Clyde, the huge crane known as Titan (☎ 07538 842596) www.titanclydebank.com ♀ G81 1BF) is both an impressive sight and a reminder of Glasgow's world-renowned shipbuilding history. The desire to construct bigger ships – and more of them – on the Clyde led to the order for Titan being placed in 1905. Two years later, Titan was aiding construction of record-breaking ships, including the *Queen Mary* in 1934. Today you can visit Titan, journey to the top of its bulky frame and even abseil from the summit for charity. Titan's shipbuilding days have long gone, but the modern-era turning point in the crane's fortunes came in 2004 when an urban regeneration company kicked off plans to transform the industrial gargantuan into a tourist attraction. It opened up three years later following a £3.75m investment and the crane is now an 'A' listed building, which puts it on the same status as Edinburgh Castle.

There are only 11 giant cantilever cranes remaining in the world – and four of them are on the banks of the Clyde in Glasgow. The most famous is Finnieston Crane, no longer used but left as a proud reflection of the city's shipbuilding industrial heritage. It's an iconic part of the Glasgow skyline and is often seen in the background in broadcasts from the BBC Scotland studios at the Pacific Quay, a regenerated dock with a geographically dubious name.

The Tall Ship

Thousands of ships were built in the Glasgow shipyards, with tens of thousands of workers helping to launch the biggest, fastest and most technologically advanced vessels of the day. Incredibly, there are only five sailing ships still afloat that started life on the Clyde. One of them, the *Glenlee*, is the main attraction at The Tall Ship museum (☎ 0141 357 3699 www.thetallship. com ♀ G3 8RS). The *Glenlee* was launched as a cargo carrier in 1896 and sailed around the world four times before being sold to the Spanish Navy in 1922. The ship served in various training roles until being retired in 1981 and largely forgotten. The *Glenlee* was spotted by an eagle-eyed naval architect in 1990, prompting the Clyde Maritime Trust to pay £40,000 and bring her home.

Getting here

As Scotland's biggest city and home to 600,000 people, Glasgow is well connected. The motorway network includes the M8, M73, M74 and M77. The train station has regular links east to Edinburgh, north to Fort William and south to London.

◁ One of our most famous ships the *Waverley* can be seen on the Firth of Clyde.

Full steam ahead!

Getting the chance to see the world's last seagoing paddle steamer is a real treat. The *Waverley*, which was launched in 1947 and then began a long career taking passengers up and down the Firth of Clyde, may be spotted outside the Glasgow Science Centre. Donations to carry out repairs to get the *Waverley* sailing again have topped £2.2 million (www.waverleyexcursions.co.uk). The *Waverley* was one of several paddle steamers on the Clyde that were owned by rail companies and provided a vital link between villages on the coast and the start of the rail line.

On air!

One of the most significant buildings on the banks of the Clyde today is the shiny headquarters of BBC Scotland. It's also one of the most important employers and a symbol of new, skilled jobs coming to the areas of former shipyards. It's always fun going to look around a TV studio and there are certainly some interesting things to learn about Scottish TV shows on the two-hour BBC tour – as well as some fun activities (https://www.bbc.co.uk/showsandtours/tours/bbc-scotland-pacific-quay ⊙ G51 1DA).

Stay a while

🛏 Glasgow Guest House, 56 Dumbreck Road, Glasgow, G41 5NP. ☏ 0141 427 0129 www.glasgow-guest-house.co.uk

🧳 Premier Inn, Pacific Quay, Glasgow, G51 1DZ. ☏ 0141 2128837 www.premierinn.com

⛺ West Highland Way Campsite, Milngavie, Glasgow, G63 9AW. ☏ 07488 261730

△ Glasgow's waterfront is home to the HQ of BBC Scotland.

MULL OF KINTYRE

MY DESIRE IS ALWAYS TO BE HERE

Why visit?

★ Sing the famous song by Paul McCartney and Wings that put this remote part of Scotland on the map

★ Enjoy a stroll on the beach and enjoy the sight of the castle and ruined abbey

★ Stand at the tip of the Mull of Kintyre by the lighthouse to gain an inspirational viewpoint to Northern Ireland

Shine a light

At the Mull of Kintyre's tip stands the second oldest lighthouse in Scotland. Completed in 1788, it became a warning beacon for ships sailing close to the coast of Scotland and Northern Ireland. The adjacent cottages at this stunning location used to provide accommodation for the lighthouse keeper and assistants. That was before automation took place in 1996 and operation was carried out remotely from Edinburgh. The lighthouse is reached via a lengthy single-track road that winds south from the village of Southend. On a clear day, when the mist is not rolling in from the sea, it's possible to gaze across and see the County Antrim coast.

The Mull gives you wings

It's easy to see why this drooping peninsula of beautiful coastline inspired Paul McCartney both to live here and write an anthem in homage to it. The promotional video for the Wings classic features McCartney wandering along the coast with his guitar, later joined by the Campbeltown Pipe Band on the beach at Saddell. It finishes with locals coming together for a sing-song on the beach, a blazing fire keeping them warm and the landmark Saddell Castle in the background. One of the most iconic videos of all time, the success of the single put this relatively unknown corner of Scotland on the map and spread its name around the world. Released in

△ The coastlines in these parts have inspired artists for decades.

Getting here

Although it's not too far from Kilmarnock as the crow flies, getting to this remote peninsula is trickier than you might think. By car, you'll need to head north of Glasgow and then loop around back south on the A83. An alternative is to take the ferry from Ardrossan.

November 1977, 'Mull of Kintyre' sold over 2 million copies, rocketing up the charts to be Christmas number one and staying there for nine weeks. Leaving aside charity releases, it remains the UK's best-selling single. You simply can't visit this neck of the woods without giving it a listen. The song is, of course, a love song to the area's natural charm and the way it allowed Paul and Linda McCartney to escape the media glare. This was very much their spiritual home, the place they returned to again and again and the area they settled to raise their four children. While living in Kintyre, they played an active role in the community, attending the annual agricultural show and local cinema.

△ You're sure to find your own special place when in the Mull of Kintyre.

Memorial garden

A quiet memorial garden with a bronze statue has been established in memory of Linda McCartney in Campbeltown, on the eastern coast of the peninsula. Check opening times before visiting at www.lindasgarden.co.uk. It's a calm, inspirational place to pay respects and spend some quiet time.

Saddell Bay

A nice beach to take a walk and spend an afternoon on, Saddell is a sheltered area with beautiful sands. It's also a landscape that's part of pop history. There are two prominent buildings here, and both featured in the 'Mull of Kintyre' video. Linda McCartney emerges from the white house, although the gate that Paul McCartney sings on is no longer there. Further along the coast, Saddell Castle is wonderfully lit up in the background of the video; it's now a holiday home you can rent out from the Landmark Trust (www.landmarktrust.org.uk). Look out for the thought-provoking Antony Gormley sculpture found in the bay. The human figure gazing out over the Kilbrannan Sound towards Arran is called *Grip* and was one of five placed around Landmark Trust sites to mark their 50th anniversary. The other four were removed as planned in 2016, but an anonymous donor bought this one and gave it a permanent home.

Abbey ruins

Overlooking Saddell Bay, the ruins of a Cistercian monastery are an atmospheric place to wander around. Saddell Abbey was founded in 1207 and occupied by Irish monks from Mellifont Abbey. It was in use for 300 years before falling into disrepair and became a scheduled ancient monument in 1975.

△ Sunset greets the harbour at Tarbert, on West Scotland's Kintyre Peninsula.

All about Kintyre

Journey back through the millennia to discover the history of Kintyre at Campbeltown Museum on Shore Street (◉ PA28 6BS). Archaeological discoveries stretch back to the Bronze Age, with more recent exhibits including a Liverpool lamp from the Mull of Kintyre Lighthouse. A seascape by William McTaggart is among other items that explore the natural and social history of the region.

13

OBAN
A TOWN FUELLED BY WHISKY

Oban Distillery – the tipple at the heart of the town

Located beneath a steep cliff and just a stone's throw from the sea, Oban's iconic and easily recognisable distillery has been synonymous with the town since the 18th century. Oban grew up around the distillery and is proud of its whisky-producing heritage. Local merchants and entrepreneurs John and Hugh Stevenson sowed the seed for Oban's whisky roots when they opened the business in 1794. The distillery stayed in the family for decades before being sold

△ There are adventures to be had on sea as well as on land.

△ A whisky tour tells you how the town has thrived on the hard stuff.

on, by which time the role of Oban as a major whisky producer was well established. Despite suffering from fires, a crash in the whisky market and a space-restricting town-centre location, the distillery has gone from strength to strength and today produces bottles of the golden spirit that has a hint of salt and complements seafood dishes. Whisky-lovers can take a tour, spend time in the shop and enjoy samples in the visitor centre on Stafford Street (☎ 01631 572004 obanwhiskey.com ♥ PA34 5NH).

Plenty to sea

The wildlife and islands found in the waters off Oban make it the perfect place to hit the waves and view the coast from the sea. There are several boat companies running a wide range of adventures from Oban and whether you want a lengthy trip out to Mull or a more leisurely idle around calmer waters, you'll find something to tempt you off the land. One of the most popular trips makes a pilgrimage to the Isle of Iona, where you can visit the famous abbey, enjoy lunch in a café and experience what life is like in this isolated community. Make sure your sea voyage includes a visit to the volcanic island of Staffa, where you can get an up-close perspective of magnificent hexagonal basalt columns and maybe even a peek inside the awe-inspiring Fingal's Cave. Wildlife tours go on the lookout for seals, whales, dolphins, basking sharks and sea eagles. Every trip is different and you never know which animals you'll spot.

War and Peace in Oban

The history of this important west-coast port is explored in the Oban War and Peace Museum (📞 01631 570007 www.obanmuseum.org.uk 📍 PA34 5PX). As its name implies, there are exhibits about how Oban fared during times of conflict and also in more prosperous times. A small museum run by local volunteers, this great destination has its origins in a 1995 display that was established to mark the 50th anniversary of the Second World War coming to an end. Oban played an active role in the war, with flying boats operating from the bay and aircrew from Australia, Canada and the United States being based here. The display about the war proved so popular with locals and visitors alike that the decision was made to make it permanent and the museum was established in 1996 with artefacts added from other eras.

🔔 Stay a while

🛏 Fàilte Bed and Breakfast, Rockfield Road, Oban, PA34 5DQ. 📞 01631 570219 www.failtebandb.com

🧳 Perle Oban Hotel, Station Square, PA34 5RT. 📞 01631 700301 www.perleoban.com

⛺ Oban Caravan and Camping Park, Gallanachmore Farm, Gallanach Road, Oban, PA34 4HQ. 📞 01631 562425 www.obancaravanpark.com

🚏 Getting here

An important port on Scotland's west coast, Oban is well connected via road and rail. The A85 and A816 meet in the town, providing different options to approach it over the mountains. Trains arrive at the town centre station, which is ideally placed for ferry connections.

McCaig's Tower

The unmistakable amphitheatre-esque, curving stone structure on the hill overlooking the coast dominates Oban's townscape. McCaig's Tower, named after local banker John Stuart McCaig, is visible from most places in the area and easily the town's most iconic landmark. Building of the tower started in 1895 and took five years. The project was McCaig's philanthropic attempt to both provide work for local stonemasons and create a lasting monument to his family. The gardens within the tower's wall are well worth a visit, but the chief draw here is the view. Peering out from the granite stone, the scenery over the town and out to sea is awesome. McCaig designed the tower himself after being inspired by Greek and Roman architecture. He wanted the tower, which has a circumference of 200 metres (656 feet), to take on the look of the Colosseum. It's one of the most unusual and unforgettable structures you'll see on the coast.

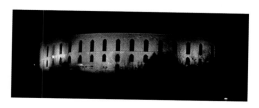

△ The Romanesque McCaig's Tower is iluminated after darkfall.

14

FORT WILLIAM
ALL ABOARD FOR MALLAIG!

Why visit?

★ Take the rail route made famous in the Harry Potter movies to enjoy the quaint port of Mallaig

★ Walk a section of the Caledonian Canal and see boats tackle the impressive Neptune's Staircase

★ Get kitted out for a memorable hike up to the highest mountain in Britain

Fort William

While it may not be the prettiest town in the world, Fort William does a sterling job in marketing itself as the gateway to the Highlands. It is, without doubt, a premier outdoor destination and pulls in visitors from all over the world. There are so many adventurous activities to enjoy within driving distance from Fort William, you could spend a month here and still have plenty of things to tick off. It's no wonder that many people choose the town as a base for a thrilling Scottish trip.

▽ Ben Nevis, the highest mountain in Britain, is one of many adventures to be had near Fort William.

The mightiest mountain

Providing a formidable backdrop to Fort William and Loch Linnhe, Ben Nevis towers 1,345 metres (4,412 feet) high. It's the highest peak in Britain and, make no mistake, it's a tough climb. You're setting off close to sea level so there's a lot of mountain to hike up. Allow around 7 hours to get up and down the mountain, with the most popular starting point being at the Ben Nevis Visitor Centre (☎ 01349 781401 ♥ PH33 6ST www.highlifehighland.com/bennevis). In the summer months you'll encounter people racing up and down on their way to try and complete the Three Peaks Challenge – Ben Nevis, Scafell and Snowdon in 24 hours.

△ The incredible Neptune's Staircase allows boats to navigate the steep incline to the Caledonian Canal.

Getting here

On the shores of Loch Eil, Fort William has good road and rail links considering its location. Follow the A82 from either Glasgow or Inverness to get here in the car or take a train to arrive in the town centre.

Neptune's Staircase

An incredible feat of 19th-century engineering, the series of eight canal locks at Banavie allows barges to tackle a 20-metre (66-foot) incline in just a quarter of a mile. Negotiating this series of canal elevators might take up to 90 minutes, but Neptune's Staircase plays an essential role at the Caledonian Canal's southern tip for those boats travelling between east and west Scotland. It's an awesome sight that's best viewed from a distance, at the other side of the road and train track. This is the biggest staircase lock on the British canal network and those who travel up and down it can complete a floating coast-to-coast journey.

△ Visiting Neptune's Staircase at night is an illuminating experience.

One of the world's greatest railway journeys

Any list of scenic railway journeys worth its salt will include the beautiful line that winds from Fort William to Mallaig. Many argue the 135km (84-mile) round trip on the edge of the Scottish Highlands is without peers. Regular services run to Mallaig and, of course, offer the same views as special services. But if you're going to make a once-in-a-lifetime journey along these famous rails, why not embrace the Age of Steam? West Coast Railways (www.westcoastrailways.co.uk) have daily services during the holiday months that see the famous steam engine The Jacobite pulling carriages over viaducts and alongside lochs. There's nothing quite like experiencing a nostalgic journey by steam engine in such remarkable surroundings. It's a bombardment on the senses. Seeing the plumes of steam rise from the engine before you as it rounds a corner is matched by the hypnotic smell of burning coal and the spine-tingling peep of the whistle. The highlight of the trip has to be the 21-arch Glenfinnan Viaduct that the engine chugs over. Overlooking Loch Shiel and the Jacobite Monument, this gorgeous structure was made famous in the Harry Potter films as the Hogwarts Express sped back to school for the new term. On the final stretch into Mallaig, keep an eye out for the River Morar. At less than 1km (half a mile) in length, this is one of the shortest rivers in the country, flowing from the western edge of Loch Morar and into the sea. When the train comes to a stop in Mallaig, Loch Nevis – the deepest of all the seawater lochs – is just a stone's throw away and adds an enchanting element to the west coast scene.

Mallaig – sailing to the Small Isles

Hidden away on the western coast and surrounding beautiful coastal and mountain landscapes, Mallaig can be a bit of a shock. The charming little port is not what many expect. Although there is an undoubtedly quaint aspect to Mallaig and plenty of photo-friendly scenes, this is a busy, vibrant place that has plenty of people passing through. The well-serviced train line and regular ferry services to Skye and the Small Isles ensure there is plenty of hustle and bustle about the place. Fishing boats coming and going add to Mallaig's dynamic character. If you have longer to spend in this beautiful corner of Scotland, jump on a Caledonian MacBrayne ferry (www.calmac.co.uk) to explore the isles of Eigg, Rum, Muck and Canna – collectively known as the Small Isles. It's possible to visit one or more of these unique communities in a day trip.

Stay a while

🛏 Torcastle House, Torcastle, Banavie, Fort William, PH33 7PB. ☎ 01397 701633
www.torcastlebandbfortwilliam.co.uk

🧳 The Garrison, High Street, Fort William, PH33 6EE. ☎ 01397 602021
www.thegarrisonhotel.co.uk

⛺ Glen Nevis Caravan and Camping Park, Glen Nevis, Fort William, PH33 6SX.
☎ 01397 702191
www.glen-nevis.co.uk/campsite

15

KYLE OF LOCHALSH
STAR OF THE SCREEN

Why visit?

⭐ Enjoy picturesque views you may recognise from blockbuster films and TV shows

⭐ Take a selfie at Eilean Donan Castle – one of the most photographed scenes in the country

⭐ Go that little bit further and take a trip over the Skye Bridge to experience island life

Eilean Donan – there can be only one

Driving along the coast to the Kyle of Lochalsh, the A87 brings you to one of the most iconic and oft-photographed scenes in Scotland. Eilean Donan Castle (☎ 01599 555202 www.eileandonancastle.com ⚲ IV40 8DX) sits on an island at the point where three beautiful sea lochs meet – Loch Alsh, Loch Long and Loch Duich. The setting is sublime and the castle gets an A grade in aesthetics during all weathers. Eilean Donan – or Isle of Donan – is named after the sixth-century Irish saint, Bishop Donan, who is thought to have formed a community on the island. The first fortifications were built in the 13th century and various changes were made to the buildings down the centuries. After lying neglected and ruined for 200 years, the fortune of Eilean Donan changed for the better when Lt Colonel John MacRae-Gilstrap bought the island in 1911 and began a programme of restoration that followed earlier plans and was finished in 1932. Five decades later, the castle's most famous moment came when it featured in the *Highlander* series of films starring Christopher Lambert and Sean Connery. Stepping across the bridge exploring the castle is a journey through centuries of history and culture.

▽ Eilean Donan – the 20th-century castle has been featured in several films and TV shows.

The other Macbeth…

If the scenery around Plockton looks familiar, it may be because you've seen it before on the small screen. All three series of *Hamish Macbeth* were filmed here, following the career of the titular police officer played by Robert Carlyle and his terrier, Wee Jock. The small village has much to offer those coming here for the peace and solitude they've seen on TV. Secluded bays with coral beaches offer stunning views. Abundant bird and marine life provide plenty of reasons to bring your binoculars. A National Trust for Scotland Conservation Village, Plockton does well to balance its heritage and natural beauty with tourism. Be sure to check out the gallery while you're there; it's a showcase for the local artistic talent that takes advantage of the many inspirational scenes.

Getting here

Follow signs for the Isle of Skye, taking the A87 as it heads west and reaches the shores of Loch Alsh. A regular train service from Inverness terminates at the station close to the shore of the loch.

First and last...

The whitewashed buildings of Kyle are home to a busy little village when you think about its remote location. This is the last stop on the mainland before tourists from all over the world make their way to the Isle of Skye. For many, it's a place to get cash from the bank and pick up provisions before delving in to island life on Skye or beyond on the Western Isles. Most people will simply cruise straight by Kyle, but it's worth exploring the pier and shoreline to sample the magnificent views across the loch. Several boat companies based near the railway station offer trips out on to the sea, spotting marine life and enjoying the mountains that tower up high above the water.

Standing at Skye's edge

Just 500m (1,640 feet) across the loch from Kyle of Lochalsh, you can see the goings-on in Kyleakin on the Isle of Skye. Until the 1990s, a local ferry service was the only link between the two communities and travellers had to queue up to make the five-minute journey. Work started on the famous Skye road bridge in 1992, opening up to traffic three years later. But rather than being celebrated as a way of shortening the journey time and increasing convenience, the bridge became the focus of much controversy because of the tolls charged. The cost of a round trip rose to over £11 by 2004 and many locals staged protests by refusing to pay the charge. Hundreds were arrested over the years and over 100 were convicted. At the end of 2004, the Scottish government bought the bridge and tolls were immediately removed. Today, it's free to take the short journey from Kyle of Lochalsh over to the Isle of Skye.

Stay a while

🛏 Conchra House, Kyle, IV40 8DZ.
📞 01599 555233
www.conchrahouse.com

🧳 Tingle Creek Hotel, Erbusaig, Kyle, IV40 8BB. 📞 01599 534430
www.tinglecreek-hotel.co.uk

⛺ Shiel Bridge Caravan Park and Campsite, Shiel Bridge, IV40 8HW. 📞 01599 511221
shielbridgecaravanpark.co.uk

△ The tidal loch is framed by magnificent mountain and forest scenery.

16

ULLAPOOL
A FISHING TOWN OF BEAUTY ON THE NC500

Why visit?

★ One of the highlights of the popular North Coast 500 road trip

★ Linger amid the quaint streets and specialist shops to appreciate Ullapool's charming character

★ Spend an afternoon fly-fishing in a coastal loch to wind down from our fast-paced lives

NC500

Since being launched by Scottish tourism marketers in 2015, the North Coast 500 has exploded in popularity and breathed a new lease of life into many remote Highland destinations. With over 500 miles (830km) of stunning scenery and heritage to explore, the newly promoted route has pulled in people from all over the world. It's been listed among the best road trips to take on the planet and become known as the 'Scottish Route 66'. Starting and ending at Inverness Castle in the capital of the Highlands, those making the pilgrimage pass through the Black Isle, Easter Ross, Caithness, Sutherland and Wester Ross. Calling at mountains, beaches, rivers and towns, this circular route has earned a fabulous global reputation for a reason. If you're wanting a UK road trip, there's nothing that can match the NC500.

Experience Ullapool

It doesn't take long to walk around Ullapool's town centre. An hour or two should leave plenty of time to browse gift shops and enjoy a drink at the harbour. But expect to spend a lot longer in Ullapool if you're going to get a real feel for this calm and relaxed Highland community, perched on the coast with whitewashed buildings surrounded by mountains. The idyllic setting gives Ullapool the romantic air of a Nordic fishing village by the fjords, a charming characteristic that can be

Getting here

On the banks of Loch Broom and a gateway to the Summer Isles and Lewis, Ullapool is found at the north-western extremes of the A835 leading from Inverness.

△ The fishing industry has been important to Ullapool for centuries.

appreciated at every turn. The longer you stay, the more you'll be able to immerse yourself in the easy-going coastal lifestyle and enjoy the outdoor activities tourists flock here for.

The boom on Loch Broom

A golden era of mackerel fishing attracted the attention of many European fishermen between the 1970s and 1990s. The klondyking era saw the Ullapool community living alongside crews of Eastern Bloc countries, who would come to the sheltered waters of Loch Broom to spend the winter months. A flotilla of factory-processing fishing boats would be a common sight in the loch. Some fascinating photographs of this period in the town's history are on display at Ullapool Museum on West Argyle Street (☎ 01854 612987 ullapoolmuseum.co.uk ♀ IV26 2TY). A pair of leather sea boots and a collection of other items from the klondyking period are on display, alongside other key items that celebrate the links Ullapool has with the ocean. These include a pair of pistols given to Robert Melville, the merchant from Dunbar who helped to establish Ullapool as a fishing station in 1788. Emigration to Nova Scotia is another important theme explored at the museum. Ullapool was the last place seen by many who became displaced during the clearances and decided to start a new life in a distant land.

Cast away day-to-day stress

For many people, nothing quite gets them away from the humdrum of day-to-day life like the

🔔 Stay a while

🛏 Creagan Guest House, 18 Pulteney Street, Ullapool, IV26 2UP. ☎ 01854 612397 www.creaganguesthouse.com

🧳 Ceilidh Place, 14 West Argyle Street, Ullapool, IV26 2TY. ☎ 01854 612103 www.theceilidhplace.com

⛺ Clachtoll Beach Campsite, 134 Clachtoll, IV27 4JD. ☎ 01571 855377 www.clachtollbeachcampsite.co.uk

peace and tranquillity of fishing. On a beautiful day, with a stunning mountainous backdrop, you can be alone with your thoughts, birdsong and the ripple of the water. Those trying their luck fly-fishing in these parts could encounter Atlantic salmon, Arctic char, sea trout and wild brown trout. Finding the right place where you're able – and allowed – to spend a day fishing can be tricky, but local experts such as James Curley (☎ 01854 666232 www.jamescurley.org ♀ IV27 4HH) are on hand to help plan the perfect day by the water, whether you want personal solitude or a family adventure.

CAPE WRATH
AT WORLD'S END

17

Why visit?

★ An adventure involving a small ferry and a bus to take you to the remotest spot on the mainland

★ Stand beneath the most northerly lighthouse in Britain – designed by the grandfather of Robert Louis Stevenson

★ Pick up a snack in the café and imagine sailing away to Iceland or the Faroe Islands, the next countries you'd reach

Cape Wrath

You can often feel you're at the end of the world when standing on the edge of the coast, gazing out to endless sea. But Cape Wrath is different. Knowing you're as far north-west as you can go on the British mainland leaves you with an exhilarating feeling. The fact that this place is so remote and accessed by a small ferry just adds to the senses.

When your feet are planted on the clifftop at Cape Wrath, you're part of the north-west corner that makes up the jigsaw of Britain. With only water between you and the Arctic, the feeling of isolation is not matched anywhere else in Britain. The cape comprises 277 sq km (107 sq miles) of wild moorland. But it's the furthermost tip that grabs all the attention. The iconic lighthouse was built in 1828 by well-known designer Robert Stevenson and was manned until 1998 when operation became automatic. Standing atop a huge cliff, the light is 122 metres (400 feet) above sea level and in clear weather should be visible from 40km (25 miles) away. Foggy, rainy and misty conditions – so rife in this part of the world – often restrict the light's reach. In the early 20th century, a lower beam of light was planned to deal with the weather, but it was never completed.

▷ **The most extreme part of Britain's coastline – getting to Cape Wrath is an adventure in itself.**

The long and winding road...

Getting to such a remote outpost as Cape Wrath is never going to be an easy task. But if you find yourself on the north coast of Scotland, it would be rude not to go the extra few miles and reach this north-western extremity. Standing on the edge and gazing out to sea gives you an uncommon feeling even if you are familiar with travelling around the British coast. Here, 1,176km (731 miles) from London, you would reach the Faroe Islands and Iceland if you sailed across the waves to the north-west. Even if you're in the vicinity and are due to pass on the North Coast 500, don't think you can simply nip over to Cape Wrath without thinking it through. It's a complicated journey involving a ferry and a minibus that needs to be well timed. But you'll be glad you put in the effort to stand on the clifftop and gaze out from Cape Wrath.

△ A dramatic coastline, full of stacks, stumps and caves.

There are three steps to heaven...

Step 1: Drive to Keoldale and get ready to begin your trip. From Durness on the north coast, follow the A838 south-west until the picturesque Kyle of Durness comes into view. There'll be ferry signs guiding you to the right, down a small country road. At the bottom, all those making the homage to Cape Wrath wait for the small ferry to sail back across.

Step 2: There's not much to be found at Keoldale, just space to park your car and some information about crossing times. It's not a year-round service, so check out in advance when this small boat operates (www.visitcapewrath.com). The crossing only takes around ten minutes, giving you the chance to enjoy some fabulous views from the middle of the water as you head across. Pay the ferryman during the journey to the other side.

Step 3: You'll be greeted by a minibus waiting for you as the boat gets in. There is a separate fare payable for this service, which is the only way to get to Cape Wrath and back for a day visit. Buckle up and get ready for the bumpy ride along the 18km (11-mile) track. To try and cut down on the white-knuckle factor, the drivers take it easy and don't go above 24kph (15mph). They also provide an informative and entertaining commentary on the way up, pointing out local landmarks and wildlife.

When to visit?

Getting to Cape Wrath is dependent on the ferry and minibus. The operating season runs from Easter until mid-October, avoiding the poor weather over winter. Days where conditions are too stormy may also cause services to be cancelled. Look on the Cape Wrath website for other days when there may be cancellations. The Ministry of Defence using the area and the

△ Cape Wrath's lighthouse provides a warning for ships out to sea and a nearby café welcomes intrepid explorers.

Highland Games programme in Durness have led to disruption in previous years.

The café that never sleeps

Spend a weekend in the Big Apple and you'll be used to eateries that never close their doors; however, it's not what you might expect in the wild Highlands around Durness. But the Ozone Café, found near the tip of the land in the shadow of the lighthouse at Cape Wrath, prides itself with its round-the-clock opening hours. Not that there's a rush on at 3 a.m. on a Wednesday morning, but the door is always open. Unless it's too cold, that is.

Stay a while

🛏 Bae Seren, Smoo, Durness, IV27 4QA.
☎ 01971 511437
www.baeseren.wixsite.com

💼 The Old School, Inshegra, Lairg, IV27 4RJ. ☎ 01971 521383
www.oldschoolklb.co.uk

⛺ Sango Sands Oasis, Sango Bay, Durness, IV27 4PZ. ☎ 07838 381065
www.sangosands.com

BALNAKEIL

A CRAFTY BIT OF COASTLINE

Why visit?

★ A wonderful beach on the northern coast of Scotland, it's the ultimate place to get away from it all

★ See the tumbling waterfall in Smoo Cave, where a river crashes through a hole in the ground into a stunning natural feature

★ Explore craft shops in a village established in buildings intended for use in the Cold War

Smoo Cave

Looking mysterious enough from the surface to tempt most passers-by to investigate, Smoo Cave consumes the Allt Smoo river as it tumbles down from a loch in the hills. Watching the flow of water cascade into the unknown is mesmerising and the journey down the steps to the cave itself is revealing. The huge entrance drips with rainwater that has permeated through the few metres of land above your head. The real jewel in this Scottish cave lies inside, where the Allt Smoo's waterfall drops majestically 21 metres (69 feet) through the pothole into a freshwater lake hidden away from the coast. In the summer months, tours of the cave can be taken and it's even possible to get up close to the waterfall on a boat trip. Smoo Cave is found just to the east of Durness village (☎ 01971 511704 ♀ IV27 4QB).

△ Smoo Cave contains a picturesque waterfall and is a carnival for the senses.

Balnakeil Beach

This is simply one of the best places to unwind along the entire coast of the UK. Balnakeil Beach (♀ IV27 4PX) is a fabulous sandy stretch, so remote that you're unlikely to encounter too many people while you're here. The mighty dunes at the back of the beach are a powerful nod to the strong winds that batter this coast at times and build them up into the formidable landscape they are. A small car park sits next to the dunes, while the location is perfect for the golf course 300 metres (1,000 feet) down a track. Balnakeil Beach is cared for by locals and it's a very clean environment. Visitors are asked to

🔔 **Stay a while**

🛏 Hillside B&B, Hillside, Durness, IV27 4QA. ☎ 01971 511737

🧳 Smoo Cave Hotel, Lairg, IV27 4QB. ☎ 01971 511227 new.smoocavehotel.co.uk

⛺ Sango Sands Oasis, Sango Bay, Durness, IV27 4PZ ☎ 07838 381065 www.sangosands.com

△ Expect the beaches on the north of Scotland to be quiet, with the chance of seeing military drills at Balnakeil.

pick up a piece of plastic if they see one and place it in a dedicated bin. The isolated nature of this northern coast means there's not a great deal of variety when it comes to staying over, but if you can build an overnight here into your itinerary, it will be long remembered.

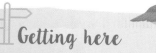

Getting here

Head along the Scottish north coast, following the A838 west from Tongue. Balnakeil Beach is a short distance down the road from Durness. Smoo Cave sits on the A838 east of Durness.

Northern craft

As the Cold War was hotting up in the 1950s, a number of odd-looking buildings were constructed in the remote Highlands with the intention of housing a nuclear missile early-warning system. But the Ministry of Defence facility was never commissioned and by the 60s the small village at Balnakeil started to host a much more creative industry. Advertisements were placed in the national newspapers offering skilled craftspeople a place to work for minimal rent and a new society was introduced to the north coast. Without power or running water, initial conditions were very basic, but the artists started arriving to transform Balnakeil into a thriving art scene. Today it's still home to many creative folk, including a glassmaker, woodturner, painter, hairstylist and masseuse (♥ IV27 4PT).

A mountain of chocolate

Every family needs a nice café to make a day at the beach perfect, whether it's to escape a rainy spell, have a rest from playing or warm up with a coffee. The wild coastline of northern Scotland can bear the full brunt of some unwelcoming weather and its remote location means facilities are few and far between. Fortunately, Balnakeil has a top-quality place to spend a chocolatey hour. A short distance from the beach at Balnakeil, at the entrance to the craft village, you'll find Cocoa Mountain and the tasty treasures it holds within (📞 01971 511233 www.cocoamountain.co.uk ♥ IV27 4PT). Drinks with chocolate spilling over the edge, flavoured chocs on the side, delightful pastries and chocolatey cakes are just some of the sweet treats on offer. The noticeboard serves as a wealth of local information and the small shop tempts you with delicious souvenirs to take home.

EAST SCOTLAND

Far up in the north-eastern corner of the country, John O'Groats is one of the best known and most significant points on our coastal map. The antithesis to Land's End in Cornwall, hundreds of adventures both started and wound up here as people on bikes, in cars and on foot made the journey between our coastal extremes.

Just north of Inverness, the small coastal community of Cromarty is the place to head to for a thrilling RIB ride to glimpse seabirds and dolphins. As you reach Spey Bay – a great place to sample a wee dram of Speyside whisky – you may be lucky

enough to see dolphins from the shore. The Aberdeenshire coast serves up all kinds of treats, from the castle that inspired Dracula to one of the best seal colonies in the country. Scotland is, of course, well known for extravagant Hogmanay celebrations, and the east coast of Scotland is one of the world's top destinations at the end of December. The fireball-swinging ceremony at Stonehaven is often heralded as one of the best ways to welcome in the New Year on the entire planet, let alone in Britain. The best cure for a New Year's Day hangover is to take an early morning dip in the Firth of Forth at South Queensferry. (Fancy dress

is optional.) Scotland's east coast is, of course, a delight to explore all year round. New galleries have seen a punchy revival in Dundee, castles and wildlife havens are to be discovered at regular intervals and the student city of St Andrews is forever popular among golfers, movie buffs and those seeking the place where William met Kate. No eastern Scotland coastal voyage would be complete without going inside the Kelpies and walking by the coast-to-coast Forth and Clyde Canal to the Falkirk Wheel. Whatever you get up to in Scotland, take time to sample the local cuisine – be it fish soup, a glorious plate of fish and chips or a deep-fried Mars Bar – and make sure your days out build in time to spot dolphins and huge bird colonies.

Don't miss

- ✓ Making the far-flung trip up to John O'Groats and gazing out to Orkney
- ✓ Seeing in the New Year with Stonehaven's fireball swingers
- ✓ Teeing off on some of the world's most famous golf courses
- ✓ Running along the sand at St Andrews to recreate the famous scene from *Chariots of Fire*
- ✓ Touring the Royal Yacht *Britannia* to see where the rich and famous were entertained

▽ The dramatic scenery of Slains Castle is the inspiration behind a certain blood-sucking vampire.

19

JOHN O'GROATS
TO THE END OF THE EARTH

Why visit?

★ Stand on the northernmost point on the classic route from Land's End and imagine those setting out 874 miles away

★ Explore one of the Queen Mother's favourite castles and learn how it was renovated

★ Try a tipple of an alcoholic spirit you don't normally associate with Scotland

Castle of Mey – a favourite of the Queen Mother

To the west of John O'Groats sits a royal castle the Queen Mother took a shine to and lovingly restored in the 1950s. The Castle of Mey, or Barrogill Castle as it was then known, was in a poor state of repair until it came under royal ownership. Once restored, the Queen Mother would spend three weeks here every August and come back for ten more days in October. Today, the castle is open for tours of the rooms and a chance to wander around the gardens and enjoy the sea views before unwinding in the café (☎ 01847 851473 www.castleofmey.org.uk ♥ KW14 8XH).

🪧 Getting here

Head north on the A9 from Inverness, taking the A99 from Wick. John O'Groats and other local destinations are signed from the main road.

▷ Duncansby Head is a place of unmatched beauty in this north-east corner of Scotland.

▽ The historic Castle of Mey was a favourite coastal retreat of the Queen Mother.

John O'Groats

Compared to the carnival of attractions available at Land's End, those arriving at the other end of the famously epic 874-mile (1,407km) slog are in for a relatively calm experience. There's still a collection of gift shops vying for your Scottish pound and the famous signpost beckons for an obligatory photo. But there aren't the crowds here that flock to the tip of Cornwall. Critics may say the area is in need of some care, attention and investment to bring it up to the mark, but there's also a charming absence of commercialism about the place. As the coach parties roll up and people are allowed a 30-minute stop, there's a 'been there, done that' element to John O'Groats that suggests some people are here simply to tick it off their list and go home with a souvenir. Fishing boats, sculptures and an inn add to the landscape, but on a clear day the real views lay across the sea, where Orkney lures you to continue your adventure. Boats for the islands leave further along the coast at Scrabster (☎ 0845 6000 449 www.northlinkferries.co.uk ⊙ KW14 7UT).

Duncansby Head

John O'Groats may steal the limelight on this stretch of coastline, but for the real jaw-dropping view and, indeed, to get to the true north-eastern extreme of Scotland, you need to go to Duncansby Head. The lighthouse is at the end of a country track that leads off from John O'Groats and a short walk to the south brings you to the scenic wonder that is the natural rocky arch called Thirle Door. Beyond are the Stacks of Duncansby, jutting up from the sea. It's a stunning landscape that seems to change and evolve with every step you take along the clifftop path.

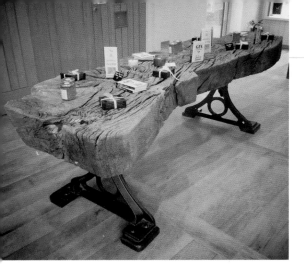

△ Scotland isn't just about whisky, as you'll learn at Dunnet Bay gin distillery.

Scotch gin

Although world famous as a whisky-producing nation, this corner of Scotland is developing the market for specialist gin and vodka. Martin Murray and his wife, Claire, set up Dunnet Bay Distillery (☎ 01847 851287 www.dunnet baydistillers.co.uk ♥ KW14 8XD) in 2014 and its range of flavoured spirits have gone on to win nationwide awards. Northern Scotland tipples such as Rock Rose Gin and Holy Grass Vodka are now tempting buyers on the international market who want to broaden their horizons when sampling a Scottish short.

Thurso

Although it's only a small town, arriving in Thurso has a 'bright lights, big city' feeling after travelling around this remote stretch of northern coastline. If you're after services such as High Street shops, supermarkets, cafés and restaurants, Thurso is going to be your best bet. If you're just passing through, it's a pleasant place to while away an afternoon. Be sure to stroll along Janet Street, which has a great vantage overlooking the River Thurso and the town's main bridge. The historic Meadow Well is worth a visit; it was here that Thurso residents accessed fresh water for hundreds of years. The circular building was built around the well in 1823 and it remained in use until a more sufficient supply from Loch Calder became used. Be sure to pop in and see Ian Pearson's Glass Creations on Riverside Road to gain an insight into how glass can be made into sparkling sculptures (☎ 07816 762601 www.glasscreationsthurso.co.uk ♥ KW14 8BU).

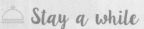

🔔 **Stay a while**

🛏 Hamnavoe, Roadside, John O'Groats KW1 4YR ☎ 01955 611776 www.johnogroatsbnb.com

🧳 Seaview Hotel, County Road, John O'Groats, KW1 4YR. ☎ 01955 611220 www.seaviewjohnogroats.co.uk

⛺ John O'Groats Caravan and Camping, County Road, John O'Groats, KW1 4YR. ☎ 01955 611329 www.johnogroatscampsite.co.uk

△ Tourism and fishing combine to dominate the local economy at John O'Groats.

20

CROMARTY
WILDLIFE AND THE
GHOSTS OF INDUSTRY

Why visit?

★ Speed across the Moray Firth on a boat in search of dolphins and basking sharks

★ Gaze out at the huge oil rigs that are towed here when not needed at sea

★ Visit a quaint museum to dig out information about fossils

Dolphins and ocean spray

Speeding away from Cromarty on a RIB in search of marine wildlife is an activity you'll never forget. It's also one to wrap up warm for. No matter how much the on-land temperature may lure you into a false sense of security, hitting the open waves at a fair pace is usually a chilly affair. Fortunately, the trips put on by Cromarty-based EcoVentures (☏ 01381 600323 www.ecoventures.co.uk ♀ IV11 8YE) include all the weatherproofing equipment you'll need. There's a wealth of wildlife to spot when out on the Moray Firth. Bottlenose dolphins tend to be the most often encountered, but keep an eye out for basking sharks and pilot whales as well. There's no guarantee of seeing them, of course; these are wild creatures, not animals trained to perform. But the skipper knows the best places to look and the noticeboard in the office is full of recent sightings. Another highlight of the trips is the visit to the seabird breeding colony at North Sutor, where you'll get the chance to view razorbill, shag, kittiwake, guillemot and fulmar. Expect splashes as you speed across the waves and prepare to see plenty.

△ There are spectacular dolphin-watching opportunities to be had from the small town of Cromarty.

△ The Cromarty Firth is the place where huge rigs come to be repaired and retired.

🔔 Stay a while

🛏 The Factor's House, Denny Road, Cromarty, IV11 8YT. ☎ 01381 600394 www.thefactorshouse.com

🧳 Royal Hotel, Marine Terrace, Cromarty, IV11 8YN. ☎ 01383 600217 www.royalhotel-cromarty.co.uk

⛺ Rosemarkie Camping and Caravanning, Ness Road East, Rosemarkie, IV10 8SE ☎ 01381 621117 www.campingandcaravanningclub.co.uk

Graveyard of the rigs

In such an exceptionally beautiful environment, the queuing oil rigs on the Cromarty Firth paint a strangely stark picture as they wait their turn to be towed away. These once productive industrial giants that have been placed in storage off Cromarty are, ironically, one of the most hypnotic and fascinating features on this stretch of the Scottish coast. The four-legged beasts, complete with living facilities, helicopter landing pads and huge cranes, were once at the centre of North Sea oil and gas production. The rigs stored here are waiting to be repaired, scrapped or redeployed. The number of rigs sitting off the coast here can reflect the ups and downs of the global oil industry. When demand is booming, the old rigs off Cromarty could be put to use once more. A downturn, however, can lead to a lengthening of the line waiting to be worked on. Many of the sightseeing trips out to sea will take you up close to these hulks. Some have now become an important home for seabirds.

Hugh Miller's Cottage

Inspirational geologist, fossil hunter and author Hugh Miller was born in Cromarty in 1802. The cottage where he spent his early years is open for visitors and adjoins an informative museum that tells the story of how Miller began work in a quarry and developed an interest in geology (☎ 01381 600245 www.nts.org.uk ⚲IV11 8XA). Run by the National Trust for Scotland, there's a great collection of Miller's tools, fossils and manuscripts in the museum, along with a sundial pedestal he carved that now sits in the Lydia Garden – named after his wife. Visitors can take an audio tour around the cottage or, if booked in advance, arrange a guided tour delivered by an expert. Much of the commentary on the self-guided audio experience is in Miller's own words as he wrote about the place he was born and the garden he played in as a child.

Across to Nigg

Across the Cromarty Firth at Nigg, you'll be able to see the Fabrication Yard where workers are busy refurbishing oil rigs. It's here where oil

△ Have a splash on one of the high-speed wildlife tours.

is piped in from the Beatrice Oil Field in the Moray Firth. The development of the North Sea oil industry created many jobs for skilled workers in and around Nigg, leading to an improvement in local infrastructure. Two bridges took the A9 across the Cromarty and Beauly Firths in the early 1980s, cutting down the driving time for those heading north from Inverness. The small ferry from Cromarty still heads across to Nigg during the summer months, carrying foot passengers and a maximum of two vehicles.

Getting here

Cromarty is at the tip of the Black Isle and is reached by heading north from Inverness on the A9 before taking the A832 and following it east until you run out of land.

SPEY BAY
A DOLPHIN'S TALE

21

Why visit?

★ Stand on the shoreline in wonder at dolphins playing in the Moray Firth

★ Enjoy an afternoon walking on the coastal path and snap a picture of the incredible Bow Fiddle Rock

★ Work up an appetite for a steaming bowl of Cullen skink – there's nothing better to warm you up!

Grace of pod

Bring your binoculars to Spey Bay and head straight for the Scottish Dolphin Centre for some casual spotting from the shoreline (📞 01343 820339 dolphincentre.whales.org 📍IV32 7PJ). Your chances of seeing some of the world's largest bottlenose dolphins are good in the summer months as they gracefully swim and jump in the Moray Firth. Various boat trips are available from Inverness and Cromarty to view these magnificent creatures on the water, but don't underestimate the sheer joy of seeing a pod from the pebble-strewn coast. During the summer months, talks are regularly given by the staff at the Scottish Dolphin Centre and there's

Getting here

The northern coast of Aberdeenshire and Moray is not heavily populated. Towns and villages strewn along this rugged edge of Scotland don't benefit from a steady stream of passing trade; it's not a place you pass on the way to anywhere. Even the A96 heading east from Inverness cuts the corner off instead of heading all the way around the coast. But those negotiating the local roads and branching out from Inverness, Aberdeen and Fraserburgh will be rewarded with some amazing natural wonders.

△ Bow Fiddle Rock, which also looks a bit like a toothbrush.

the chance to go on a dolphin-spotting walk with them as they regularly monitor how many are in the area. Leave time for the Icehouse tour, which takes you beneath the surface of the 19th-century salmon-fishing industry. In this underground storage area, huge quantities of Spey Bay salmon were packed in ice brought from nearby before being transported down to London markets. It's an informative glimpse into the region's heritage.

When to visit

The Scottish Dolphin Centre has seasonal opening times and there is more opportunity to sign up for activities in the summer months. Check times with the centre before you set off.

On the fiddle

Having stopped in a nondescript car park and followed a muddy path to the well-signed Bow Fiddle Rock at Portknockie, some may have low expectations of this being anything out of the ordinary. But this fabulous quartzite feature, home to thousands of gulls, has jaw-dropping appeal. Best viewed from the small, pebble-covered bay at the end of the footpath, standing before Bow Fiddle Rock is a mesmerising experience it's difficult to pull yourself away from. Non-musical tourists may struggle to see the exact resemblance to a bow fiddle and notice other obvious shapes in this magical formation. But Tooth Brush Rock just doesn't have the same ring to it.

Local delicacy

Make it your mission to try a bowl of Cullen skink. The best place to order your serving of this fishy soup is in Cullen itself, the home of the Cullen Skink World Championships. Lily's Kitchen on Seafield Street (☎ 01542 488816 📍AB56 4SH) has been a winner and the Cullen

skink there is something to behold! If you're peckish at the western end of this stretch of coast, head to the Bandstand Restaurant at Nairn (☎ 01667 452341 www.braevalhotel.co.uk 📍IV12 4NB). With cracking views, a good range of seafood meals, vegetarian options and over 100 types of whisky to choose from, this is a popular place to eat.

△ This rugged coastline is fabulous for taking walks all year round.

🍽 Stay a while

🛏 The Rest B&B, The Rest, Spey Bay, IV32 7PJ. ☎ 01343 821608 www.therestspeybay.co.uk

🏨 The Garmouth, South Road, Garmouth, is a 3-star hotel on the other side of the Spey, IV32 7LU. ☎ 01343 870226 www.garmouthhotel.co.uk.

⛺ The Speyside Camping and Caravanning Club Site is found slightly inland at Aberlour, AB38 9SL. ☎ 01340 810414 www.campingandcaravanningclub.co.uk

22

PETERHEAD
THE BLOO TOON!

Fishing with conviction

Perching on the most easterly point of mainland Scotland, Peterhead is home to nearly 19,000 people – the biggest settlement in Aberdeenshire. Because of the blue stockings originally worn by local fishermen, Peterhead is often called the 'Bloo Toon' and the folk who live there the 'Bloo Tooners'. You'll find all kinds of 'Blue Toon' businesses in Peterhead, from a small microbrewery to a fish and chip shop and car valeting company. Fishing has been at the heart of Peterhead for centuries – the first harbour here was built in 1593 – and it remains important today. Despite pressures from imports and government fisheries' policies, over 500 fishermen are still employed in Peterhead. The harbour is a busy place with many large fishing boats coming and going. Measuring more than 120 hectares (300 acres), it was created by two large breakwaters and built in part by convicts from the local prison. The visually stunning jail is now open as a museum, highlighting what life was like for those serving time there between 1888 and 2013. It's an amazing place that will deliver stories of inmates inside the prison walls and explain the importance it had in the local community (📞 01779 482200 www.peterheadprisonmuseum.com 📍AB42 2ZX).

Getting here

Head north from Aberdeen on the A90 to access Peterhead and other attractions along this part of the Scottish coastline.

Inspiring horror

Cruden Bay was a popular haunt for Bram Stoker and he returned many times, seeking solitude and inspiration to write his much-loved stories. On a return visit to the bay in 1895, his famous *Dracula* novel started to take shape. His imagination was fired by Slains Castle, which stands atop a dramatic clifftop. Stormy days in Cruden Bay conjure up blistering sea conditions that can be terrifying to gaze upon. It's thought that on one of these squally occasions, Bram Stoker sat near the castle on the cliff as his

△ There's gothic horror within the beauty of Slains Castle.

characters and events fell into place. And so we have the classic image of Count Dracula emerging from the castle window and climbing down the steep wall, spider-like, while a 'dreadful abyss' loomed below.

Where Bram Stoker stayed...

The accommodation chosen by the creator of *Dracula* is still open today and a popular destination for lovers of the Gothic tale. It was 1894 when Bram Stoker first checked in to the Kilmarnock Arms. You can see the legendary author's signature in the Victorian guest book. After his stay he wrote *The Watter's Mou*, a tale based around Cruden Bay that actually features the manager of the Kilmarnock Arms at the time, James Cruickshank. Bram Stoker was certainly impressed with his visit. His guest-book entry reads: 'Delighted with everything and everybody and hope to come again.'

Barrels of Cruden oil

You won't see any evidence of it as you wander around Cruden Bay, but beneath your feet is an important 177km-long (110 mile) oil pipeline. It is pumping the black gold from the Forties oil field in the North Sea on to the mainland. From below Cruden Bay, the pipe heads to nearby Whinnyfold and then enters an overground pipe taking it to Grangemouth.

Seal of approval

Experience the wonder of viewing a seal colony at close hand a few miles south of Cruden Bay, at Newburgh. From the car park at the end of Beach Road, take one of the paths over the dunes to the sandy banks of the River Ythan. Across the water is a colony of over 400 seals, and they look stunning basking in the sun if you're lucky

enough for it to be out. On any given day, the whole stretch of the river will be dotted with seals, diving around and popping up for a nosy at who is on the banks. Just remember that this is a conservation area designed to give the seals a place to rest. Don't get too close because it can cause them unnecessary stress. It's not just the seals that make this a worthy place to go for a walk, though. The long, sandy beach is a great spot to take off your shoes and socks and embrace nature. The extensive dune network provides a picturesque backdrop and you're sure to encounter some of the eider ducks, diving terns and oystercatchers that call this ecosystem home.

△ A lonesome seal can sometimes show crazy levels of curiosity.

🔔 Stay a while

🛏 Trinity Boutique, 104 Queen Street, Peterhead, AB42 1TY ☎ 07805 824211 www.trinityboutiquebb.com

🏨 Kilmarnock Arms Hotel, Bridge Street, Cruden Bay, AB42 0HD ☎ 01779 812213 www.kilmarnockarms.com

⛺ Ythan Valley Campsite, Smithfield, Ellon, AB41 7TH. ☎ 01358 761400

23

STONEHAVEN
GREAT BALLS OF FIRE!

Why visit?

★ Stay up to welcome in the New Year with people from around the world, watching Stonehaven's swinging fireballs

★ Spend time in Aberdeen and pay a visit to the Maritime Museum

★ Stroll along the cliffs from Stonehaven to the picturesque clifftop castle at Dunnottar

△ The swingers of fireballs in Stonehaven keep this age-old tradition ablaze.

A swinging New Year

Search online for the best things in the world to do on New Year's Eve and you're sure to find a visit to this small Scottish harbour town in the Top Ten. Thousands of merrymakers line the streets on 31 December from 10pm in readiness for one of Britain's most bizarre and spectacular traditions. Local men and women known as swingers emerge before midnight with specially made spherical metal cages packed with burnable household objects. The fireballs are attached to a handle so they can be swung around the swingers' heads. In the dying minutes of December, they set fire to their load and parade up and down the street after the bell tower rings in the New Year. The balls of fire are whirled around with passion and precision for 20 minutes before the flames start to die down. With a cheer and a drum roll, each of the fireballs are hurled into the harbour to douse the flames. Pubs are on hand to serve drinks throughout the night and bagpipers add to the lively atmosphere, all rounded off with an impressive fireworks display. It's a Hogmanay you'll not forget.

 Fish, chips and ice cream

For some of the finest fish and chips in Scotland, head to The Bay on Beach Promenade (☎ 01569 762000 www.thebayfishandchips.co.uk ● AB39 2RD). Once voted the best in the nation, fresh fish here is cooked to order and there's even information on the wall about which boats supplied the catch of the day. Next door, Aunty Bettys is the perfect place to follow up with some delicious ice cream (☎ 01569 763656 ● AB39 2RD).

Prison of the past

For a glimpse into Stonehaven's history, head to the Tolbooth Museum that sits on the harbour (☎ 07512 466329 www.stonehaventolbooth.co.uk ● AB39 2JU). Exhibits from the town's past include a hand-powered washing machine and a tattie masher that survived being in a New Year fireball. But it's the tales from this building's past life as a prison that are most intriguing. As well as the original cell door, there are also historic seven-hole stocks and a stomach-churning punishment device called the crank.

Dunnottar – the castle on the cliff

A stunning walk along the clifftops south of Stonehaven brings you to Dunnottar Castle, a magical fortress perched on a rocky outcrop (☎ 01569 766320 www.dunnottarcastle.co.uk ◉ AB39 2TL). It's only a mile away from the town, but it seems like this journey takes you back in time to a different world. Dunnottar has been the scene of Viking battles and visits from many key Scottish figures, including William Wallace, Mary Queen of Scots and King James VI. More recently, Dunnottar was the film setting for *Hamlet*, starring Mel Gibson.

△ It's a climb to reach Dunnottar Castle – ay, there's the rub!

Home of the deep-fried Mars bar

In 1995, a snack from The Haven in Stonehaven became the stuff of legend. Now known as The Carron Fish Bar, you'll easily spot this well-known eatery on Allardice Street thanks to the banner declaring it the birthplace of deep-fried Mars bars. It may not be good for the diet, but there are plenty who are eager to sample deep-fried delicacies (☎ 01569 765377 ◉ AB39 2BN).

Getting here

The town of Stonehaven is home to around 11,000 people and there's plenty to do in the area for a couple of days. Reach it by heading south of the great Scottish city of Aberdeen and taking the turning off the A90. Stonehaven's train station has direct links with Aberdeen, Edinburgh and Glasgow.

For Auld Lang Syne

William Burns, the father of Scotland's well-known bard, was born in the Stonehaven area, prompting the town to brand itself as Burns' Fatherland. The poet himself visited the land of his forefathers in 1787 and today you can seek tranquillity in the charming Burns Memorial Garden on Belmont Brae. It's a great place to relax with a book of his finest works.

When to visit

There are events to enjoy all year round in Aberdeen, including the Jazz Festival in March and the TechFest in late summer. The key time to be in Stonehaven is New Year's Eve to experience the fireball swinging – but you'll need to book accommodation well in advance.

△ Aberdeen's Maritime Museum, in the heart of the Granite City, teaches about fishing and oil industries – and more!

Stay a while

🛏 Shorehead Guest House, 14 Shorehead, Stonehaven, AB39 2JY.
📞 07753 746043
www.shoreheadguesthouse.co.uk

🍴 The Ship Inn, 5 Shorehead, Stonehaven, AB39 2JY. 📞 01569 762617
www.shipinnstonehaven.com

⛺ Wairds Park Campsite, Beach Road, Johnshaven, DD10 0EP. 📞 01561 362395
www.johnshaven.com/accommodation/wairds-park-campsite

Along the coast to Granite City

A trip up the coast to Aberdeen should include a visit to the brilliant free-to-enter Maritime Museum (📞 01224 337700 www.aagm.co.uk 📍AB11 5BY). With displays exploring the history of the famous 'Granite City', there's plenty to learn here about how local people have had a close relationship with the sea over many centuries. There's good coverage of the city's history, from when the fishing boom started hrough to the exploration of fossil fuels in the North Sea. Not to be missed is the model of an oil rig that takes centre stage across all floors. There's a pleasant café and awe-inspiring views out over the harbour.

24

DUNDEE
DISCOVER A PROUD
INDUSTRIAL HERITAGE

Why visit?

★ Wrap yourself up in the history of textiles

★ Load up memories of 1980s video games

★ Tuck into the region's much-loved Arbroath smokies

This great Scottish city has gone through many industrial changes over the centuries and has contributed a great deal towards the nation's progress. Today, Dundee is home to world-class visitor attractions that chart the changing fortunes of trade by the Tay.

Hey Jute

Shipbuilding and whaling played an important role in the industrial development of Dundee, but the city is best known for jute – the natural fibre that went into rope and sacks. Over 40,000 people were once employed in Dundee's textile trade, leading to the city being known

△ The shipping heritage of Dundee is explored at Discovery Point.

△ When night falls, ambitious lighting transforms the Dundee waterfront.

as 'Juteopolis'. The best way to wrap yourself up in the rich textile history is to visit Verdant Works (☏ 01382 309060 www.verdantworks. com ◉ DD1 5BT), a refurbished and extremely atmospheric mill very much at the centre of the industry. Verdant Works not only focuses on the significance of the jute industry in Dundee, it plots the growing and manufacturing process from start to finish. Local companies' important links to India are explored as you learn about how jute was grown in tropical climates. There's information about how vital Dundee's docks were in the process and you'll see how the textile fibres were created and made into products that benefited a range of other industries. It's a self-guided tour that allows you to move around at your own pace. During a visit, take in the working beam engine that dates back to 1801, hear the bewildering noise of the machines and see how workers spent what little leisure time they had.

The three Js

As well as jute, Dundee is well known for jam and journalism – leading to its 'City of the three Js' nickname. Legend has it that a local woman called Janet Keiller invented marmalade here in the 18th century and so transformed tastes at the nation's breakfast table. Her son, James, went on to launch the city's Keiller jam factory, producing palate-pleasing preserves for decades until the business was sold and moved to England. Jam and jute may be confined to Dundee's history, but there's still a large number of people employed by the third 'J' – journalism. The family firm DC Thomson is known throughout the world for printing comics loved by children and adults alike. Every *Beano* and *Dandy* comic starts life here, along with regional and local newspapers.

Loading… Please wait…

If you're old enough to remember the joys of playing Manic Miner or Jet Set Willy, you owe a debt of gratitude to computer designers based in Dundee during the early 1980s. The Sinclair ZX81 and Spectrum machines were made here, introducing basic graphics gameplay to a generation and using only 16k of memory. See examples in the McManus Gallery in Albert Square (☎ 01382 307200 www.mcmanus.co.uk ⚲ DD1 1DA).

The V&A's northern outpost

Dundee's hugely improved waterfront has the V&A Museum of Design as a focal point (☎ 01382 411611 www.vam.ac.uk ⚲ DD1 4EZ). Housing collections from London's Victoria and

△ The Museum of Design's ship-like, iconic beauty is a work of art in itself.

Albert Museum, it features examples of Scottish designers such as Charles Rennie Mackintosh. The building itself is noteworthy – an ambitious addition to the cityscape from Japanese architect Kengo Kuma.

Stay a while

- The Shaftesbury, 1 Hyndford Street, Dundee, DD2 1HQ. ☎ 01382 669216
- Apex City Quay Hotel and Spa, 1 West Victoria Dock Road, Dundee, DD1 3JP. ☎ 01382 202404 www.apexhotels.co.uk
- Greenacres Campsite, Dronley Road, Dundee, DD2 5QR. ☎ 07740 506076 www.caravanclub.co.uk

The Tay Bridges: Disaster and development

The opening of the Tay Bridge in 1878 was a pivotal moment for industry in Dundee, allowing people and goods to reach Edinburgh and London far faster than before. But three days after Christmas in 1879, disaster struck when the first version of the bridge collapsed and a train heading to Dundee plummeted into the Firth of Tay, killing an estimated 75 people. The bridge was not built strongly enough to handle the strong winds that often batter the region. Extensive testing took place on the replacement bridge before trains could once again enter Dundee in 1887. Cars could avoid the long detour around the Firth of Tay from 1966 when the Tay Road Bridge opened, replacing the old Tay Ferry and being one of the longest bridges in Europe at the time.

Arbroath smokie

Venture north to Arbroath to sample one of Britain's finest regional foods. The Arbroath smokie gained its Protected Geographical Indication from the European Union in 2004. To be called an Arbroath smokie, haddock must be smoked in the traditional manner no more than 8km away from the town. Make your way to the But 'n' Ben restaurant to sample Arbroath smokies in a great setting (☎ 01241 877223 www.thebutnben.com ♥ DD11 5SQ).

△ The Tay Road Bridge is an impressive way to arrive in Dundee.

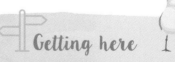

Getting here

Both the A90 and A92 head into Dundee, the latter crossing on the Tay Road Bridge. The railway station is located on the banks of the Tay, close to the V&A Museum.

25

ST ANDREWS
TIME FOR A HIGH TEE

The home of golf

Few places are so synonymously linked with a sport as St Andrews. The Scottish seaside town is known as the 'Home of Golf', with records of games dating back to 1552. The place has golf flowing through its veins. Stay for a few hours and you're sure to see people making their way around St Andrews with golf bags as they excitedly head for a round on some of the most famous courses in the world. There are no fewer than seven golf courses on the western approaches to St Andrews, each with a fearsome reputation. Tee-off times can all be booked online at www.standrews.com, though prices and availability differ depending on the course's status. The most renowned of them all is the Old Course, lovingly referred to as the Home of Golf. The Open Championship has been held on these 18 holes countless times, with winners including Jack Nicklaus, Seve Ballesteros, Nick Faldo and Tiger Woods. You can get an up-close experience of the Old Course without playing a round by booking in for a walking tour of the key features. The guided walk is led by an expert and takes in the 1st, 17th and 18th holes of the world-famous course. Significant landmarks and key events from major championships are all covered in the tour. It gives you an amazing chance to tread in the footsteps of golfing legends and see the fairways from a player's point of view.

△ Can you hold your nerve during a round at the Home of Golf?

△ The sandy beach is ideal for playtime, or recreating award-winning movie scenes!

Chariots of Fire

One of the most iconic moments of any British film was shot on West Sands, jutting out from St Andrews across the mouth of the River Eden. The famous beach scene features athletes kitted out in white shirts and shorts as they train for the 1924 Olympics. *Chariots of Fire* was nominated for seven Academy Awards, scooping the prize for best picture, best original screenplay, music and costume design. If you feel like grabbing a piece of the action, head to West Sands at the beginning of June for the annual charity beach race. The coast will then be packed with hundreds of runners taking part in a 5k event, every single one wearing 1920s-style gear and feeling like they're in the movies. The famous soundtrack by Vangelis even plays as the athletes are starting and finishing the largely flat course by the sea. Advance registration is essential as the places always fill up.

When William met Kate...

Any aspect of royal history proves popular with tourists, and the interest peaks when Prince William and Kate Middleton are involved. St Andrews is where the royal couple first met, both coming here to study at university. The place where their eyes first met is the North Point Café on North Street (☎ 01334 473977 ♀ KY16 9AQ), and it's a nice place to pop in for a snack. You can simply go for coffee or try adding a fry-up to your order. Expect the royal meeting place to be busy; it's a regular haunt for local students and there are lots of visitors wanting to see where the magic kicked off.

Getting here

Heading north from Edinburgh, leave the M90 and take the A91 towards St Andrews.

△ The incredible ruins of St Andrews Cathedral have so many stories to tell.

St Andrews Cathedral

Once the centre of the Roman Catholic Church in Scotland, the ruined cathedral in St Andrews is an impressive sight and awash with history. Like the nearby castle, which housed Scotland's leading bishops, it was built on a grand scale and thrived until the days when conflict between Catholics and Protestants became inflamed. The gargantuan cathedral dates to the middle of the 12th century and its ruins suggest it was the largest church ever constructed in Scotland. After being the focus of Catholicism in the country for hundreds of years, pressure grew in the 16th century for the Catholic stronghold to make closer political ties with King Henry VIII's Protestant England. In charge of the cathedral at the time, Cardinal David Beaton resisted and had a Protestant preacher burned in front of the castle. This did not go down well. Protestant nobles occupied the castle and assassinated Cardinal Beaton, leading to a famous siege, which saw significant damage inflicted on the castle. Ironically, it was this siege that also created some of the best-loved and most remarkable features of the castle. Mines dug by those on both sides of the conflict are some of

the most unusual remains of medieval warfare and give the site a truly unique feel. During the Scottish Reformation, when Catholic mass was made illegal and bishops were banned, the cathedral and castle quickly fell into disrepair. Today they give a fascinating insight into this period of Scottish history and are overseen by Historic Environment Scotland (www. historicenvironment.scot).

Stay a while

🛏 No 12 Bed and Breakfast, 12 Grange Road, St Andrews, KY16 8LF.
📞 07545 068748
no12bedandbreakfaststandrews.co.uk

🧳 Old Course Hotel, Old Station Road, St Andrews, KY16 9SP. 📞 01334 474371
www.oldcoursehotel.co.uk

⛺ Nydie Caravan and Camping Site, Strathkinness, St Andrews, KY16 9SL.
📞 01334 850828 www.nydie.co.uk

British Golf Museum – a fair way to spend an afternoon

Anybody who has swung a golf club and teed off on an 18-hole journey will be blown away by the wealth of exhibits in the British Golf Museum (📞 01334 460046 www.britishgolfmuseum. co.uk 📍 KY16 9AB). Beginning in the 16th century and running right up to the present day, the history of golf is explored in a range of displays and interactive attractions. Almost every conceivable angle of Scottish golf is explored, from the world's oldest Major to some of the colourful characters who have played the much-loved sport. There's also a busy programme of events and lectures that runs throughout the year.

26

FALKIRK KELPIES
SPIRITS OF THE WATER

The Kelpies

Mythological shape-shifting beasts that possess the strength and stamina of ten horses, kelpies seemed the ideal analogy to reflect the transformational power of Scotland's inland waterways. Sculptor Andy Scott's vision for the steel pieces of art also factored in the role of the horse in the region's industrial past, pulling the barges and coal ships that helped to develop the area. The result is a gritty, powerful image that is inspirational to stand beneath. Each of the two Kelpies weighs in at 300 tonnes and stands 30 metres (100 feet) tall. They're fabulous to look at from a distance and are eye-catching as you drive past. But nothing can compare with strolling along the canal and gazing up from within their shadow. Book in at the visitor centre (☎ 01324 590600 www.thehelix. co.uk ♥ FK2 7ZT) to enjoy the 30-minute tour that takes a peek inside one of the kelpies – the largest horse sculpture in the world.

The Helix

A £43m regeneration project to transform the landscape around this important coast-to-coast canal network, The Helix is now one of the most visited destinations in Scotland. Families in the surrounding regions and tourists from further afield enjoy the miles of paths available for walking, running and cycling close to the waterway. Close to where the River Carron runs into the Firth of Forth, a visitor centre provides information about the project and a café sells much-needed supplies for those who have been

active. Families enjoy the adventure playground and the energetic set out on the towpath for the journey to the Falkirk Wheel. The Helix was designed as a hub to bring communities and places together and even on a short visit you can see it's doing exactly that.

Getting here

The Kelpies can be spotted right next to the M9 by those travelling between Edinburgh and Stirling. There is plenty of parking at The Helix, which is well signed around the Falkirk area.

△ The Kelpies are one of the largest and most recognisable modern sculptures.

Coast to Coast – via a canal

Back in 1790, the industrial prospects of central Scotland were boosted by a 56km (35-mile) canal linking the Firth of Forth with the Firth of Clyde. The cross-country route linked the east and west coasts of Scotland at the narrowest point of the nation's neck. Boats could join the Forth & Clyde Canal from the River Forth at Grangemouth and transport materials across to the River Clyde at Bowling. A little inland at Falkirk, a vital connection with the Union Canal allowed vessels to reach central Edinburgh. Switching canals used to involve a time-consuming 11-lock challenge to manage the tricky topography, but this stopped being an option in the 1930s when the locks were dismantled. The engineering wonder that is the 1,200-tonne Falkirk Wheel means boats can now manoeuvre between the two canals in one swift movement. Attracting half a million tourists a year, the majestic Falkirk Wheel has connected the two canals once more, as well as rekindling a public fascination with the Scottish waterways.

Grangemouth

A short distance from the green surroundings of The Helix is one of the most significant industrial centres in Scotland. Grangemouth is the largest container port north of the border, handling 9 million tonnes of cargo each year. The oil refinery at Grangemouth has been in operation since 1924 and is responsible for the futuristic industrial landscape of chimneys, flames and pipes near the coast. The nearby refinery, which is the region's major employer, is the only one in Scotland working with crude oil and quenches most of the country's thirst for petrol.

△ The Falkirk Wheel allows an easier route across the country.

27

SOUTH QUEENSFERRY
BUILDING BRIDGES

Why visit?

★ Travel along the Firth of Forth by train, taking in one of the world's best-known bridges

★ Make a splash by diving into the cold waters on the morning of New Year's Day

★ See where the rich and famous dined on the waves on a visit to the Royal Yacht *Britannia*

Dominated by bridges crossing the Firth of Forth, most people bypass South Queensferry, but they are missing out on spectacular views, charming buildings, interesting heritage and some mouthwatering spots to eat.

Bridging the gap

Standing at the water's edge in South Queensferry, the huge Forth Bridge never fails to impress. The magnificent feat of Victorian engineering looks mighty fine on pictures, but when it's actually in front of you it's simply awesome. The Forth Bridge has a gritty, industrial feel that reflects its northern roots in both the design and materials used. Construction was taking place at the same time as Tower Bridge in London, which was given a much prettier, more decorative appearance. As you gaze up at the hulk of the huge cantilever bridge, you'll see trains travelling back and forth between South Queensferry and North Queensferry. The scale of the bridge makes them look tiny. It's an inexpensive journey and the best way to get up close to the colossal structure, which is a UNESCO World Heritage Site.

The Forth Road Bridge was opened in 1964, replacing the historic ferry service that had taken vehicles across the Forth for hundreds of years. As

△ Trains regularly criss-cross the epic, breath-taking Forth Bridge.

THE FORTH BRIDGE IN NUMBERS

- Opened in 1890
- 2,467 metres long
- 53,000 tonnes of steel
- 6.5 million rivets
- 200 trains cross every day
- 3 million passengers use it each year
- 240,000 litres of paint used to cover the bridge

Getting here

On the outskirts of Edinburgh, South Queensferry is extremely well-connected because of the major routes heading north over the Firth of Forth bridges. The M90 and A9000 head across the water from here and trains from Edinburgh and Perth arrive in the small station close to the centre of town.

more and more traffic started to use the bridge, it was recognised that demand was outstripping the capacity it was designed for and a replacement was needed. Work started on the Queensferry Crossing in 2011, with the first cars making the journey across it in 2017. With the Queensferry Crossing now carrying all the private vehicles, the original Forth Road Bridge is designated for buses, taxis, cycles and pedestrians. There is a footpath on either side of the Forth Road Bridge and a walk across it is exhilarating, providing outstanding views of both the Queensferry Crossing and the rail bridge.

Fancy a dip?

If you're nursing a hangover from Edinburgh's exuberant Hogmanay celebrations, South Queensferry is the place to come on New Year's Day. The 'Loony Dook' came about in 1986 as a fun cure for overindulging at New Year parties. Participants rid themselves of a sore head by diving into the chilly waters of the Firth of Forth. Many wear fancy dress, giving the early-morning event a carnival atmosphere. In its first year, only three people took the plunge, but they decided to repeat it and raise money for charity 12 months later. When the annual dip started to gain media attention, it gained in popularity and is now included as an important part of Edinburgh's Hogmanay celebrations. Expect to see a thousand revellers celebrating the arrival of 1 January, with thousands more looking on. The Dookers are greeted by bagpipers after parading through the town in their costumes, then fed a bowl of warm porridge before running into the sea. Their crazy antics have made a splash – raising thousands of pounds for local charities.

◁ P-p-p-pick up a picture while having a New Year's Day dip.

△ The Royal Yacht Britannia is a rare glimpse into celebrity catering.

Elegance on the waves

Travel eleven miles east along the coast to Leith and you'll have the chance to step on board the famous royal vessel where the likes of Winston Churchill, Liz Taylor, Frank Sinatra and Nelson Mandela dined. Commissioned in the 1950s, the Royal Yacht *Britannia* was in service for 44 years and completed the equivalent of an around-the-world trip during each 12-month period. Used for royal tours, honeymoons and business meetings, the yacht called at over 600 ports in 135 countries. Boasting a rich history that includes evacuating British nationals from a civil war in Yemen, a visit to *Britannia* includes an audio tour that brings some of the famous events to life (☏ 0131 555 5566 www.royalyachtbritannia.co.uk ♥ EH6 6JJ).

Go Forth and eat

Haggis, whisky, Cullen skink, Scottish mussels – all are on the menu at The Rail Bridge, which serves up an amazing view of the Forth Bridge to complement the local dishes. With an emphasis on local suppliers, there's a distinctly Scottish feel about this bistro, which is located in the shadow of the famous bridge and has plenty of iconic pictures on its walls (☏ 0131 331 1996 www.therailbridgebistro.com ♥ EH30 9TA).

Stay a while

🛏 The Queens Bed and Breakfast, 8 The Loan, South Queensferry, EH30 9NS. ☏ 0131 331 4345 www.thequeensbandb.co.uk

🧳 Orocco Pier Hotel, 17 The High Street, South Queensferry, EH30 9PP. ☏ 0131 331 1298 www.oroccopier.co.uk

⛺ Beecraigs Caravan and Camping Site, Linlithgow, EH49 6PL. ☏ 01506 284516 www.westlothian.gov.uk

NORTH-EAST

The north-east coast of England provides wonderful opportunities to dive into the nation's history. The tidal island of Lindisfarne – or Holy Island – was the site of the first Viking raids on home soil. A little further down the Northumberland coast is the medieval splendour of Bamburgh Castle, a brilliantly preserved castle with a stunning outline that features in one Britain's most famous views.

A day out at Craster is a treat for the tastebuds, with famous crab sandwiches and smoked kippers on the menu. The recently built offshore breakwater at Newbiggin-by-the-Sea doubles up as a modern work of art thanks to the sculpture making it yet another must-visit destination on this coastline. Visit Whitley Bay's Spanish City for a coffee before enjoying a wander around one of the most popular day-trip destinations for the folk of Newcastle. This stretch of coastline is often buffeted by strong winds coming in from the North Sea, something that water-sports enthusiasts in Redcar thrive on. Surfing, kite surfing and other wind-dependent activities are popular on the long beach here, which sits close to unlikely nature reserves in former industrial zones. Or if art is more your scene, the galleries of Staithes possesses all you need for an ideal day out. Anybody familiar with Bram Stoker's *Dracula* will have a soft spot for Whitby, which is the setting for part of the Gothic horror. A visit to this fabulous north-east town should include a climb up to the abbey, which featured in the tale, and it's best when coinciding with the colourful, jaw-dropping Gothic festivals held here. One of the UK's best coastal cycle routes – the Cinder Path – is found in the north-east; be sure to stop off at Ravenscar to enjoy the National Trust and wander down the steps to see the seal colony stretched across the rocks on the beach.

Bamburgh Castle is a formidable sight to behold, from all angles and in all weathers.

Don't miss

✓ Checking the tides and heading out to atmospheric Holy Island

✓ Enjoying one of the nation's most beautiful coastal views at Bamburgh

✓ Brushing up on your Dire Straits lyrics at Whitley Bay's Spanish City

✓ The spectacle of being in Whitby during Gothic and Steam Punk festivals

✓ A stroll among the breathtaking seal colony at Ravenscar

28

HOLY ISLAND
WATCH THE TIDES!

Why visit?

★ Gaze out to sea and imagine formidable Viking longships coming into view when monks lived on the island

★ Indulge in the speciality foods of Holy Island, including locally roasted coffee and traditional mead

★ Stay on Holy Island during the high tide to experience life when all the tourists have gone home

Before you go

A trip across the causeway to the Holy Island of Lindisfarne is one of the most rewarding journeys to make around the whole coast of Britain. But this is an excursion that needs planning ahead. The road to the island is completely cut off twice a day as the tide rises and if you don't respect the travel advice, you may find yourself cut off for several hours, needing emergency rescue and losing your car to the sea. It is essential to check the safe crossing times. They are displayed on a board at the entrance to the causeway, along with photographs of cars almost covered in salty water, which have been strategically placed to let you know how badly things could turn out. The safe crossing windows are also available online at www.northumberland.gov.uk. As you journey over to Holy Island, it's worth parking up and having a look around to soak up the seaweed encroaching on the road and the sands that shift every few hours. Climb the slippery steps to the wooden emergency shelter and imagine being trapped here as the sea closes in a few feet below.

Getting here

Follow the signs from the A1 to Holy Island, which you'll find between Alnwick and Berwick-Upon-Tweed. Follow the twisting lane and head over the rail tracks to get to the causeway.

▽ High tide brings an atmospheric wonder to Holy Island, shutting it off from the mainland.

Lindisfarne Priory

Dating back to the 12th century and thought to be built on the same site as an Anglo-Saxon church, the ruined priory on Holy Island oozes history (☏ 01289 389200 www.english-heritage.org.uk ♥TD15 2RX). Now managed by English Heritage, remains of this ancient building are breathtaking. Look out for the incredible Rainbow Arch, a rib of the crossing vault that remained intact even when the tower fell down.

A restored castle

Out of action for an 18-month restoration programme, 16th-century Lindisfarne Castle reopened in 2018 (☏ 01289 389244, www.nationaltrust.org.uk ♥TD15 2SH). Costing £3 million, the improvements combatted 100 years of damage caused by the elements. In the early 20th century, the castle was converted into a private holiday home for Edward Hudson, who founded *Country Life* magazine. In such a commanding position, the castle is one of the most recognisable sights on Holy Island.

The Vikings are coming!

The troubled arrival of Viking invaders on this island and the impact it had on the local religious community is explored at Lindisfarne Heritage Centre (☏ 01289 389004 www.lindisfarne-centre.com ♥TD15 2SD). The Viking attack here in the late eighth century hit the nation hard, striking as it did at the heart of religious beliefs at the time. This is the place where St Cuthbert was made bishop in 685 and his legacy was hugely important. Cuthbert became one of the most revered Anglo-Saxon saints after his death and huge importance was placed on his remains. Fearing a Viking invasion in 875, monks carried St Cuthbert's body away from Lindisfarne, along with treasures including the

△ The arch of Lindisfarne Priory is just one of the wonders to see here.

celebrated Lindisfarne Gospels. The dedicated monks journeyed around northern England and southern Scotland for seven years. Fenwick Lawson's stunning sculpture, *The Journey*, shows the monks in careful procession with the coffin of St Cuthbert; find it in the church of St Mary on Church Lane. It's a jaw-dropping piece of art, made from seven elm trees, and shows monks carrying their heavy load to protection.

△ The stunning Lindisfarne Castle was transformed in a 20th-century restoration.

△ Lindisfarne is a small island with more than its share of historical treasures.

Drink like Beowulf!

The favourite tipple that connects the hero of England's oldest surviving long poem and the priest from Chaucer's *Canterbury Tales* is, of course, mead. A blend of honey, local water and fermented grape juice, the drink coined 'nectar of the gods' is still made at St Aidan's Winery on Lindisfarne. There are samples to taste and plenty to buy at the mead shop (☎ 01289 389230 www.lindisfarne-mead.co.uk ♥ TD15 2RX).

Take a break…

You might well smell the coffee before you see Pilgrims Coffee House because the owners roast it in the garden. There are lovely tables to eat inside and out and souvenirs to buy from their small shop (☎ 01289 389109 www.pilgrimscoffee.com ♥ TD15 2SJ). The old post office is now the 1st Class Food café, where fresh crab and lobster is sought after (☎ 01289 389271 www.1stclassfoodholyisland.co.uk ♥ TD15 2SQ).

A new day, a new opening time

The opening times of the facilities on Holy Island are likely to change every day. If the tide comes in late afternoon, expect shops and cafés to close as the tourists leave and mainland workers rush to get home.

🛎 Stay a while

🛏 Bamburgh View, Holy Island, TD15 2SR. ☎ 01289 389212 www.bamburghview.co.uk

🧳 Lindisfarne Hotel, Holy Island, TD15 2SQ. ☎ 01289 389273 www.thelindisfarnehotel.co.uk

🔺 Old Mill Caravan Site, West Kyloe Farm, Berwick Upon Tweed, TD15 2PF. ☎ 01289 381295 www.westkyloe.co.uk. NB No camping is allowed on Holy Island itself.

BAMBURGH
A VIEW TO INSPIRE

Why visit?

★ Bamburgh Castle serves up superb views from the outside and incredibly rich history on the inside, while nearby Seahouses is the picture-perfect north-east fishing village

★ Discover the story of a 19th-century heroine who saved lives at sea and became a Victorian celebrity

★ Admire the view of the castle from Bamburgh's beach – it's one of the most loved in the country

★ Save room for a meal of smoked kippers in Seahouses – it's a local institution

Our best-looking castle?

When the nation was asked to vote for its favourite view as part of a TV series, the iconic setting of Bamburgh Castle overlooking the long, golden beach was up there in the shortlist. Sitting proudly above the small town, Bamburgh Castle (☎ 01668 214208 www.bamburghcastle.com 📍 NE69 7DF) dominates the landscape and has a commanding presence about it. One of the largest inhabited castles in the UK, a tour around its interior reveals how this has been an important stronghold through several key eras in British history. After becoming strategically important in medieval times, Bamburgh Castle was the scene of an important siege as the War of the Roses reached its finale. In the 20th century, the castle took on the role of a vital surgery, dispensary and respite home. Self-guided tours shed light on the people who have called this part of the world home over the last 10,000 years.

△ The view of Bamburgh Castle is one of the best in the country.

A 19th-century heroine

In the heart of Bamburgh, the free-to-enter Grace Darling Museum is run by the RNLI and tells the story of a local woman who famously risked her life to save others at sea (☎ 01668 214910 www.rnli.org ♥ NE69 7AE). Born in Bamburgh, Darling was the daughter of a lighthouse keeper and from humble beginnings went on to make history on a global scale. At an early age she moved with her family to live in the cottage connected to Longstone Lighthouse on the Farne Islands. Her life-changing moment came in September 1838 when the steamship *Forfarshire* ran aground on nearby rocks. Darling rushed out to help them, setting off across stormy waves to rescue nine lives. The story hit the headlines and Grace Darling became a Victorian media celebrity, decorated with several awards.

Putt away your worries

No trip to nearby Seahouses is complete without paying a visit to The Bunker for a round of mini golf! With sea views out to the Farne Islands providing a beautiful backdrop, there's lots of fun to be had as you struggle to knock the ball through castles, lighthouses and other coastal obstructions (☎ 01665 721402 www.thebunker-seahouses.co.uk ♥ NE68 7SW).

 Fish and chips

Pinnacles Restaurant in Seahouses has a solid reputation among locals. Find it on Main Street (☎ 01665 720708 www.pinnaclesfishandchips.com ♥ NE68 7RE).

△ The coastal scene at Bamburgh, with the castle overlooking a beautiful scene of dunes and farms.

Smokin' home of the kipper!

For a true taste of fishing history in Seahouses, head to Swallow Fish and experience seafood that has been smoked in the same way since the Victorian era (☎ 01665 721052 www.swallowfish. co.uk ♥ NE68 7RB). The Fisherman's Kitchen is home to this traditional company and uses the original smokehouses that were first brought on site in 1843. Using oak sawdust that is free of any additives, the natural flavours give the fish a familiar taste. This iconic building is thought by some to be the place where the kipper was invented, and it proves to be one of the most popular products today. It's not just about the smoked fish; the company specialises in crab, lobster and oysters as well. The shop is open to buy produce and look around at the collection of historic fishing photographs. You can also have a pack of kippers sent to your home to provide the perfect breakfast treat.

△ Fishing is a valuable part of the economy for places like Seahouses, where old smoking methods thrive.

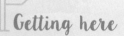

Getting here

North of Newcastle, Bamburgh and Seahouses are located just to the east of the A1. Take the B1340 to head into Seahouses and the B1342 for Bamburgh.

Birders' paradise is not Farne away

The Shiel family has been operating boat trips to the nearby Farne Islands for over 100 years, primarily to just a few keen twitchers after the morning's fishing had been completed. But in the 1930s the business started to grow and Billy Shiel's business has expanded to include ten boats and a RIB. Thousands of wildlife enthusiasts have now travelled to observe the important nesting site, where seabirds such as puffins, razorbills, shags and common terns can

be spotted. Keep your eyes peeled for plenty of seals, too. If you're taking a trip that lands on one of the islands, take some cash to pay the National Trust fee (☎ 01665 720308 www.farne-islands. com ♥ NE68 7RN).

Stay a while

🛏 The Bamburgh Castle Inn, Seafield Road, Seahouses, NE68 7SQ.
☎ 01665 720283
www.bamburghcastlehotel.co.uk

🏨 Longstone House Hotel, Main Street, Seahouses, NE68 7UA. ☎ 01665 721202 www.longstonehouse.co.uk

⛺ Budle Farm Campsite, Budle Bay, Bamburgh, NE69 7AJ. ☎ 01668 214357

CRASTER
OF CRABS AND CASTLES

Historic harbour

Protection from the rough seas is provided by the harbour walls at Craster. During the centuries before it was built, local fishermen hauled their vessels on to land with only a couple of offshore rocks to break the waves. When built by the Craster family in 1906, the two walls provided shelter for the important local fishing boats; today, it still serves boatmen well and adds a touristic charm to this delightful little village. The two harbour walls are dedicated to the memory of Captain John Craster, who was killed in Tibet. Taking a walk to the end of the walls allows you to turn around and get a great view of Craster, which seems to squeeze into a tiny space. At the end of the southern harbour wall, there's a clue to another important industry of yesteryear. Until the 1930s, here stood one of three large wooden structures that stored crushed limestone, transported in along an overhead bucket system from a nearby quarry.

🔔 Stay a while

🛏 Jubilee House, W.T. Stead Road, Embleton, Alnwick, NE66 3UY. ☎ 01665 576839 www.bedbreakfast-northumberland.co.uk

🧳 Dunstanburgh Castle Hotel, Embleton, Alnwick, NE66 3UN. ☎ 01665 576111 www.dunstanburghcastlehotel.co.uk

⛺ Dunstan Hill Camping and Caravanning Club Site, Alnwick, NE66 3TQ. ☎ 01665 576310 www.campingandcaravanningclub.co.uk

Foodie specialities

There are two essential places to visit if you want to enjoy a taste of Craster while you're in the north-east, so it might be worth planning meals accordingly. Pop into The Jolly Fisherman on Haven Hill for lunch (☎ 01665 576461 www.thejollyfishermancraster.co.uk 📍NE66 3TR). There are plenty of tasty options on the menu, but this pub is famed for the crab sandwiches it serves up. Save some room for the famous Craster kippers that have been smoked in the same way for generations at L. Robson & Sons (☎ 01665 576223 www.kipper.co.uk 📍NE66 3TR). When smoking is taking place, the fishy scent wafts through the village and puts you in the mood to sample some of the kippers and salmon they have become well known for.

△ The charming harbour at Craster is well known for sourcing crabs.

△ A stunning walk along the cliff top is the only way to reach Dunstanburgh Castle's atmospheric ruins.

Dunstanburgh Castle

High on a prominent Northumberland headland, historic Dunstanburgh Castle's ruined walls house centuries of intriguing and often violent history (www.english-heritage.org.uk ♀ NE66 3TT). Work started on the castle in the early years of the 14th century. It became a stronghold for Thomas, Earl of Lancaster, who had Dunstanburgh built on a grand scale to show his resistance to King Edward II. Relations between Lancaster and the king continued to deteriorate and soon led to open conflict. Lancaster led military action against the king in the early 1320s but was captured as he attempted a retreat to Dunstanburgh. He was put on trial and later executed near Pontefract Castle. Later in the century, the castle fell into the hands of John of Gaunt and significant improvements were made. After an eventful time switching sides in the Wars of the Roses, the castle started to fall into disrepair; it was too expensive to maintain a castle of this size and importance. A highlight of a visit to the castle is seeing the two impressive towers of the keep, as well as taking in the clifftop location. Car parking is available at Craster and the castle is then accessed via a 2km (1.3 mile) footpath.

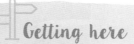

Getting here

Reach Craster by taking the B1340 or B6347 from the A1, just north of Alnwick. The walk to Dunstanburgh Castle begins from the harbour.

Sporty beach

The lovely stretch of sand at Beadnell is very popular and has a heap of holiday accommodation to match demand. It's also one of the best-equipped places on the north-east coast when it comes to water sports. Surfing, windsurfing, kite surfing, sailing and scuba diving are all on the agenda for the adventurous visitors to Northumberland.

 Fish and chips

For a seafood treat, visit the Craster Seafood Restaurant on Haver Hill (☎ 01665 576230 www.crasterseafood.co.uk ♀ NE66 3TR).

NEWBIGGIN-BY-THE-SEA
A LOVELY COUPLE

New couple has a big impact

When Newbiggin's coastal defences received a boost in 2007, the town's artistic importance also took a leap forward. At the same time as a new breakwater began fighting back against the sea's erosional power, the country's first permanent offshore sculpture began its long and thoughtful life staring out to sea. *Couple*, by artist Sean Henry, features two larger-than-life people standing on the breakwater gazing out to the horizon. What they're meant to be thinking is left up to each individual who visits this small north-east town, but the addition of the two tall folk on the breakwater is certainly thought provoking. Carefully designed, the height of the town's tallest residents is deceptive as they stand looking at the ever-changing seascape. At first glance they seem life-size, but when a boat or bird passes by in the background the true scale of the installation becomes more obvious. The two people with their backs to the shore are three times bigger than the real residents of the town and took three years to bring to life. The disadvantage of Sean Henry's work, of course, is that you can only fully appreciate it when you're offshore yourself and facing *Couple*; however, those wanting to keep their feet on the land need not worry. A smaller version of the sculpture has been placed on the promenade so everybody can study the detail in these two fascinating characters. Try coming up with your own story about their lives.

△ You can only speculate about what the Couple might have to talk about...

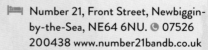

🍽 Stay a while

🛏 Number 21, Front Street, Newbiggin-by-the-Sea, NE64 6NU. ☎ 07526 200438 www.number21bandb.co.uk

🛍 Premier Inn, Queen Elizabeth Country Park, Ashington, NE63 9AT. ☎ 0871 527 8034 www.premierinn.com

⛺ Tranwell Farm, Westfield, Tranwell, Morpeth, NE61 6AF. ☎ 07947 598832 www.holidaynorthumbria.com

Getting here

Heading north from Newcastle on the A189, Newbiggin-by-the-Sea is reached by taking the B1334 at North Seaton.

A significant small town

The lengthy promenade at Newbiggin is the longest in the county, giving visitors plenty of room to stretch their legs and enjoy learning about the town's maritime history. Dotted along the coastline are wonderfully accessible information boards and blue plaques that tell the story of Newbiggin. One of the most prominent places to visit is the town's lifeboat station – the oldest one still operating in the UK. It was opened up in 1851 following the tragic disaster that saw ten local fishermen lose their lives out at sea. The Cable House is another important location and helped to boost international communication in Victorian times. The first telegraph cable between the UK and Scandinavia was placed here in 1868, vastly reducing the amount of time it took to send and receive messages. A further blue plaque proudly tells of how Newbiggin was once the third most important port for transporting corn, coming in behind London and Hull.

Geordie Banger!

A few miles up the coast from Newbiggin, the harbour shopping village at Amble is a terrific place to find tasty treats (www.amble harbourvillage.co.uk ♥NE65 0FD). Wandering around the retail pods, the smells and the offers pull you in different directions so make sure you have a good explore before deciding on where to enjoy your snack. The Geordie Banger Company is famed for its 'sausage on a stick'. Exactly as the name suggests, this bargain snack comes with a sausage served kebab-style and allows you to walk around in the sunshine enjoying one of several flavours with a north-east theme. Nearby, the Cheese Pod offers a wide range of local cheeses made close to this stretch of the seaside. If you're in the mood for something more than street food, the Old Boathouse on Leazes Street has won several awards for its seafood menu (☎ 01665 711232 www.boathousefoodgroup.co.uk ♥NE65 0AA).

△ The long arm of Amble's harbour, sheltering waters from the turmoil of the sea.

△ Fishing boats at Amble bring in a fresh catch from the sea every day.

Thou shalt have a fishy...

Although fishing is still common in the north-east, it's hard to imagine just how huge the industry was here at the end of the 19th century. At the time of the 'herring boom' in the 1880s, there were hundreds of ships, of all sizes, at work in the bay. At the centre of Newbiggin's herring industry was a building known as the Herring House, where fish preparation took place on a large scale. The town developed a successful reputation for curing and a smokehouse was a significant employer that went from strength to strength when the railway arrived. The Herring House was important for Newbiggin's fishermen right up until 1953, when it was severely damaged by a storm and demolished.

 Fish and chips

Ladhar's Fish Bar serves up a tasty fish supper you can devour while admiring *Couple*. You'll find it on Front Street (☏ 01670 852360 ladharsfishbar.co.uk ◉ NE64 6NJ).

WHITLEY BAY
GIRL, IT LOOKS SO PRETTY TO ME...

Why visit?

★ Brush up on your Dire Straits songs and enjoy afternoon tea at the Spanish City

★ Enjoy a brisk walk along the sands before visiting the lighthouse

★ Time your visit to include the popular film festival in late August

Spanish City

If a town were to be represented by just one building, there are few that would do such a sterling job as the Spanish City. This domed, shining beacon overlooking the North Sea is Whitley Bay's understated Taj Mahal or Palace of Versailles. Generations of young people in the north-east have grown up hanging out at the Spanish City, now a Grade II listed building. Opened in 1908, it served locals and the throngs

SPANISH CITY FACTS

Before the building was erected, the site was used as an open-air entertainment venue with awnings decorated in a Spanish style – hence the name Spanish City.

△ Dominating the townscape of Whitley Bay and youthful memories of the past, the famous white dome of Spanish City.

△ As well as a vibrant nightlife, Whitley Bay has lovely stretches of beaches to wander along in the day.

of tourists with a concert hall, tearoom and roof garden before a ballroom and funfair were added in later years. Two female statues on the roof represent fun times experienced inside,

🍽 Stay a while

🛏 Lighthouse Guesthouse, 20 North Parade, Whitley Bay, NE26 1PA.
📞 0191 252 2319
www.lighthouseguesthouse.co.uk

💼 York House Boutique Hotel, 106–110 Park Ave, Whitley Bay, NE26 1DN.
📞 0191 252 8313
www.yorkhousehotel.com

⛺ Bobby Shafto Caravan Park, Beamish, Co Durham, DH9 0RY. 📞 0191 370 1776
www.bobbyshaftocaravanpark.co.uk

one of them dancing with a tambourine and the other holding cymbals. Anybody with a working knowledge of Dire Straits' songs will recognise the Spanish City from 'Tunnel of Love' – the line 'girl, it looks so pretty to me, just like it always did / like the Spanish City to me when we were kids' sounds like a longing to be in the Mediterranean, but is actually rooted in the coast north of Newcastle. This iconic white building – the Spanish City – was immortalised by the north-east band in a track that pays homage to several permanent funfairs around the world that have now closed down. Those mentioned by Mark Knopfler in the song include Palisades in New Jersey (closed in 1971), Steeplechase Park in Coney Island, New York (closed 1964) and Rockaways' Playland, New York (closed 1982). The Spanish City itself entertained a period of decay in the early 2000s, when it was in much need of some vital investment. The venue did eventually close down, but was reopened in 2018 after a seven-year restoration programme. Today, it's a stunning place to enjoy some food and watch the world go by (☎ 0191 691 7090 www. spanishcity.co.uk ♥ NE26 1BG).

A film festival with some bite

Late August is a great time to visit Whitley Bay if you're a movie lover. The town's film festival was kicked off in 2010 and has grown to have hundreds of events in dozens of different venues. There are always creative, innovative ideas to wow movie buffs at the festival. One year an audience sat on the beach to watch *Jaws*, with the waves of the sea lapping just metres away. Only the brave will have ventured into the water at the end of that screening!

△ There's plenty of fun to be had on the seafront, under the gaze of St Mary's Lighthouse.

Getting here

The A1058 runs north-east from Newcastle city centre to reach the coast at Whitley Bay. The town has good local connections through its Metro train station.

St Mary's Lighthouse

Standing tall and warning ships of impending doom between 1898 and 1984, St Mary's Lighthouse is one of Whitley Bay's top attractions on what was once a very hazardous coastline. Modern navigational methods mean the light is no longer needed to guide ships and North Tyneside Council now run the former keepers' cottages as a visitor centre. You can climb the 137 steps to grab an unparalleled 360° view of the north-east coast and learn about the history of the lighthouse. Time your visit carefully, though. To get to St Mary's Island you cross a causeway that is only accessible at low tide. The danger here is real and people have needed rescuing. Opening times vary depending on the tides, so it's best to telephone ahead to check (☎ 0191 200 8650). Every year, the popular North Tyneside 10k Run sees runners making their way around the coast and finishing with a memorable, if fatigued, crossing to the lighthouse. Around the island, there's plenty of family fun to be had exploring rock pools and spotting seabirds.

Fish and chips

North of the town at Seaton Sluice is The Harbour View, a popular place where the locals dig into a fish supper (☎ 0191 237 2478 www.the-harbour-view. com ♥ NE26 4DR).

33

REDCAR
THE WINDY CITY

A history of saving souls

Launched in 1802, the *Zetland* is the oldest surviving lifeboat in the world and the star attraction at Redcar's Lifeboat Museum (☎ 01642 494311 www.zetlandlifeboat.co.uk ♥ TS10 3AH). The free-to-enter museum relies on donations and volunteers to keep the well-preserved *Zetland* on display for all to learn how many souls have been saved on the treacherous shores around Redcar. *Zetland* served the seafaring community for 78 years and helped to saved more than 500 lives put at risk when vessels got into difficulties. The *Zetland* was named after local landowner the Marquess of Zetland and has been in its current home since 1907, coming out into the sunshine just once to get a fresh coat of paint. Now part of the National Historic Fleet, this is one of the most significant old boats visitors can see in the UK.

△ The wind powers so much on this blustery north-east shoreline.

🛎 Stay a while

🛏 Edwardian Guest House, 45 High Street West, Redcar, TS10 1SF.
☎ 01642 506228
www.edwardianhouseredcar.co.uk

🏢 The Park Hotel, Granville Terrace, Redcar, TS10 3AR. ☎ 01642 490888
www.parkhotel-redcar.com

⛺ Ashfield Caravan Park, Dalton Piercy, TS27 3HY. ☎ 01429 269969

Redcar's wind power

Gaze out to sea from Redcar's coastline and you can't help but be drawn to the rotating turbines. Welcome to the Teesside Offshore Wind Farm, one of many around the coast of Britain that are playing a part in reducing our reliance on fossil fuels. The UK is one of the windiest places in Europe and Redcar is one of the breeziest spots in the UK, as you may well discover when you take a walk on the beach. This north-east town is ideal for harnessing the power of Nature. This wind farm dates back to 2012 and is home to 27 turbines, spread out in three rows of nine. There's 1.5km (just under a mile) between the nearest wind turbine and the shore, with at least 300 metres (1,000 feet) between each of them. With a capacity of 62MW, the Teesside Offshore Wind Farm can supply 40,000 homes with power – more than the number in Redcar. Importantly, those spinning towers reduce the amount of carbon dioxide entering the atmosphere by 80,000 tonnes a year.

Kite surfing

You might think it would be better suited to Hawaii or California, but kite surfing is one of the fastest growing sports in the country and Redcar is at the heart of the action. There may be more rain falling from the grey skies, the seas might be duller and the thermometers pointing to much lower temperatures, but the beach to the north of the Teesside town is one of the hottest places in the world to take to the waves. The reason is simple – conditions here are perfect. There are large, open beaches, there's not much shipping traffic in the sea and then there's the wind – the key factor that Redcar has plenty of. Beginners and experienced kite surfers take to the air in this exhilarating – but potentially dangerous – hobby.

Getting here

To the north-east of Middlesbrough, follow the A1085 out of the town to get to Redcar on the Teesside coast. Redcar has a couple of train stations – Redcar Central is the one with best access to the beach.

Seal Sands

Travel up the coast from Redcar and you'll pass through one of the most industrialised parts of the country. Chimneys and pipelines dominate the Teesside coastal landscape. It's not an area you would associate with a thriving wildlife scene, but Seal Sands gained its name for good reason. Dozens of common seals use the tidal stretch of the River Tees as a breeding ground, and when you factor in a strong bird population you can see why this is a popular place among wildlife enthusiasts. One of the most accessible places to gain a good view is on the A178 south of Seaton Carew. From the Seal Sands car park it's a short walk to a hide where seal sightings are pretty much guaranteed at high tide. Seals were first spotted here hundreds of years ago, but as industry built up in the area the population suffered because of pollution. It's only in recent decades that the seals have started to thrive again.

△ Mine! Mine! Mine! Keep your chips close to hand!

Need a chippy?

Head to the beautifully named Lobster Road for some quality fish and chips in Redcar at Sea Breeze (☎ 01642 472422 www.seabreezefishnchips.co.uk ◉ TS10 1SH).

STAITHES
CACHE OF COASTAL CREATIONS

Art in heaven

The sublime scenery in the village of Staithes, the surrounding countryside and out towards the sea has been an inspiration for generations of artists. A colony of around 25 well-known artists settled in Staithes during the 19th century, inspired by French impressionists such as Monet and Renoir. The artistic tradition of the Staithes Group continues today; many painters decide to make this popular north-east destination their base and display work in local galleries. To see a good sample of what they have produced, head to the Staithes Gallery on High Street (☎ 01947 841840 www.staithesgallery.co.uk ♥ TS13 5BH).

△ Twisting streets are home to the many galleries making Staithes famous.

A festival to inspire

Over a weekend in early September, Staithes becomes even more of a buzzing artistic hub than usual. Dozens of cottages that line the village's maze of roads open their doors and exhibit the work of local and visiting artists. The Staithes Festival is an ideal weekend to immerse yourself in the creative reputation of this fascinating seaside village. Expect to see work from over 130 artists in the best part of 100 different venues, covering everything from painting and printmaking to textiles and ceramics. There's also a programme of entertainment and busking, adding fun to the trip. For more information, go to www.staithesfestival.com.

Old Jack's Boat

Younger fans of the seaside will recognise the cobbled streets of Staithes from a CBeebies show starring Bernard Cribbins. Every episode of *Old Jack's Boat* sees the veteran actor telling fantastical stories with his faithful dog, Salty. The visually stunning and atmospheric village is the show's co-star as friends chat with Old Jack before story time begins.

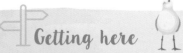

Getting here

This stretch of the coast is accessed by the A174, east of Middlesbrough. Saltburn is also served by a train station.

 Fancy fish and chips?

For the fresh local catch, head to Excelsior Fisheries on Staithes Lane, Staithes (📞 07478 735563 📍 TS13 5AJ).

△△ Small boats moored in the tidal section of Staithes Beck.

△ After a busy time looking through local arts and crafts, enjoy a drink in idyllic seafront settings.

Three reasons to visit Saltburn

Just up the coast from Staithes, you'll find another coastal gem that's worth exploring if you have a bit of extra time.

CHECK OUT IN SALTBURN

- The water-powered cliff lift that takes the strain out of climbing the steep route to and from the beach. It's a popular tourist activity and recently enjoyed a £30,000 refurb.
- Saltburn Pier, which is a lovely place to stroll out to sea and take in the views. It's 206 metres (681 feet) long and opened in 1869. After standing firm for over 150 years, it's now the only remaining pier in Yorkshire.
- The Professional Surf Tour, when folk come to Saltburn from all over the world to show off their rad moves in May.

Captain Cook

James Cook moved to Staithes when he was 16 years old and began a stint working for local grocer William Sanderson. It's said that his passion for the sea developed in the village and he would spend his spare time gazing from the shop towards the waves. After just 18 months, Cook realised he was not suited to shop life and moved to Whitby, where his career on the ocean began in earnest. Captain Cook made a name for himself exploring and mapping New Zealand and the east coast of Australia before coming to a sticky end in Hawaii. Learn all about his life and the influence of this seaside village at the Staithes Heritage Centre on High Street (☎ 01947 841454 ♥ TS13 5BQ). As well as books and letters from the 18th century, there's also a life-size reproduction of a Staithes street as it would have been in Cook's day.

△ Layered cliffs at Staithes provide a backdrop to a row of coastal houses.

A long haul

Staithes is built on a steep slope that dives down to sea level. To protect the village from becoming snarled up in traffic congestion, cars are not allowed down unless for access. There's a car park at the top of the hill. Be prepared for the steep walk down and what seems like an even steeper hike back up.

🍽 **Stay a while**

🛏 Captain Cook Inn, 60 Staithes Lane, Staithes, TS13 5AD. ☎ 01947 840200 www.captaincookinn.co.uk

🧳 St Hilda's Boutique Hotel, 3A High Street, Hinderwell, TS13 5JX. ☎ 01947 841935 www.rlsenterprises.co.uk

⛺ Serenity Camping, High Street, Hinderwell, TS13 5JH. ☎ 01947 841122 serenitycamping.co.uk

WHITBY
FULL OF GOTHIC CHARM

When to visit?

Goth Weekend, of course! For an unforgettable experience, head to Whitby on one of its biannual weekends celebrating everything Gothic (www.whitbygothweekend.co.uk). Various acts during the night entertain Goths from around the country, who make their way here in a variety of eye-opening and head-turning costumes. During the day, the streets are dominated by Goths old and young, along with a growing band of steampunk enthusiasts. Photographers snap away at folk posing in the most extravagant costumes. The cobbled walk along narrow Church Street and up the 199 steps to the abbey is the best place to go people-watching during this fabulous event. The weekends, usually in late April and late October, have increased in popularity over the years and you'll have to book well in advance if you want to stay overnight.

The legend of Dracula

Thousands of holidaymakers arrive in Whitby every year to enjoy its Gothic charm, but one particular trip in the late 19th century left a lasting impression on the town and helped to define its legacy. Bram Stoker had been working in Scotland when he decided to rest a while in Whitby, where he stayed at a guest house on the Royal Crescent. During the week before his wife and young son joined him, the legendary writer enjoyed thoughtful strolls around the town and learned of its history, piecing together the novel he was working on about a vampire. In the library, Bram Stoker read about a 15th-century

△ Fabulous wardrobes are on display every time Whitby has a gothic festival.

▽ Cobbled streets wind around the harbour and up to Whitby's historic abbey.

prince in Bucharest nicknamed 'Dracula', who would impale his victims. From here, one of the greatest ever horror legends was born. In the famous Gothic novel, Dracula arrives in Whitby aboard the sea vessel *Demeter*, adapted from the real-life *Dmitry* that ran aground here five years before Stoker's visit. No crew survived in the story and only the captain is found, tied to the ship's wheel. Dracula takes the form of a dog that leaps on to land and runs up the famously steep 199 cobbled steps to the haunting abbey. The name of Dracula's first victim, 'Swales', was inspired by a grave in the churchyard at the top of these steps, high on the East Cliff. The terrifying story of Dracula has had a lasting impression on Whitby. Guided walking tours (Dracula Ghost Walks, ☎ 01947 880485 www. whitbywalks.com), which begin beneath the Whale Bone Arch and visit the novel's key sites, are something to remember. The town's Gothic weekends also pay homage to the Victorian tale. Younger readers may have enjoyed Robert Swindells' *Room 13*, a story on a Dracula theme about a school trip to Whitby.

△ Whitby's huge whalebone arch is one of its key landmarks.

On yer bike!

Whitby is blessed with the Cinder Track, a cycle route along a disused railway that links the town with Scarborough further south along the coast.

△ The Cinder Track is an impressive route with coastal views.

🛎 Stay a while

🛏 The Shepherd's Purse, Sanders Yard, Whitby, YO22 4DU. ☎ 01947 820228 www.theshepherdspurse.com

💼 Marine Hotel, 13 Marine Parade, Whitby, YO21 3PR. ☎ 01947 605022 www.the-marine-hotel.co.uk

⛺ Folly Gardens, Green Lane, Whitby, YO22 4EN. ☎ 01947 601364 www.follygardens-whitby.co.uk

As it was designed for trains, gradients are kept to a minimum and make this an enjoyable trail that families can tackle. Although the full 69km (43-mile) route to Scarborough and back may be too much for many, there are places between these two seaside towns that allow you to dip your toe into this mainly off-road bike track. Robin Hood's Bay and Ravenscar are two places worth visiting and both have places to lock your bikes. As you glance out to sea, it's fun to imagine the steam trains carrying goods and passengers between Scarborough and Whitby. The last service trundled along here in 1965, as Dr Beeching's cuts began to bite.

Ravenscar

Seals may look cute and cuddly on posters, but in real life they are anything but. With sharp teeth and a bite worse than many dogs, they are not to be approached. Walking down to the beach area at Ravenscar may bring you face to face with these fascinating creatures, and it's an unforgettable experience. The sights and sounds you'll encounter are truly stunning. But heed the local signs and stay at least 10 metres (30 feet) away from them. A National Trust shop and café is on hand at Ravenscar (☏ 01723 870138 www.nationaltrust.org.uk/yorkshire-coast ♥ YO13 0NE), as well as the friendly Ravenscar Tea Rooms 600m down the road (☏ 01723 870444 www.ravenscartearooms.co.uk ♥ YO13 0LU).

Robin Hood's Bay

With steep cobbled streets and higgledy-piggledy houses, Robin Hood's Bay has a lovely, antiquated seaside feel. Much quieter than its neighbours, don't come here for time on a beach but instead arrive to hunt for fossils on the rocks, search in rock pools for marine life and browse around the quirky shops.

Getting here

On the eastern edge of the North York Moors National Park, Whitby sits just off the A171 between Scarborough and Middlesbrough. The centrally located railway station, close to the River Esk and a short walk from Bridge Street, has connections to Middlesbrough.

△ Whitby has a small beach by the harbour and a larger one on the north end of town.

Fish and chips

Whitby seems to have a decent fish and chip shop every few metres and in summer the town's benches will be rammed with people tucking in to the town's favourite meal. The people's favourite tends to be the Magpie Cafe (☏ 01947 602058 www.magpiecafe.co.uk ♥ YO21 3PU), a prominent white building on Pier Road, and it's quite normal to see people queuing up for both the restaurant and takeaway. If the wait to get in is too long, try out Angel Fisheries on Angel Yard, where there's a friendly welcome and some quaint indoor seating (☏ 01947 606551 ♥ YO21 1BW).

EAST COAST

With a slightly more favourable climate than the north-west coast and a varied set of destinations, there is plenty to attract folk here from the big cities of northern England. You'll still find a good nightlife, plenty of places to stay, some rides and amusements at the likes of Bridlington, Filey and Scarborough, but they have a quieter feel than many of the bigger seaside towns.

Contrasting rock types near Bempton, where huge numbers of birds find a ledge on the cliff to raise their young.

The North Bay of Scarborough is especially suited to a quieter trip to the coast. And if wildlife is what you like on a day out, the boat trip to Bempton Cliffs provides an unforgettable encounter with thousands of breeding seabirds. This coast, however, has a menacing side. The cliffs here are some of the fastest eroding in the world and millions of pounds have been spent at Holderness to protect homes and businesses. A wander down Spurn Point is to enjoy a lesson in both history and geography of the east coast's

constant battle with the sea, attempts to minimise erosion and the damage that the forces of nature can cause. The biggest city on this stretch of coast is Hull, home to some fascinating museums about its maritime history and role in ending the slave trade. An up-and-coming city, there are plenty of cool cafés and nice bars to spend relaxing afternoons and evenings. Look out for chip shops with the regional speciality 'chip spice' next to the salt and vinegar. And long before Banksy, a special piece of graffiti was memorable in Hull – look out for the 'Dead Bod' that welcomed ships back home.

If record-breaking is something you're keen to do, Cleethorpes is the place for you. At this much-loved and popular resort on the edge of the Humber Estuary, you can fill yourself up at the world's biggest fish and chip shop before washing it down with a drink at the world's smallest pub. Those who like a loud and raucous scene head to Skegness, a place that prides itself on living life to the full. Acres of caravan sites, music playing until late and a fine range of fast-food joints make for a memorable visit. Away from the urban attractions of east-coast England, there are many encounters with nature to be had. Fabulous walks around the Wash will take you on some of the lesser-trod footpaths in the country and get you up close with some of our most tranquil environments.

Don't miss

- ✓ Discovering one of the biggest bird colonies in the UK on a boat trip from Bridlington

- ✓ Feasting at the world's largest fish and chip shop and smallest pub in Cleethorpes

- ✓ Enjoying the rides and amusements pulling in the crowds at Skegness

- ✓ Learning about Hull's maritime history and sprinkling chip spice on your chips

- ✓ Enjoying a walk to Spurn Head, a dramatic natural spit

36

SCARBOROUGH
A TALE OF TWO BAYS

The castle between the bays

Perched atop Scarborough's prominent headland, the town's historic castle is an ideal place for visitors to get to grips with the area's human and natural background. Now cared for by English Heritage, the castle (☎ 0370 333 1181 www. english-heritage.org.uk ♥ YO11 1HY) had its defining days in the 12th century when it was developed by King Henry II and King John. It saw plenty of action in key moments of English history. Twice Scarborough Castle was besieged by Parliamentarians during the English Civil War, and it was also fortified in the face of the threats against the country from the Jacobites and Napoleon. More recently, the castle was bombarded by German warships during the First World War. It's obvious why this 16-acre hilltop site has been a popular location for the nation's defenders down the centuries; the view out across the North Sea gave an early warning if an invading force was on the move. Today, the views from the castle are recreational instead of strategic and give an insight into the town's distinct make-up. To the north and south of the castle's headland are large bays where the sea's erosive powers have carved away the softer rock along the coastline. The town is defined by its two bays and they have a very different feel. Both have decent beaches and a range of facilities, though the South Bay is by far the busier of the two and has more in the

▽ Scarborough Castle, keeping watch over both the town's bays.

Getting here

On the east coast of Yorkshire between Whitby and Bridlington, Scarborough is one of the country's most popular seaside resorts. The A64, A170 and A171 merge here as people head east from Leeds and York. Scarborough train station is in a central position, about 400m from the coast on the A64.

way of amusement arcades and souvenir shops. The quieter North Bay has a Blue Flag award for its beach, some major attractions such as the Sea Life Centre and a wide range of B&Bs and hotels at the top of the cliff. To make the most of a day in Scarborough, walk between both bays or take the open-top bus, noting the changes as you go.

△ The boats in Scarborough are important for both tourism and fishing.

Fish and chips

Award-winning North Bay Fisheries, on Columbus Ravine, has a great reputation and is ideally situated next to Peasholm Park. There are picnic benches, so you can tuck in outside on sunny days (☎ 01723 500073 ♥ YO12 7QZ). If you're feeling peckish in the South Bay, head to the Lifeboat Fish Bar on Eastborough, which is well worth the short walk from the seafront (☎ 07970 091083 ♥ YO11 1NJ).

Music by the sea

Scarborough's Open Air Theatre (☎ 01723 818111 www.scarboroughopenairtheatre.com ♥ YO12 6PF) has hosted the top names in the music industry over recent years and the programme of summer concerts is always impressive. Thousands of people combine a visit to the seaside with the chance to enjoy these coastal gigs, which run in June, July and August.

A walk in the park

From the South Bay, enjoy a walk along the promenade towards the North Bay, enjoying the vista out to sea and the changing face of this picturesque seaside town. When you reach the colourful row of beach huts, follow signs up the hill to Peasholm Park and you'll come to one of the best-loved public spaces in the country. Dominating the famous park is a large boating lake, which proves popular in the summer months with tourists and locals alike. The biggest decision you'll face is not whether to step into a boat, but which type of vessel to take out on to the water – choose from traditional rowing boats, canoes, dragon-headed pedalos and swan launches. Sit back and relax, listening to live music coming from the bandstand in the middle of the lake. With a sea breeze cooling your brow and a drink in hand, there are few places better to be on a sunny day.

△ Getting ready for a dip, it's the town's Bathing Belle statue.

For the adrenaline junky

There are a few fairground rides at the foot of the headland between Scarborough's North Bay and South Bay. It's called Luna Park and you'll find dodgems, a helter-skelter and a big wheel. Those seeking more of a white-knuckle adventure should head inland to Flamingo Land for a theme park experience (📞 0800 4088840 www.flamingoland.co.uk ◉ YO17 6UX). Thrill seekers will be able to have a go on the world's steepest roller coaster, a ride that flies you around like a superhero and a motorbike ride propelling you to superfast speeds in a matter of seconds. Flamingo Land combines its adrenaline-rush rides with a small zoo, giving you the chance to get up close with lions, tigers, hippos and giraffes. And don't miss the fabulous sea lion show!

🛎 Stay a while

🛏 The Toulson Court, Columbus Ravine, Scarborough, YO12 7QZ.
📞 01723 503218
www.toulsoncourtscarborough.co.uk

🧳 Crown Spa Hotel, Esplanade, Scarborough, YO11 2AG. 📞 01723 357400 www.crownspahotel.com

⛺ Scarborough Camping and Caravanning Club, Burniston Road, Scarborough, YO13 0DA. 📞 01723 366212 www.campingandcaravanningclub.co.uk

37

BEMPTON CLIFFS
CITY OF BIRDS

Pack your binoculars!

The chalk cliffs between Bridlington and Filey on the east coast of Yorkshire are home to a metropolis of birdlife. Between April and October, around half a million aves take a perch on Bempton Cliffs to lay eggs and rear their young. Cramming precariously on to ledges, gannets, guillemots, razorbills and kittiwakes contribute to the enormous population at what is the UK's largest mainland seabird colony. The main pull for many binocular-wearing tourists are the puffins carrying fish to their newly born pufflings. Their black body – usually about 30cm tall – contrasts beautifully with their white face and orange legs and beak. This is one of the most cherished bird sightings on these shores. The RSPB looks after over 5km of this valuable coastline, managing the needs of the birds and marine life while encouraging people to see the spectacle and be educated about the needs of nature. A network of clifftop paths leads out from the RSPB reserve at Bempton Cliffs (📞 01262 422212 www.rspb.org.uk 📍 YO15 1JF). They connect a series of lookout positions that allow birders to gaze over the edge at the thousands of seabirds flying out to catch fish and returning to the very same spot.

△ Gannets are one of the big pulls for birdwatchers on the east coast.

△ Puffins at Bempton Cliffs – possibly the cutest of the birds here?

Puffin cruise

The best vantage point to appreciate the enormity of Bempton's vast seabird colony is from out on the water. Starting in April and continuing throughout the summer, the well-known pleasure cruiser *Yorkshire Belle* takes bird lovers on a three-hour round trip from Bridlington, beyond Flamborough Head and up to Birdville. The sound of calling gulls, gannets and guillemots fills the senses as you start to see them dart about overhead. The smell of guano is pungent as you get up close to this colossal habitat. Photo opportunities abound as you zoom in on nesting gannets, a seldom-seen group of shags and puffins bobbing in the water. These tours are very popular and need booking in advance through the RSPB (☎ 01262 422211 www.rspb.co.uk ♥ YO15 3AN)

Flamborough Head

Jutting out to sea and visible for miles along the coast, Flamborough Head is home to some wonderful natural features and a prominent lighthouse. The first attempt at a lighthouse, dating back to 1674, still remains but was never actually lit because shipping would not contribute to funds. The current lighthouse dates back to 1806 and since 1975 has been accompanied by an electric foghorn that warns shipping in times when visibility is poor. Before this, in the 19th century, a gun and explosive rockets were fired in foggy weather. Tours of the lighthouse are available for those willing and able to scale the 119 steps (☎ 01262 673769 www.trinityhouse.co.uk ♥ YO15 1AR). A path near the lighthouse leads down to the small beach, which is a treasure trove of distinctive features caused by coastal erosion. The wave-cut platform has been carved out by the sea and is now home to many rock pools. Look out also for caves, arches, stacks and stumps that have been created over hundreds of years.

🔔 Stay a while

🛏 Swandale Guest House, 11 Swanland Avenue, Bridlington, YO15 2HH.
☎ 01262 424857
www.swandaleguesthouse.co.uk

💼 Wrangham House Hotel, 10 Stonegate, Hunmanby, YO14 0NS. ☎ 01723 891333 www.wranghamhouse.com

⛺ Centenary Way Camping and Caravan Park, Muston Road, Filey, YO14 0HU.
☎ 01723 516415
centenarywaycamping.co.uk

△ Flamborough Head is well known for its towering lighthouse.

Take a step back...

A little further up the coast from Bempton and Flamborough, Filey is an antidote to the busy vibes of Bridlington and is known for being a calmer, more laid-back place. The biggest selling point here is the huge beach. It's ideal for families to enjoy lazy days and there's so much space that it's never as crowded as nearby resorts.

 Award-winning chippy

The fish and chips served up at '149' on Marton Road have been voted the best in the country and they're proud to say their stock comes from sustainable sources (☎ 01262 678378 www.149fishandchips.co.uk ● YO16 7DJ).

Getting here

Look out for the prominent local road signs for Bempton Cliffs, which are sandwiched between Filey and Bridlington off the A165. The village of Bempton has a train station, which is just over a mile's walk away from the RSPB reserve.

Bridlington

One of the fastest options for a day at the coast from Leeds, York and Sheffield, Bridlington is a busy place to be on sunny weekends, but there's plenty of beach to go round. The small working harbour ensures there's a plentiful supply of seafood, with crabs and cockles among the treats on sale in the town's many fish kiosks. For a taste of something more sweet and crunchy, there's plenty of John Bull rock in local shops; the factory is located on the edge of Bridlington and tours of the site are available (☎ 01262 678525 www.john-bull.com ● YO15 3QY).

△ Geography field trips come to Flamborough to see the range of natural features.

38

THE HOLDERNESS COAST
LIFE ON THE EDGE

Why visit?

★ Spend time in small villages living a precarious balance between the land and sea

★ Walk to Britain's newest tidal island along a sandy spit

★ Learn how humans have battled against the elements on this coast – and often lost

From Mappleton to Hornsea – coastal erosion in action

GCSE geography students in the north of England are likely to have come across Mappleton, a tiny village on the Holderness coastline that has been ravaged by attacks from the sea. The cliffs here on the East Riding of Yorkshire consist of glacial till – or boulder clay. This is literally a glacial mash of clay and small rocks that have been compressed over time. It's incredibly soft and any pieces you find on the beach will break apart in your hands. No wonder, then, that storms can cause a huge amount of damage here in just a few hours, making it the most rapidly eroding coastline in Europe. Sand is taken from the beach by the waves and gradually moved south, weakening the natural defences around Hornsea. The sand is eventually deposited in the mouth of the Humber Estuary, forming the long, thin spit

△ You don't have to be an expert to realise that the Holderness cliffs are ripe for erosion.

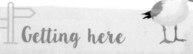

Getting here

Head east of Hull on the A1033 to reach Withernsea and Spurn Head.

known as Spurn. At Hornsea and Mappleton, huge piles of rocks have been placed in front of the cliffs to dissipate the wave's energy, but it's a difficult battle to fight. Erosion rates have been slowed where costly measures have been taken, but it tends to make the problem worse further along down the coast. The walk along the beach from Mappleton to Hornsea is a charming one. Lighthouses are visible at Spurn Point to the south and Flamborough Head to the north, and this delightful three-mile stretch of sand is rarely busy. A short walk along the front will reveal the sea's damage; fences once firmly in fields now dangle in mid-air and holiday homes at Hornsea teeter on the edge of the cliff. The battle between humans and nature in these parts is not over.

Fish and chips

Whitehead's on The Greenway at Hornsea has an awesome reputation, sourcing all fish within ten minutes' drive away and letting you know the name of your frier (☎ 01964 536954 www.whiteheadsfishandchips.com ● HU18 1SL). Expect a queue.

Spurn Head

Approaching Spurn is like taking a journey towards the end of the Earth. Settlements become few and far between and the flat landscape slowly tails off towards the North Sea. When you arrive at the entrance to this unusual landform, park up

and begin one of the most fabulous walks in the country. The stroll to Spurn Head, at the tip of the spit just beyond the lighthouse, is a six-mile there-and-back venture into the Humber Estuary. For your own safety, it's important you plan your visit to coincide with the tide. Back in 2013, a ferocious storm surge with extraordinarily high sea levels swept away a section of the spit. The result was the creation of the country's newest tidal island, with crossing restricted twice a day. Under no circumstances attempt to cross over to Spurn Point at high tide and you should take careful note of the warning signs that display the danger times.

Stay a while

🛏 Acorn Lodge, 31 New Road, Hornsea, HU18 1PG. ☎ 01964 536733
www.acornlodgehornsea.co.uk

💼 The Victoria, 39 Market Place, Hornsea, HU18 1AN. ☎ 01964 537653
www.victoriahornsea.co.uk

⛺ Hornsea Leisure Park, Atwick Road, Hornsea, HU18 1EL. ☎ 01964 535352
www.shorewoodlg.co.uk/hornsea

The shifting sands on this curious landform have always caused problems for maintaining a road to Britain's only full-time RNLI lifeboat station and the now-disused lighthouse. Some of the damage caused to it can still be seen, resembling that caused in an earthquake. Walk on the beach along the spit and you'll see a human-made treasure trove of attempts to fight back the sea, ranging from permanent groins for holding the sand in place to temporary road surfaces and bundles of bricks. In contrast to human attempts at coastal

△ The walk to Spurn Head reveals debris from ferocious storms.

management, the natural landscape provides a haven for a wide range of butterflies and birds. Be aware of the brown-tail moth caterpillars, though. In recent years, several visitors have had a serious reaction to the hairs of this creature, which can break off as barbs and lead to rashes, headaches and, in some cases, severe illness.

At the far end of Spurn Point, you're remarkably close to the ships heading in and out of the Humber Estuary. Grimsby and Cleethorpes are visible across the water in Lincolnshire and a horizon of wind turbines, docks and oil terminals sits starkly next to the peace and quiet of your immediate surroundings. The Spurn Discovery Centre (☎ 01964 650144 www.ywt. org.uk ♥ HU12 0UH) contains a bird-watching

area with information about the different species and binoculars available to borrow. A café and toilets are also on site. Those not wanting to walk to the end of the spit can join a safari-style trip on a truck that follows the route of the old road.

Withernsea Lighthouse

Only a handful of lighthouses are built inland, and Withernsea's is a fine example that you can have a tour around. The 38m-tall white building in the middle of the town no longer gives a warning to ships in the North Sea, but visitors can learn about the lighthouse's history thanks to old photographs and exhibits from the RNLI and HM Coastguard (☎ 01964 614834 www. withernsealighthouse.co.uk ♥ HU19 2DY).

39
HULL
CHIP SPICE AND A DEAD BOD

Why visit?

★ Explore a rejuvenated city with a rich history of fishing and fighting slavery

★ Take a stroll over one of the world's longest suspension bridges

★ Cover your coastal fish and chips in a spicy local condiment

To Hull and back

Like many industrial cities in the north of England, Hull has replaced industrial decay with urban renewal. After years in the shadows, Hull has bounced back from recession in a sea of cultural transformation to become one of the coolest places in the country. Nowhere is this more evident than on Humber Street near the city's marina, where rotting fruit warehouses have metamorphosed into cool bars, coffee houses, galleries, shops and restaurants. The new-look thoroughfare – a stone's throw from the Humber Estuary – won the Academy of Urbanism's Great Street Award in 2018, cementing the importance of this cobbled part of Hull's history. Take time to wander down Humber Street and see the innovative ways the old warehouses have been put to use.

△ The city of Hull has many attractive waterways.

A Dead Bod

When a couple of trawlermen had a few beers and went to the side of the Humber with a tin of white paint, they had no idea their graffiti of an upturned dead bird would become a priceless character that represented Hull. To reflect local dialect, they scribed 'A Dead Bod' beneath the drawing and there it lay to rest on corrugated iron, welcoming boats back home. It was only visible when on the river and many folk were unaware it was there, but when plans to build a new factory threatened its survival there was a large public campaign to save it. Today, the iconic bird hangs in the café space at Humber Street Gallery (☏ 01482 304453 www. humberstreetgallery.co.uk ♥ HU1 1TU). That

△ Hull's iconic graffiti contains a caption to clear up any confusion – it's a dead bod!

image of a 'dead bod' has become an unlikely symbol of the city. You can buy T-shirts and mugs with it on, as Hullensians continue to celebrate this unique piece of 1960s' graffiti.

Humber Bridge

The enormous Humber Bridge – once the longest suspension bridge in the world – is best appreciated by having a stroll across its mesmerising 2.2km length. Head for Humber Bridge Country Park (☎ 01482 395207 ♥ HU13 0HB) and take the steps up to the road before stepping on to one of the two pedestrian routes that flank the bridge. Pick a fine day if you can; it can get terribly breezy when you're high up in the middle of the estuary. The bridge constantly moves in the wind and can bend up to 3m in 80mph gusts. The main cables are made up of nearly 15,000 wires. End to end, the total length of all the wire would be 71,000km and reach around the globe almost twice!

The Deep

Educating families about conservation, local fish stocks and species from further afield, people have enjoyed diving into The Deep since it opened in 2002. In that first year it attracted more visitors than London Zoo and has continued to build on its reputation. One of the best aquariums in the country, highlights include a 10m deep underwater tunnel featuring sharks,

BRIDGING THE HUMBER

- 💡 Opened: June 1981
- 💡 Volume: Over 10 million vehicles a year
- 💡 Length: 2,220m
- 💡 Width: 28.5m
- 💡 Height: 155.5m
- 💡 Cost: £151m

an icy exhibit housing penguins and an elevator taking you up through the water. Gaze out across the Humber from the awesome viewpoint in the top-floor café (☎ 01482 381000 www.thedeep. co.uk ♥ HU9 1TU).

△ The Spurn Lightship is one of Hull's many maritime attractions.

Getting here

Head east on the M62 and continue along the A63 to reach the centre of Hull. The city's train station is found at 184 Ferensway, Hull, HU1 3QX.

Destination: history

There's no better way to learn about Hull's history than to step aboard vessels that have journeyed through it. The Spurn Lightship, found in the Marina, guided ships in and out of the Humber Estuary for nearly 50 years until it was decommissioned in 1975. (☎ 01482 300300 www.hcandl.co.uk ◉ HU1 1TJ). The *Arctic Corsair* is a trawler built in 1960 that saw front-line action in the 1970s' Cod War with Iceland. Opened up as a museum in 1999, a refurbishment programme started in 2019. The ship is due to take its place in the city's North End shipyard as part of a programme turning Hull into 'Yorkshire's maritime city'.

 Fish, chips and spice

Buy fish and chips in Hull and you'll need more than just salt and vinegar to create the perfect local meal. A visit to the United States in the 1970s by a pair of local spice blenders saw them introduced to a mix of salt and paprika that was just perfect on chips. A version of it was made in Hull and sold to the city's pioneering Yankee Burger bar, with other varieties coming online and being distributed throughout Hull's chippies. Walk into a chip shop in the city today and you'll find 'chip spice' on the counter alongside more familiar condiments. Sprinkle them on your takeaway to enjoy fish and chips Hull-style! For a good eating-in or taking-out chip shop experience, head to East Park Chippy on Holderness Road (☎ 01482 703730 www.eastparkchippy.co.uk ◉ HU9 3DT).

◁ The *Arctic Corsair* gives a unique insight to the Cod Wars.

▽ Historic vessels mix with the new in the harbour at Hull.

△ The statue for tireless anti-slavery campaigner William Wilberforce.

△ Enjoying a coffee at Thieving Harry's on Hull's Humber Street.

Ending the slave trade

One of the most influential men to hail from Hull, William Wilberforce became a Member of Parliament and tirelessly campaigned for the abolition of slavery. In a political battle that lasted decades, Wilberforce headed the Parliamentary movement that resulted in the Slave Trade Act of 1807 and later supported the passing of the Slavery Abolition Act 1833. He died just days after knowing this bill would pass through Parliament and was buried in Westminster Abbey. The birthplace of this famous Hull native is now the Wilberforce House (☎ 01482 300300 www. hcandl.co.uk/museums-and-galleries/wilber force-house ◉HU1 1NQ), telling the horrific story of the slave trade and the role the MP played in bringing it to an end.

Fancy a coffee?

It's the locally roasted blends and weekly rotated guest beans that make a visit to Thieving Harry's a must for coffee fans. The Humber Street venue is also a great place for breakfast (☎ 01482 214141 www.thievingharrys.co.uk ◉HU1 1TU).

CLEETHORPES
WHERE SIZE MATTERS

All features great and small

The joys of Cleethorpes are found in both large and tiny record breakers. The magnificent building on the pier has been a source of fun for generations, hosting stand-up from comedy legends, gigs by rock bands and student club nights. Cleethorpes Pier entered the record books in 2017 when the world's largest fish and chip restaurant opened. Able to cater for up to 500 people at a time, all of them eating their way through the nation's favourite dish, Papa's Restaurant is especially popular (☎ 01472 601501 www.papasfishandchips.com ♀ DN35 8SF). Most people sitting down to a fish supper will have ornate chandeliers above their head, with the old stage and a grand piano helping to set the decadent scene. It blends modern-day facilities with a nod to yesteryear and, with the tide ebbing and flowing below you, it's hard to imagine a more appropriate setting.

Getting here

Almost directly across the mouth of the estuary from Spurn Point, Cleethorpes kitsch is the perfect antidote to its more industrial neighbour, Grimsby. Follow the A180 from Doncaster or the A46 north of Lincoln to reach these symbiotic towns that huddle on the Humber. Cleethorpes has a good train service, too. The station is a stone's throw from the beach and well connected to Doncaster, Sheffield and Manchester.

In contrast to the grand opulence of the nation's largest chippy, Cleethorpes is also home to the tiniest pub on the planet. As fantastically homely

▽ The pier at Cleethorpes is home to the world's biggest fish and chip shop.

△ Enjoying a big rest at the smallest pub.

All aboard!

The beachside at Cleethorpes is a lengthy walk to tackle, but thankfully two trains chug along to help you out. Cleethorpes Coastal Light Railway (☎ 01472 604657 www.cclr.co.uk ♥ DN35 0AG) takes you on a lovely four-mile route by the seaside, leaving from the café at Lakeside Station to the Signal Box Inn and out towards the Greenwich Meridian line. Linking the light railway with the northern Promenade, the deliciously named Lollipop Road Train (☎ 07808 645858 www.lollipop-road-train-cleethorpes.co.uk ♥ DN36 4NX) hands lollies out to all children. They can be seen quietly licking away when the service runs along the seafront every half hour.

as it is cramped, The Signal Box Inn (☎ 01472 604657 www.cclr.co.uk ♥ DN35 0AG) measures just 8ft by 8ft but still manages to pack a hefty punch when it comes to providing a wide range of ales and ciders. There's music and a TV to entertain drinkers, but don't expect to be able to sit in comfort; there's hardly enough room to swing a cat in this signal shed located at the coast light railway. Expect to queue out of the door, but don't miss the quirky cosiness of this tiny public house.

🧺 Fish and chips

Aside from the huge restaurant on the pier, there are plenty of other spots to indulge in the traditional seaside dish. Steels Corner House Restaurant (☎ 01472 692644 www.steelscornerhouse.co.uk ♥ DN35 8LY) has been a local institution since it opened in 1946. Across the road on Market Street, Beckett's is a popular chippy with a traditional feel (☎ 01472 691234 ♥ DN35 8LY).

△ All aboard! The light railway helps people get up and down the seafront.

△ Kids love the elaborate waterfall and bird statue near the front at Cleethorpes.

Grimsby tales

Head to Alexandra Dock in Grimsby to tackle the story of the town's fishing heritage (☎ 01472 323345 www.fishingheritage.com ⚐ DN31 1UZ). Discover what life was like for local trawlermen in the 1950s, experiencing the sights, smells and sounds of the day. You can also dive into the town's colourful past in the old police cells at the Time Trap museum (☎ 01472 324109 www.nelincs.gov.uk ⚐ DN31 1HX). The twists and turns through this unusual building are full of exhibits telling the story of Grimsby's industrial and cultural journey.

When to visit

Morris dancing and music combine with all kinds of fermented juice at the annual Folk and Cider Festival that has put Cleethorpes on the events map. It takes place in late May at the Cleethorpes Coast Light Railway and features three days of bands and dancing. In mid-September, the Rail Ale and Blues festival is home to more live music and almost 100 different ales and ciders. In the height of the summer holidays, the Coastal Family Festival at the Meridian Showground is home to diverse music, food and drink.

🛎 Stay a while

🛏 **Jedburgh Guest House,**
26 Albert Road, DN35 8LX.
☎ 01472 508092
www.jedburghguesthouse.co.uk

🧳 **Premier Inn, Meridian Point, King's Road, Cleethorpes, DN35 0PN.**
☎ 0871 527 9470
www.premierinn.com

🏕 **Thorpe Park Holiday Centre,**
Cleethorpes DN35 0PW.
☎ 01472 813395
www.haven.com

SKEGNESS

WELCOME TO FABULOUS SKEGVEGAS!

Why visit?

★ Pack in all the fun of seaside – don't forget the slots, the chippy and the funfair!

★ Stay at the first ever Butlin's, a monument to early mass tourism

★ Chill out on a wildlife afternoon at nearby Gibraltar Point

Glitzy home of the Jolly Fisherman

Thousands of kids in Lincolnshire and the North Midlands have grown up enjoying day trips to 'Skeggy' – a vibrant seaside town of just 20,000 people that punches well above its weight when it comes to fun. Skegness was firmly placed on the tourist map thanks to a famous railway poster designed by John Hassall in 1908. It featured a larger than life 'Jolly Fisherman' skipping along the beach beneath the now well-known slogan 'Skegness is SO Bracing'. That same fisherman is still a symbol of the town, with statues and T-shirts reminding townsfolk of their background. Just like in those early days, the function of Skegness today is to entertain. It does it well with chippies, a good beach, pubs, clubs and plenty of neon-lit amusements – all helping to earn it the nickname 'Skegvegas'. A major draw for families escaping to the east coast is Bottons Pleasure Beach (☎ 01754 763697 www. pleasurebeachskegness.com ♥ PE25 2UQ). Right on the seafront, this is the place to go for classic seaside rides like the ghost train, cups and saucers, pirate boat and giant wheel.

The first Butlin's

Further north along the Lincolnshire coast, Ingoldmells is the seaside town chosen by legendary tourism pioneer Billy Butlin to build his first holiday camp. In the 1930s he ploughed £100,000 into building the large site, which contained hundreds of chalets and a range of entertainment facilities. The grand opening took place over Easter in 1936, with famous pilot

△ The Big Wheel is an iconic sight at Skeggy's Pleasure Beach.

 Fish and chips

Conveniently located close to the seafront, Trawler's Catch is a popular spot serving up hearty portions in a large restaurant with a nautical theme (☎ 01754 611400 ♥ PE25 2UG).

Amy Johnson doing the honours. Adverts were place in national newspapers and holidaymakers were soon flocking to Butlin's for a week-long full board break at bargain prices. Several refurbishments later, Butlin's is still thriving on the Lincolnshire coast and the famous redcoats will be there to greet you. The modern facilities are very different from those that housed people in the 1930s; you can still see one of the original chalets, now a preserved grade II listed building providing an insight into the early days of mass tourism (☎ 0330 100 6648 www.butlins.com ♥ PE25 1NJ).

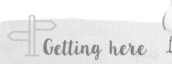

Getting here

On the east coast, just to the north of The Wash, Skegness sits at the end of the A158 and A52. The train station is in the centre of town on Wainfleet Road.

Wind power

The view out to sea at Skegness is dominated by two huge offshore wind farms, producing power that is transmitted to the national grid along cables that run beneath the golf course by the north shore. The first wind farm here was completed in 2008 and made the UK a world leader in offshore power; the Lynn and Inner Dowsing farms have 54 turbines, which cover an area of 20km² and have a capacity of 194MW. Construction work started in 2011 on the even bigger Lincs wind farm, which sits a little further away from the coast to the east. With the sea up to 15m deep there, it took two years to get the 75 turbines in place at this 270MW wind farm.

△ Powering the bright coastal lights, the huge offshore wind farm near Skegness's coast.

△ A popular rollercoaster at the Pleasure Beach provides white knuckle thrills.

Gibraltar Point – a wildlife haven on The Wash

If the razzmatazz of Skegness gets too much, there's a perfect antidote within walking distance to the south of the town. Gibraltar Point Nature Reserve covers a large stretch of fantastically unspoilt coastline that begins on the edge of Skegness and continues south to The Wash. There are many opportunities to walk and cycle along the trails of the reserve, but make sure you factor in a stop at the visitor centre and café. This is an intriguing place for birders to hang out, given that it was one of the first bird observatories to be established, back in 1949. The wildlife changes with the seasons at Gibraltar Point, enticing people back at different times of the year. Whether it's viewing skylarks in summer or spotting brent geese in winter, pack your binoculars and plan to spend some time here.

🔔 **Stay a while**

🛏 The Aldor, 19 Scarborough Avenue, Skegness, PE25 2SZ. ☎ 01754 766963 www.thealdor.co.uk

🧳 The Westdene, 1 Trafalgar Avenue, Skegness, PE25 3EU. ☎ 01754 765168 www.westdenehotel.com

⛺ Crooked Willow Campsite, Burgh Le Marsh, Skegness, PE24 5JD. ☎ 01754 890480 www.crookedwillowcampsite.co.uk

42

THE WASH
ENGLAND'S BIGGEST BAY

The Sir Peter Scott Lighthouse

Three miles into the tidal marsh of The Wash from Sutton Bridge, an historic building has been a vital beacon for shipping in this area. Built in 1830, the Sir Peter Scott Lighthouse (📍 PE12 9QS) has helped vessels navigate the cutting of the River Nene that drains the surrounding low-lying fens. Occupied by a string of local families for its first century, the lighthouse was also a customs hailing station in the days before ship-to-shore radio. This involved somebody speaking to the crew through a megaphone to find out what the cargo was and where they were heading.

Peter Scott, son of the legendary Antarctic explorer, came to the house in 1933 and spent time here developing his reputation as an artist and writer. Over the decades, this iconic fenland lighthouse has experienced difficult times and maintaining it has been a struggle. It was requisitioned by the army during the Second World War and almost had the top cut off to house a gun platform. After falling into disrepair in the 1940s and suffering heavy vandalism in the 1970s, restoration work is ongoing and plans to build a visitor centre are afoot, so the public can experience this extraordinary part of coastal history for themselves. There is a free car park close to the lighthouse and a footpath that leads you by the side of it, and beyond into the mesmerising nature reserve. A recent Ordnance Survey poll indicated this area has some of the least used footpaths, so you may well spend time here without seeing a soul.

🔔 **Stay a while**

🛏 The Beeches, 2 Guanock Terrace, King's Lynn, PE30 5QT. ☎ 01553 766577
www.beechesguesthouse.co.uk

🏨 Globe Hotel, King Street, King's Lynn, PE30 1EZ. ☎ 01553 668000
www.jdwetherspoon.com/hotels

⛺ Pine Cones Caravan and Camping, Dersingham, King's Lynn, PE31 6WL. ☎ 01485 544224
www.pineconescc.co.uk

▽ The historic Sir Peter Scott Lighthouse, a former customs hailing station.

△ Birds on the Wash create incredible patterns as they dance in the air.

The Wash National Nature Reserve

A stunning coastal walk that is as remote and desolate as it is charming and invigorating, the open access path named after Sir Peter Scott is the best way to see the fenlands of England's biggest bay. Pretty and harsh in equal measure, this 10-mile walk links Sutton Bridge with King's Lynn via a momentous loop along a grassy defence wall built to hold back the sea from vulnerable farmland. Connecting the River Nene with the Great Ouse, this is a fabulously atmospheric path. There are buses that connect King's Lynn with Sutton Bridge, helping you to complete the full length of the walk. When stepping out into the nature reserve, it's important you stick to the route because of nearby quicksand and marshland. It's a flat and accessible route that will take you close to mudflats and salt marshes – all the time enjoying the vista of open water in the distance. Expect to see migrant birds such as grey plovers, oystercatchers and dunlins as they come here to feed on the mudflats during the autumnal months. Over the winter, it's time for waders to flock in.

 Getting here

The A17 between King's Lynn and Sutton Bridge is the best place to access the minor roads that head to The Wash National Nature Reserve.

Don't panic!

Occasionally, a peaceful stroll through the nature reserve may be disturbed by the alarming sound of gunfire and bombing. Further east along The Wash, an extensive area of mudflats and salt marsh is used by the RAF and NATO aircraft to practise dropping bombs and firing aircraft weapons. The noise can come as a shock if you're not used to it, although people living in the region have long since become accustomed to the activities. Bombing times are published in advance on the gov.uk website.

Fish and chips

Close to the bridge over the River Nene in Sutton Bridge, Baxter's Fish Shop will serve up a hearty meal to those who have explored the fens (☎ 01406 350335 ♥ PE12 9SF).

△ The paths around the Wash are some of the quietest in the country.

43

NORTH NORFOLK
THE INCREDIBLE SHRINKING COAST

Why visit?

★ Take a trip on an amphibious vehicle to view seals on nearby sandbanks

★ Sample local seafood by tucking into a delicious Cromer crab

★ Observe cliffs infamous for their destructive rate of erosion

Seal city

West of Cromer, a long section of the north Norfolk coast is under the protection of Areas of Outstanding Natural Beauty and Nature Reserves. There are many places along this beautiful coastline, approaching the entrance to The Wash, that make great places to take a walk and set up for a few hours of wildlife spotting. At the western edge of this ecological haven, Hunstanton sees a return to bright lights, candyfloss stalls and amusements. It's a typical and very popular coastal haunt, boasting a smattering of attractions for those day-tripping here. It's also one of the best places to embark on a marine-life tour to see some of the 3,000 common seals that call The Wash their home. Head for the amphibious vessels at Searles Sea Tours for a truly unique perspective of this fabulous area (☎ 01485 534444 www. seatours.co.uk ♥ PE36 5BH). The Wash Monster, brightly decorated with a mouthful of teeth at the front, takes you from the beach, out into the sea and heads towards sandbanks in The Wash, getting as close as possible to the seals. On some trips, it's even possible to get out on to remote patches of sand in the middle of the water, providing a bizarre and surreal opportunity for photographs. When the sun goes down, folk in west-facing Hunstanton can enjoy the lovely sight of the sun setting below the sea on the horizon – something that is highly unusual on the east coast.

Getting here

From Hunstanton in the west to Cromer in the east, destinations along the north of Norfolk are reached by driving along the A148. Sheringham, West Runton and Cromer are accessible by rail.

▽ Wide-open beaches offer plenty of room for stretching your legs.

Fish and chips

There's no shortage of fish and chip shops along the coast of north Norfolk, with one of the favourites among locals being Mary Jane's Fish Bar on Garden Street, Cromer (☎ 01263 511208 www.maryjanes. co.uk ♥ NR27 9HN).

Erosion hotspot

This section of the English coast is renowned for the frightening rate of erosion the cliffs suffer at the hands of the North Sea. In recent decades, homes, hotels and caravans alike have been lost to the sea as waves eat away at the soft boulder clay found here. It's not uncommon for several metres of land to be lost each year, although management techniques including groynes and rip-rap have held back the destructive process at settlements such as Cromer and Happisburgh. Projections for future levels of erosion indicate there are tough times ahead for some property owners living by the sea. One of the most dramatic examples of erosion in the 20th century saw the grand Overstrand Hotel, built in 1903, lost to the sea in the post-war years. Today, no trace of the once-thriving business remains. A walk along the beach in many parts of north Norfolk will reveal evidence of the battle between humans and nature. It's common to see debris washed up on the shore from buildings that once stood tall here.

Cromer

Don't leave this famous north Norfolk seaside town without sampling Cromer crab, which, along with lobsters, provides the bulk of the local fishing income. There are plenty of ways to sample the local delicacy, thought by some to be the best crabs available in the UK. For some of the tastiest crab treats, check out the Jetty Café on the High Street (☎ 01263 513814 ♥ NR27 9HG) and the suitably named Crabpot Café on Hamilton Road (☎ 01263 514023 www. crabpotcafe.co.uk ♥ NR27 9HL).

◁ **Management techniques such as groynes are deployed to try and stop coastal erosion.**

Lavender's in the air!

Just a couple of miles from the seaside at Hunstanton, the scent of lavender beckons you in to the world-famous gardens and oil distillery at Heacham (☎ 01485 570384 www.norfolk-lavender.co.uk ⚲ PE31 7JE). Norfolk Lavender was founded in 1932 and since then has grown in popularity and expanded the services on offer. As well as garden products and lavender-based household goods, the children's playground makes this a good place to spend an afternoon with the family. Tours give the history of Norfolk's lavender trade and there's the chance to pick up a fragranced souvenir to remember your time along this coast.

🛎 *Stay a while*

🛏 Danum House, 22 Paul's Lane, Overstrand, NR27 0PE. ☎ 01263 579327 www.danum-house.weebly.com

💼 Cliftonville Hotel, 29 Runton Road, Cromer, NR27 9AS. ☎ 01263 512543 www.cliftonvillehotel.co.uk

⛺ Cromer Camping, Hall Road, Cromer, NR27 9JG. ☎ 07771 971933 www.cromercamping.com

△ The north Norfolk coastal area is famous for its lavender scents.

SOUTH-EAST

Days spent on the East Anglian coast around Lowestoft offer opportunities to unwind and relax. There really are few ways of spending a day along the coast than sitting in a canoe on the tidal Norfolk Broads and then heading to the seafront for fish and chips. A little way further south than brings you to one of the beating economic hearts of the nation. Felixstowe is the largest container port in the country and a walk along the coast path will allow you to see some of the world's biggest ships up close and imagine what's inside the thousands of containers that have just arrived from Europe, Asia and beyond.

There's plenty of opportunity for traditional family days out along this south-eastern coast of Britain. Enjoy a lengthy walk to the end of Southend's pier, the longest in the world, and then have fun sampling rides, cockles and contemporary art works at rejuvenated Margate.

Visitors to England may not think of London as being a coastal attraction, but the Thames is a tidal river and the city was once one of the biggest shipping ports in the world. Getting out on to the river is one of the best ways to take a tour of the capital, either on a high-speed RIB or on a slower-paced cruise. The flood barrier beyond Greenwich is a reminder of how Londoners are more than aware of their relationship with the coast.

Standing on the White Cliffs of Dover on a clear day, you get a great understanding of just how close our European neighbours are. From here, a 30-minute train journey or 90-minute ferry

sailing will take you to the French coast. While the trip across the Channel to enjoy croissants and French wine may seem romantic today, the proximity to Calais has brought more than its fair share of anxiety and horror. When the country has been at war, the south-east has often borne the brunt of it. The coast in this corner of England is dotted with fascinating insights into conflicts, from the Dunkirk tunnels in Dover and the civilian shelter in Ramsgate to the Battle of Britain museum in Folkestone and the primitive early-warning system that listened for planes at Dungeness. Look out also for the line of Martello towers that were built to protect England from Napoleonic forces. Some of them have been adapted to give tourists a much more friendly experience.

Don't miss

✓ The longest pier in the world that stretches out to sea from Southend

✓ Stepping back through many periods of history at Dover Castle

✓ Learning about the Battle of Britain in Folkestone, where the war raged overhead

✓ Discovering how the waste material from the Channel Tunnel has attracted wildlife

✓ The narrow-gauge railway ride across Romney Marsh

Of all the natural landforms around the coast of Britain, none has the symbolism and stature of the White Cliifs of Dover.

44

LOWESTOFT
MY SWEET BROAD

Why visit?

★ Venture to the most easterly town in England and be the first to see the sun rise

★ Take a boat out on the Norfolk Broads and spend the whole day on the water

★ Amble over the narrow tracks on the clifftop known as The Scores

Our most easterly town

Get up early when you visit Lowestoft and you'll be among the first people to see the sunrise. This is the most easterly town in the United Kingdom and gets the first rays of light every day. Many see Lowestoft as an unlikely place to take a break and historically it has tended to lose out in the tourism stakes to nearby Great Yarmouth. But there is plenty of eastern delight to be had in Lowestoft, from cheesy seaside amusements to excursions on the internationally significant Broads. Visit here for a couple of days and you'll have a diverse range of options open to you, from playing on an award-winning beach to paddling along on a canoe.

▽ Lowestoft is the most easterly town in the British Isles.

Fish and chips

Close to the train station and harbour, Perry's Fish and Chips on Suffolk Road has a good reputation among locals. (☎ 01502 513918 ● NR32 1DZ).

Getting here

To reach this East Anglian outpost, follow the A143 from Bury St Edmunds or take the A146 from Norwich. Taking the train to Lowestoft will bring you right next to the harbour, while Oulton Broad is serviced by two stations, one on the northern side and one to the south.

△ Flocking overhead, seabirds feature in Lowestoft street art.

What's The Scores?

Along the cliff you'll find a unique feature of Lowestoft known as The Scores. These narrow tracks have been made by people walking between the High Street and the beach over the years and it's a nice place to spend time having a stroll. Every year, the annual Scores Race sees hundreds of energetic runners take part in an event that twists and turns over hundreds of steps and small paths. For scores of a different kind, check listings at the Marina Theatre (☎ 01502 533200 marinatheatre.co.uk ♦ NR32 1HH) to see when the Royal Philharmonic Orchestra are due to play. The orchestra has long used the theatre as one of its residencies. As well as playing popular classical tunes to many delighted audiences, it carries out a lot of community work in and around Lowestoft.

🔔 *Stay a while*

🛏 Somerton Guest House, 7 Kirkley Cliff Road, Lowestoft, NR33 0BY. ☎ 01502 565665
www.somertonguesthouse.co.uk

🧳 Ivy House Country Hotel, Ivy Lane, Lowestoft, NR33 8HY. ☎ 01502 501353
www.ivyhousecountryhotel.co.uk

⛺ The Hollies Camping and Leisure Resort, London Road, Lowestoft, NR33 7PQ. ☎ 01502 507030
www.thehollieskessingland.co.uk

137

Spending a day on the Broads

Follow the inner harbour up towards Lake Lothing and you'll reach Oulton Broad. On the edge of Lowestoft, this village makes a great base for exploring the 300km² (115-sq-mile) network of rivers and lakes that make up The Broads National Park. Until the 1960s it was thought that the Broads was a natural feature, but research showed this to be a man-made area of beauty. During the Middle Ages, huge amounts of peat were cut from the area and used as fuel in surrounding towns and cities. This lowered the height of the land and, combined with a rise in the sea level, resulted in the flooded landscape we see today. Although drainage wind pumps and dykes were built to try and control the flooding, the inundation continued and created the marshes and reed beds that today attract wildlife and tourists. The Lowestoft ferry runs between the town and Oulton Broad and is a good way to get a feel for the area. At the Lowestoft end the ferry is a short walk from the

△ Elegantly designed buildings on the seafront give Lowestoft an ornamental edge.

usual seaside amusements, while shops and cafés await passengers getting off at Oulton Broad. If you fancy being more adventurous, there's plenty to discover by taking a boat out on to the Broads. Oulton Dayboats (☎ 01502 574903 ⚲ NR33 9JS) enable you to become the captain for a few hours when you take a boat out on to the water. Or visit the Waveney River Centre (☎ 01502 677343 www.waveneyrivercentre.co.uk ⚲ NR34 0DE) to pick up a kayak or Canadian canoe for a voyage on the water that will bring you up close to the reed beds and wildlife.

The devastating North Sea flood of 1953

Like many stretches of the North Sea coastline, Norfolk paid a high price when a treacherous storm led to a devastating flood at the end of January 1953. High winds and a spring tide led to sea levels 5 metres (16 feet) higher than normal, overwhelming flood defences and surging inland. Lowestoft was sliced in two by the floodwaters. One of the town's fishing trawlers and its 11-man crew had left the town to search for herring the day before the storm, never to be seen again. It was one of eight ships to disappear that night. In nearby Great Yarmouth, seawater crashed through hotels along the Golden Mile. Small boats from a holidaymaker's boating lake were used to rescue people from bedroom windows. Across Norfolk, 100 people lost their lives that night as the sea caused devastation along the coastline of the entire county. The picture in other countries bordering the North Sea was even more catastrophic. The Netherlands lost 1,836 people in the floods and a total of 361 people were killed at sea. Altogether, the ferocious storm led to 2,551 people losing their lives and saw governments committing to ambitious flood defence projects to protect the coast from future extreme weather events.

FELIXSTOWE
THE PORT OF BRITAIN

A resort recharged

The seafront at this Suffolk seaside town is a pleasant place to take a walk, passing dozens of groynes designed to keep the sand in place, cool coffee shops and a row of cared-for beach huts that are popular in the summer. At the end of the A14 beyond Ipswich and not particularly on the way to anywhere, some might think Felixstowe would be more run-down than it is. But far from harking back to Britain's golden age of seaside resorts, Felixstowe is a smart, forward-looking town that is attracting new investment and has a lovely promenade. The cranes of the port dominate the area, visible from almost every point along the coast here, but are a symbol of resurgence in the region rather than one of oppressive industry.

Container your excitement!

The Port of Felixstowe markets itself as The Port of Britain, a name it proudly uses to reflect its status as the busiest container terminal in the nation. Benefiting from having deep water close to the shoreline and good rail links, the port can cater for some of the world's largest ships – and around 3,000 of them dock here every year. They bring in goods from all over the world, stacked up high in the four million multicoloured shipping containers unloaded annually. Nearly half of Britain's containerised trade arrives at Felixstowe. Huge cranes on the side of the port lift the containers on and off ships, moving them around in seconds and making each heavy load look like a lightweight piece of Lego. As well as a significant industry employing around 3,000 people, the Port of Felixstowe's whirring cranes and huge, slow-moving vessels are now a popular

△ The Port of Felixstowe can house enormous container ships, bringing in goods from all over.

△ Wherever you go in Felixstowe, the presence of the port is not far away.

▷ The harbour wall at Felixstowe sees the world's biggest ships come and go.

tourist attraction in their own right. Brown signs point drivers towards a viewing area at the side of the port where people can gaze at the intricate transport operation that runs throughout the week. Bring your binoculars to get the most out of your trip and take a look in the visitor centre to learn more about the area's history. Bring sturdy boots to take advantage of the walkway that goes to the beach, keeping your eyes on the horizon for one of the huge container ships heading in from Rotterdam and beyond.

Military might

With the ports of Felixstowe and Harwich being of such strategic importance, this is an area of Britain's coast that has needed defending over the centuries. Landguard Fort (☎ 01394 675900 www.landguard.com ♥ IP11 3TW) was created to do just that and has protected the East Anglian shoreline since the 17th century. Some of the first key action it saw involved warding off an attempted Dutch invasion in 1667. Royal

Marines based on this Felixstowe peninsula repelled the offensive in just one battle. The current fort was built in the 18th century and saw considerable development in the 19th and 20th centuries, cementing its role as a national military asset. Forces manned Landguard Fort throughout both World Wars and in the 1950s two old gun casemates were adapted to become a Cold War control room. After being closed in 1956, the fort was eventually handed over to English Heritage and visitors can today enjoy guided tours that explore how this stretch of the coast has been so important to the defence of the nation.

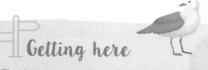

Getting here

The A14 runs east from the A1(M) until it reaches the sea at Felixstowe. There is also a well-served train station in the centre of the town.

46

CLACTON-ON-SEA
PIER TO FRATERNITY

Why visit?

★ Stroll down Clacton's historic pier and dare yourself to go on a roller coaster above the sea

★ Admire the artwork on display in the town's well-kept Martello tower

★ Enjoy a night at a traditional, much-loved theatre on the coast

This stretch of the English seaside is marketed as the Essex Sunshine Coast and if you're lucky enough to get good weather, everything is here for a traditional day out. With a pier, plenty of rides at the funfair, several arcades and a range of pleasant beaches, thousands of people head for Clacton when the forecast is favourable.

Art in the tower

Clacton's Jaywick Martello Tower is one of the 29 that were built along the south-east coast to defend England against Napoleon (℡ 01255 822783 www.jaywickmartellotower.org ♥CO15 2LF). Dating back to 1809, the tower is now a community arts hub run by the local council. There's a mixture of permanent and rotating displays along with regular music events, all giving this historical landmark an important purpose in the 21st century.

Choose your event!

Whenever you roll into Clacton, there's sure to be plenty of fun going on. The pier, especially, is a hotbed of events (℡ 01255 421115 www.clactonpier.co.uk ♥CO15 1QX). Most summer weekends there is a wealth of family entertainment taking place and the range of activities is often overwhelming. From car shows

▽ There's all the fun of the fair to be had at the helter-skelter on Clacton Pier.

and music concerts to donut eating contests and magic performances, check in advance what's going to be taking place when you go. The pier is also a great place to visit if you're wanting to enjoy traditional seaside rides. Try out the classic Waltzer or go for Stella's Revenge, a ride with a nod to the Steel Stella ride that was destroyed by fire in 1973. If that's not your thing, the old-fashioned helter-skelter is sure to please! On the promenade you'll also come across dodgems and a carousel, among many other attractions.

△ A stripy lighthouse is one of many family attractions on the front at Clacton.

PIER FACTS

- 360 metres (1,180 feet) long
- Opened in 1871
- Originally built as a landing platform for industry
- In the 1970s and 1980s, killer whales were kept on display here

🔔 Stay a while

🛏 The Adelaide Guest House, 24 Wellesley Road, Clacton-on-Sea, CO15 3PP.
📞 01255 435628
www.adelaide-guesthouse.co.uk

💼 The Kingscliff Hotel, 55 Kings Parade, Clacton, CO15 5JB. 📞 01255 818800
www.thekingscliffhotel.co.uk

⛺ Grange Farm Campsite, Station Road, Thorpe-le-Soken, Clacton, CO16 0HG.
📞 01255 861208
www.grangefarmcampsite.co.uk

A planned resort

If Clacton-on-Sea seems ideally focused on providing tourists with a great day at the seaside, this is no coincidence. The whole town was established as a seaside resort in 1871 and the first building to occupy the skyline was the pier, constructed to allow raw materials to be brought in by boat. This landing area soon became the focus of Clacton's coastal attractions and the rest of the town developed to support the needs of the thousands of visitors who were shipped in. The accessibility of the pier became an issue during the Second World War as it provided a potential landing opportunity for German soldiers, so it was breached and rebuilt when hostilities stopped. Like many of our proud historic coastal resorts, Clacton ran into trouble when the package holiday market to Spain started to flex its sun-drenched muscles. Regenerative investment in the 1990s started to reverse the decline and the development of several new housing estates saw the town expand.

△ No visit to Clacton-on-Sea is complete without a game of crazy golf and a wander by the sea.

Getting here

To drive to Clacton-on-Sea you'll need to go south-east from Colchester, taking the A133 to the coast. The train station is centrally located, also near the A133, just a short walk from the beach.

The battle on the beach

In the mid-1960s, seaside confrontation between moped-driving mods and motorbiking rockers became an unpleasant fixture at several coastal towns in the south of England. Clacton didn't escape and a notorious 'invasion' took place in 1964, when the two opposing styles rode in on two wheels. Labelled 'riots' and 'battles' in the media, this may have been an exaggeration, but there were certainly fights on the sand. Clashes between the two groups saw punches thrown and deckchairs used as weapons. Skirmishes also broke out across the Thames Estuary in Margate.

A night at the theatre

When you're planning your visit to Clacton, head to the Princes Theatre website to see if anything takes your fancy. There's something quintessentially British about going to see a performance at the seaside, a well-loved family tradition that goes back over a century. There are plenty of celebrity performances going on at the Princes Theatre, a beautiful building dating back to 1931 that can hold over 800 people (☎ 01255 686633 www.princestheatre.co.uk ♥ CO15 1SE).

47

SOUTHEND-ON-SEA

RETHINK YOUR IDEA OF A PIER

Why visit?

⭐ Take a stroll or catch a train to the end of the world's longest pier

⭐ Get involved with the art galleries and cockle sheds on the cobbled streets of Old Leigh

⭐ Go wildlife spotting on nearby beaches and mudflats

△ Rollercoasters on Southend's seafront offer elevated views of the world's longest pier.

The world's longest pier

You may well have heard about the record-breaking pier at Southend before you make your visit to this corner of the Essex coast. Even if you've been told it's a whopper, nothing really prepares you for the sight of this staggering structure disappearing off into the distance. If you're going to walk to the end, get ready for a 4km (2.6-mile) there-and-back adventure, passing attractions along the way and winding up at the café, sun deck and gift shop on the Pier Head. Unsurprisingly, a structure this

long heading out into the sea has had its fair share of troubles, including ships running into it, swirling storms battering the boards and destructive fires threatening its existence. A blaze in 2005 severely damaged the end of the pier; it's now restored to its former glory and pulling in the crowds once more. The journey is so far to the head of the pier, there's a train to take you there or bring you back – or both. It's an impressive ride. Standing on the seafront watching the carriages chug towards the coast is more like watching a Victorian service rattle over a huge bridge than a tourist train on a pier.

Getting here

Follow the A127 east and it will bring you to the centre of Southend-on-Sea. Two train stations service Southend and your arrival point will depend on the region you set off for. You'll either come into Southend Central or Southend Victoria. For those visiting Leigh, there is a separate station for Leigh-on-Sea.

Pier Museum

Holding a wealth of information and exhibits about the 2,158-metre (7,080-foot) pier, the Southend Pier Museum is worth a visit (☎ 01702 611214 www.southendpiermuseum.co.uk ♥ SS1 1EE). You'll find it in the old workshops beneath the train station at the shore, proudly telling the story of the structure that juts out into the Thames Estuary and has come to define the town. There's plenty of nostalgia on display here, and some for sale in the museum shop as well. The experience will appeal to many generations who grew up with trips to the pier, along with first-timers wanting to find out more about this remarkable landmark.

> The Pier is Southend, Southend is the Pier.
> *Sir John Betjeman*

Old Leigh

To the west of Southend is a charming area that has maintained much of its antiquated appeal and offers an antidote to the hustle and bustle of funfairs and amusements. Step on to the cobbled streets of Old Leigh to experience a wonderful atmosphere, admire the local art galleries and pick up a seafood treat at the cockle sheds.

A place to nurture nature

It's not all about the razzmatazz of bright lights and thrilling rides at Southend. There's a wealth of wildlife on this part of the UK's coast, some of it lingering around the supporting posts of the pier. Sponges, sea anemones and at least 12 different kinds of crab shelter around them. A little further west along the coast, the mudflats around Two Tree Island (www.essexwt.org.uk/nature-reserves/two-tree-island ♥ S59 8GB) are home to a rare underwater eelgrass, which in turn pulls in brent geese because they love to feed on it. Up to 40 per cent of the world's brent goose population comes here at some time during the year. The Thames Estuary supports up to 153,000 birds at any one time. And at every low tide there'll be thousands of lugworms, ragworms, cockles and razor shells burying into the sandy mud on the shore. The pools that form beneath the pier are worth exploring if you want to see what kind of life can be found on these shores. Keep your eyes peeled for sponges, sea squirts and crabs.

Stay a while

🛏 The Moorings, 172 Eastern Esplanade, Southend-on-Sea, SS1 3AA. ☎ 01702 587575 www.themooringsbedandbreakfast.com

🏨 Roslin Beach Hotel, Thorpe Esplanade, Southend-on-Sea, SS1 3BG. ☎ 01702 586375 www.roslinhotel.com

⛺ The Lake at Nine Acres Camping and Caravan Site, Nine Acres, Flemings Farm Road, Leigh-on-Sea, SS9 5QT. ☎ 01702 747723 www.thelakeatnineacres.co.uk

48

LONDON
SPACE TO BREATHE
IN THE BIG SMOKE

The Thames at speed – shaken, not stirred!

There are many ways to see the sights of our capital city. You could head to the London Eye, take a walking tour around Westminster or Whitehall, hop in a black cab or jump aboard a red bus. But nothing will deliver the views and take you on such a whirlwind tour of British history as a ride down the River Thames. Once hosting the largest collection of docks in the world, this hugely important tidal river reveals the social and economic development of the city as you glide past the Palace of Westminster, St Paul's Cathedral, the Tate Modern, the Globe Theatre, the Tower of London, Tower Bridge

Getting here

London is well connected when it comes to rail and road links. The Underground is a great way to get about the city. Use Embankment tube station for the Thames RIB Experience, North Greenwich for Up at the O2 and Canary Wharf for West India Docks. For Greenwich attractions, use the Cutty Sark for Maritime Greenwich DLR station.

and the East End docks. A journey along the Thames allows time and space to enjoy seeing such famous sights. One of the best ways to take a Thames tour is to follow the lead of Pierce Brosnan in *The World is Not Enough* and mirror 007's high-speed chase from Westminster to the Millennium Dome. Thankfully you won't have to put up with villains shooting at you or crash through fancy restaurants like in the film, but Thames RIB Experience does let you enjoy the fun bits of the journey (☎ 020 3613 2311 www.thamesribexperience.com ♥ WC2N 6NU). The tour guide points out key sights all the way down to Tower Bridge and then on comes the James Bond music as the speed increases. Bump over waves, feel splashes against your face and enjoy the thrill of being twisted on sharp turns as you remember the company's adrenaline-infused motto – Hold On Tight!

△ Sightseeing at high speed along the tidal Thames – Hold On Tight!

Up and over: a unique view at the O2

It occupies pride of place next to the River Thames, features in a James Bond film and gets a starring role during the opening credits to *EastEnders*. The Millennium Dome attracted controversy when it was built because of spiralling costs and low visitor numbers to the year-long exhibition it housed in 2000. Today it's one of the capital's most recognisable landmarks and houses the O2 Arena and a string of eateries. The design of the dome, sitting so close to the Meridian, is laced with symbolism. There are 12 yellow spires representing hours of the day and months of the year. The diameter of the dome is 365 metres and it's 52 metres high; it's virtually a walk-in calendar.

△ A spooky-looking O2 Arena, all aglow with the city behind it.

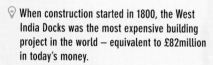

WEST INDIA DOCKS: A BRIEF HISTORY

- ♀ When construction started in 1800, the West India Docks was the most expensive building project in the world — equivalent to £82million in today's money.

- ♀ An Import Dock allowed ships to unload before sailing to get new cargo at the Export dock.

- ♀ The West India Docks had capacity to deal with 600 vessels at any one time.

- ♀ By the 1960s, the West India Docks were in decline. There was a fall in demand for local raw materials and a growth in shipping containers that could not be catered for at this type of dock.

- ♀ In 1980 the docks closed, the government took control of the land and a major programme of regeneration started.

- ♀ It is now home to the skyscrapers of Canary Wharf, one of the biggest financial centres in Europe.

There's now the chance to scale this beacon of the East End to get a bird's-eye view of the Thames meandering through docklands and regeneration (☎ 020 8463 2680 www.theo2.co.uk ♀ SE10 0DX). Hiking up a specially built, springy walkway, dome explorers deal with a 30° slope to reach the top and then have time for selfies and champagne. The tidal river leads to the city in one direction. In the other, the Thames Estuary opens up to the North Sea and you're reminded how London grew because of its trade links with the rest of the world.

Time starts here

Just as the equator divides the world into the northern and southern hemispheres, the Meridian Line through Greenwich splits the planet into east and west. At the Royal Observatory (☎ 020 8312 6608 www.rmg. co.uk ♀ SE10 8XJ) you can stand on the Prime Meridian at 0° longitude, with one foot in the east and one in the west. This line is also the reference point for Greenwich Mean Time, the international time standard adopted in the

△ Get on board the Cutty Sark to explore the last Victorian tea clipper.

19th century as trade and communications developed. Before Greenwich was chosen to keep time for the world, most cities kept their own time and there was no agreement about the length of hours or days. At night, a green laser shoots across the sky to mark the Prime Meridian.

🔔 Stay a while

🛏 Number 37, Burney Street, Greenwich, SE10 8EX. 📞 020 8265 2623 www.burney.org.uk

🧳 Novotel, 173–185 Greenwich High Road, Greenwich, SE10 8JA. 📞 020 7660 0682 www.accorhotels.com

⛺ Abbey Wood Caravan Club Site, Federation Road, London, SE2 0LS. 📞 020 8311 7708 www.caravanclub.co.uk

Also in Greenwich...

If you are fortunate enough to be able to spend a few days near the Thames, there's no shortage of attractions to remind you about the importance of Greenwich as a seafaring community and somewhere quite literally at the centre of time. Climb aboard the *Cutty Sark* to find out what life was like on the last surviving 19th-century tea clipper (📞 020 8312 6608 www.rmg.co.uk 📍SE10 9HT). The National Maritime Museum is the largest of its kind anywhere on the planet and has some incredible exhibits – including the uniform Admiral Nelson was wearing when he was killed in the Battle of Trafalgar (📞 020 8312 6608 www.rmg.co.uk 📍SE10 9NF). And explore the Old Royal Naval College, housed in the magnificent building designed by Sir Christopher Wren (📞 020 8269 4799 www.ornc.org 📍SE10 9NN). A little further to the east, learn how the Thames Flood Barrier protects 125km² (48 sq miles) of London from potentially catastrophic tidal surges by closing ten steel gates, each weighing 3,300 tonnes (📞 020 8305 4188 www.gov.uk/guidance/the-thames-barrier 📍SE18 5NJ).

DOWN TO
MARGATE!

Why visit?

★ Remember your childhood hobbies at the Hornby Visitor Centre, where the train and racing track models are off the charts

★ Immerse yourself in the paintings of Turner at Margate's new world-class gallery

★ Attempt to figure out the mystery of the grotto where over four million shells create amazing patterns

Don't forget your buckets and spades and cossies and all!

Immortalised by Chas and Dave in their 1982 rockney single, 'Margate' tells the story of a family coach trip to the popular Kent seaside town. It was in the charts for four weeks and used in a TV advert for Courage Best Bitter. Many typical features of a trip down to Margate are sung about, including eating jellied eels, collecting winkle shells, having a beer and digging in the sand.

All aboard the Hornby train set!

Anybody who has enjoyed playing with the Scalextric or building a model railway needs to set course for the Hornby Hobbies Visitor Centre (☎ 01843 233524 www.hornby.com ● CT9 4JX). Exhibits help you to trace the early history of Frank Hornby's business, when he would make railway toys at home. But the real draw here are the incredibly addictive railway and racetrack models, encompassing the full range of products that are on sale to

▽ Margate has a fantastic beach and all the facilities of a traditional seaside town.

△ Explore the mystery of the subterranean Shell Grotto.

collectors. The attention to detail is stunning and will inspire many people to go home and dig out their old collections. Of course, there's an extensive shop where you can stock up on a wide range of products from well-loved brands. Check the website for a list of events before you travel.

Spitfire in the sky

To get an idea of the huge role played by the famous Spitfire in the Battle of Britain and other times in the Second World War, head to the airfield on Manston Road (☎ 01843 821940 www.spitfiremuseum.org.uk ♀CT12 5DF). You'll get a chance to see one of the few surviving Spitfires with a wartime record – Supermarine Spitfire TB752 – and learn about her raids on German road and rail targets. The historic plane suffered damage on a landing in 1945 and over the years started to corrode away. But

a restoration in the 1970s saw her transformed after 15,000 working hours were spent on bringing her back to glory. TB752 shows the wolf insignia of 403 (Wolf) Squadron. She was one of over 20,000 Spitfires manufactured between 1936 and 1948.

The mystery of the shells

The most bizarre thing about Margate's surreal underground cavern of shell mosaics is that nobody is really sure how it got there! The legend is that in 1835 a young boy investigated a hole formed when a duck pond was being built – and ended up wandering into the phenomenal subterranean wonderland that is the Shell Grotto (☎ 01843 220008 shellgrotto.co.uk ♀CT9 2BU). In the 21 metres (70 feet) of winding passages and the main chamber, there are an estimated 4.6 million shells stuck on to the walls to make

Stay a while

🛏 The Warwick, 27 Warwick Road, Margate, CT9 2JU 1SD.
☎ 01843 227525

🏨 Crescent Victoria Hotel, 25–26 Fort Crescent, Margate, CT9 1HX.
☎ 01843 230375
www.crescentvictoria.co.uk

⛺ Quex Holiday Park and Campsite, Park Road, Birchington, CT7 0BL.
☎ 01843 841273 www.keatfarm.co.uk

incredible swirling shapes. This unusual seaside attraction was never on any of Margate's old maps and has to be seen to be believed. Several theories have been put forward about the grotto's origins – ranging from pagan altars to storehouses – but we may never know anything about the people behind this great place. Except that they had a lot of time on their hands. And they loved shells.

Artistic hotspot

Margate may not seem like an artistic beacon, but one of the country's hottest galleries is located here and visitors can explore it free of charge. Since Turner Contemporary opened its doors in 2011, over three million people have admired the work of in excess of 500 artists (☎ 01843 233000 www.turnercontemporary.org ♥ CT9 1HG). Turner Prize winners Antony Gormley and Grayson Perry have had work on display here, along with nominees Karla Black and Tracey Emin. The biggest pull is the collection of Turner's work – over 700 of the English painter's pieces are here. What's more, it's estimated that the gallery has resulted in £68 million being ploughed into the local economy and safeguarded 101 jobs.

Enter Dreamland

Take the family flying up and down, whizzing around and shrieking for joy at Dreamland, the long-standing favourite for ride-lovers on the Kent coast (☎ 01843 295887 www.dreamland.co.uk ♥ CT9 1XJ). There's plenty to do at this famous landmark to keep kids of all ages on the edge of their seat.

△ Life is a rollercoaster at fun-filled Dreamland.

Getting here

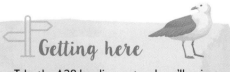

Take the A28 heading east and you'll arrive at Margate on the north coast of Kent. The train pulls into the station on the eastern side of the town, close to Dreamland.

151

DOVER
AT THE HEART OF THE BATTLE

Why visit?

★ Walk high above the sea on the White Cliffs of Dover, gazing out across the Channel towards France

★ Enjoy a tour of the National Trust's South Foreland Lighthouse.

★ Learn about Britain's history in the castle that has been at the heart of many military campaigns

Dover Castle

The premier attraction at Dover and the thing you should absolutely not miss out on is a trip to the castle on top of the hill. Dover was heavily bombed during the Second World War, as you can imagine from its proximity to mainland Europe. But the castle went untouched. Some historians reckon this is because Hitler had his eye on it for use as his British headquarters. It's easy to see why. The prominent position of the castle and the iconic buildings have seen it sit at the heart of military campaigns for centuries. It's now maintained by English Heritage (☎ 01304 211067 www.english-heritage.org.uk ♥ CT16 1HU), with free admission for members, and there is a wealth of adventures to be had here.

▽ Dover Castle keeps and eye on the town and is packed with history.

DOVER CASTLE TO-DO LIST

💡 Visit the Fire Command Post and learn about the First World War, when the area around the castle was declared a fortress and acted as the headquarters for the campaign in the trenches.

💡 In the Second World War, underground tunnels were turned into a military hospital and the immersive tour is stunning.

💡 The rescue of troops from the beaches at Dunkirk was one of the key moments of the war and it was overseen from the castle. A superb visitor attraction tells the tale of how the small boats contributed to the war effort.

💡 Medieval tales are told in the Great Tower, the centre of this nationally important castle that has been the scene of many a royal visit down the centuries.

△ Few natural features symbolise the coast of Britain more than the White Cliffs of Dover.

The White Cliffs

You'll struggle to find a natural feature that has more symbolic meaning to Britain than the White Cliffs of Dover. The imposing chalk cliffs rise from the sea and are the first thing visitors see of the country when they are travelling by boat from the continent. The gleaming white landmark has been a natural metaphor for hope and courage over the years – especially in the Second World War, when troops were ferried back home after being rescued from Dunkirk. Today, they're the natural wall that welcomes people to England, visitors and returning residents alike. The walk along the top of the cliffs is regarded by some as one of the best strolls in the country. Head for the National Trust visitor centre and read up about the local area before setting out (☎ 01304 202756 www. nationaltrust.org.uk/the-white-cliffs-of-dover ♥ CT6 1HJ). Dame Vera Lynn, of course, made 'The White Cliffs of Dover' a popular and rousing wartime anthem. But don't expect to see any bluebirds over the White Cliffs of Dover when you look up to the skies; that lyric was penned by American Nat Burton, who didn't realise the birds weren't found over here in Blighty.

South Foreland Lighthouse

The tour of this National Trust lighthouse is really something, packed with detail and the memorable view from the top (park at the White Cliffs of Dover visitor centre and follow the 3.2km/2-mile waymarked clifftop trail). Five generations of the same family once ran this geographically important lighthouse, which was also home to scientific experiments and inventions. Make time to enjoy a snack at Mrs Knotts tearoom (☏ 01304 853230 ♦ CT15 6HP) – sitting outside in the sunshine with a cream tea is a delight. There are often outside games lying about, or you may want to have a go at flying a kite.

Banksy

It once rivalled the White Cliffs as the most-photographed landmark in Dover. The huge Banksy mural showing a worker chiselling a gold star from the EU flag was inspired by the nationwide debate over Brexit. First appearing in May 2017, it was seen by thousands of people from their cars as they made their way along the A20. Mystery surrounds who was responsible for whitewashing the work of art, and what will appear on the wall in the future.

△ Shining like a temple on the cliff, South Foreland Lighthouse.

Getting here

The A2 and M20 both provide routes into Dover, while the Dover Priory train station is centrally located.

Good Deal

A little further north along Deal Road is a charming seaside destination with a long and renowned relationship with the sea. Lord Nelson is known to have many connections with Deal and often came here to stay in the Royal Hotel, claiming in 1801 that it had to be 'the coldest place in England'. We can only presume the famous seafarer was exaggerating as this is not a meteorological claim to fame many Deal dwellers will agree with.

Sandwich, anyone?

Head north of Dover and Deal to Sandwich for one of their well-known festival weekends. Two of the most popular are Le Weekend, which sees many French food sellers coming over the channel to set up stalls, and Le Medieval Weekend, celebrating the town's reputation as one of the best-preserved medieval towns in England. For more details, head to https://sandwichevents.org.uk.

Stay a while

🛏 The Churchill House, 6 Castle Hill Road, Dover, CT16 1QN. ☏ 01304 204622
www.churchillguesthouse.co.uk

🧳 Travelodge, St James St, Dover, CT16 1QD. ☏ 0871 984 6532
www.travelodge.co.uk

⛺ Hawthorne Farm Campsite, Martin Mill, Dover, CT15 5LA. ☏ 01304 852658
www.keatfarm.co.uk

FOLKESTONE
MORE THAN JUST A HOLE IN THE GROUND

Channel rubble

Folkestone has long been a popular spot from which to hop over to France. Journeys were initially made on the ferries leaving from the harbour but today, those heading to Europe from here do so aboard Eurotunnel, which first departed in 1994. The rail route beneath the sea dives underground just north of the town, trains coming up on the other side of the English Channel around 30 minutes later. An incredible feat of engineering, excavating the tunnel provided the major headache of what to do with all the rubble from rocks beneath the sea. After considering 60 sites, a land reclamation project was chosen to the east of Folkestone. The result is Samphire Hoe (☏ 01304 225649 www.samphirehoe.com ♀ CT17 9FL). Accessed via a road tunnel through the chalk cliffs, the car park is next to an education centre and small food kiosk. The further you head out from here on the network of paths, the more wildflowers and birds will be spotted – over 200 types of plants are found here, along with 123 species of birds and 30 different butterflies. Take a picnic in this man-made refuge, and make sure you stroll by the anglers, where the sea laps against the wall. If you fancy tackling an afternoon of sea angling from here, day tickets are available from the tea kiosk.

▽ An inspirational mix of wildflowers, birds and butterflies away at Samphire Hoe.

△ The blue lighthouse at Samphire Hoe.

The Creative Quarter

A short walk from the harbour, Folkestone's Creative Quarter is a much loved and respected artistic neighbourhood. Home to talented people who paint, write, film and craft imaginative pieces, the cobbled High Street is a place you can lose yourself in for an afternoon. Started in 2002 to regenerate the town through creative arts, the colourful area is thriving with cool businesses and houses, a mix of new building designs and shops that have preserved historic facades. The Creative Quarter has a great vibe to it, often filled with chatter and buzzing with exciting ideas and plans. There are also some very cool places to enjoy coffee and a cake while you consider which artistic gems you'd like to take home.

Battle of Britain Museum

On a peaceful afternoon in Folkestone, it's hard to picture the furious and all-important fight that raged overhead during the Second World War. The Battle of Britain was a pivotal moment in the war that took place over Kent between July and October 1940. People living in the south-east could see events taking place in the skies, on tenterhooks about whether a German invasion was on the cards. Winston Churchill famously summed up the victorious events by saying: 'Never was so much owed by so many to so few.' Learn about the fight in the air at the Kent Battle of Britain Museum (☏ 01303 893140 www. kbobm.org ♀ CT18 7AG). It houses the world's largest collection of related artefacts, including items recovered from a staggering 700 different crashed aircraft.

△ One of the iconic spitfires on display in Folkestone.

Phoenix from the trains

While the Channel Tunnel has provided an economic boost in some areas, it had a crippling impact on the town's ferry operators. While boats still leave for France from next-door Dover, the underground link dealt a crippling death blow to Folkestone's ferries. There are no services leaving from the harbour now and that left a town-planning quandary about what to do with such an important part of the town. The result is the revitalised Harbour Arm. The town's all-important harbour wall was once the scene for warships, fishing boats and steam packets to France. Today it's a hive of business meetings, people getting together to chat and those wanting to enjoy a drink sitting out in the sunshine. When you're on the Harbour Arm, it's hard to picture the passenger and freight trains disappearing into a hole in Folkestone's suburbs and whizzing beneath your feet on their way to Calais. The Channel Tunnel brought mixed fortunes to the town, but the Harbour Arm has breathed in new life after the final departure of the ferries.

🛎 Stay a while

🛏 Seabrook House, 81 Seabrook Road, Folkestone, CT21 5QW.
☎ 01303 269282
www.seabrookhouse.co.uk/en-GB

🏨 The View Hotel, 30–32 Clifton Road, Folkestone, CT20 2EF. ☎ 01303 252102 www.viewhotelfolkestone.co.uk

⛺ Folkestone Camping and Caravanning Club Site, The Warren, Folkestone, CT19 6NQ. ☎ 01303 255093 www.campingandcaravanningclub.co.uk

🪧 Getting here

Very well connected because of the importance of the Channel Tunnel and the nearby Port of Dover, Folkestone is found is south-east Kent, where the A20 meets the M20. The Folkestone Central train station is located between Kingsnorth Gardens and Radnor Park.

The Leas

Folkestone's unique promenade runs along the clifftop rather than next to the sea. Designed in the mid-1800s, the planner behind it was Decimus Burton – the man behind creations at London Zoo and Kew Gardens in the capital. It's a fine place to walk along, enjoying the local views and architecture. Events take place at the bandstand during the summer and there's a good children's playground to pass the time for little ones.

△ The British Channel Tunnel entrance takes travellers from Folkestone to France.

52

DUNGENESS
ON THE RIGHT TRACKS

Why visit?

★ A landscape like no other in Britain, where a low-lying shingle promontory is home to wildlife and nuclear power

★ Explore the history of lighthouses that have needed replacing due to the changing coastline

★ Ride on one of the most famous narrow-gauge railways in the world on a 22km (13½-mile) seaside trip

Exploring the Marsh

Romney Marsh has a centuries-long natural history of being created and changed by the sea, while humans have reclaimed sections from the English Channel, fought against storms and attempted to drain the wet land. The result is a surreal low-lying landscape of shingle plants tolerant of a coastal life. Take the journey from New Romney to Dungeness – preferably by train – to see the promontory becoming wilder and more remote as the busy world of England is left behind.

Maintain the wall

'Honour the King, but first maintain the wall' may sound like something Jon Snow would proclaim in *Game of Thrones*. This phrase – so appropriate for Romney Marsh – is from a local novel of 1935 called *The Scarecrow Rides* and describes the historical importance assigned to looking after Dymchurch Wall. There's been a protective wall at Dymchurch since Roman days. Today's wall cost £60 million to build and is part of a wide flood-defence scheme to protect 2,500 homes in the area.

△ Miles of shingle beach on this stretch of coast provide opportunities for crunchy walks and skimming stones.

△ Beach huts are available for those wanting to spend a full day by the sea.

The fifth continent

Though technically on very dodgy geographical ground, Romney Marsh became known as 'the fifth continent' in the 19th century when author Richard Barham wrote that the world is divided into Europe, Asia, Africa, America and Romney Marsh.

World-famous miniature railway

Few narrow-gauge or heritage railways have the international recognition or foreign visitor appeal of this 22km (13½-mile) gem. Racing driver and millionaire landowner Captain Jack Howey was the railway enthusiast who set the wheels for the Romney, Hythe and Dymchurch Railway in motion (☏ 01797 362353 www.rhdr.org.uk ♀ TN28 8PL). After exploring other parts of the country, the 15" gauge railway was established between Hythe and New Romney in 1927 and one year later it was extended all the way to Dungeness. It proved instantly popular and remains one of the top attractions on the south coast today. Between Hythe and Dungeness, four other stations provide good places to stop off and each is within walking distance of the beach.

△ Make tracks to Dungeness on the railway, passing the old lighthouse.

Getting here

It's the A259 that hugs the coast in this part of the south-east, with Romney Road leaving it at New Romney to head all the way down Romney Marsh to Dungeness. The best way to get to Dungeness is to take the narrow-gauge railway, picking it up at Hythe near Folkestone.

Dungeness – remote, yet busy – nature, with industry

Although at the far end of Romney Marsh, it's here where you can get a true appreciation of its unique setting. Don't expect to be alone in the summer months, though. The Romney, Hythe and Dymchurch Railway was extended here in 1928 and brings in over 100,000 visitors each year. Practically at sea level, you can understand how life here is intertwined with the sea and the weather. Look around, however, and you'll see plenty of people who choose to call Dungeness 'home'. The collection of unusual homes is worthy of inspection in itself. Look out for the houses that have been converted from old railway carriages and dragged here along the shingle. Dominating the skyline are the two nuclear power stations, the nearest one being built in the 1950s and 1960s. Decommissioning started on this in 2007, though the second power station continues to provide enough energy for 1.4 million homes. Summer brings out an abundance of wildlife in the area; keep an eye out for the yellow horned poppy, bumblebees and a range of butterflies.

Shifting sand, shifting lighthouses

With the coastal process of longshore drift moving sand, shingle and pebbles along the seafront, the land at Dungeness has changed remarkably over the centuries. The first lighthouse here was constructed in 1615, but this and subsequent warning beacons have needed rebuilding as the shoreline advanced into the sea and the light became obscured. The large black lighthouse – the fourth to be built – was opened in 1904 but the nuclear power station obscured much of its scope. An automatic lighthouse – the large black-and-white one – has now been placed closer to the shore, but the old lighthouse is open for a tour around (☎ 01797 321300 www.dungenesslighthouse.com ♥ TN29 9NB).

Martello tower

When the threat of French invasion was at its height in the early 19th century, a series of Martello towers was built along the south coast. The best preserved of these forts to survive is number 24 at Dymchurch, now looked after by English Heritage. Opening times are limited, but admission is free (📞 01797 212507 www.english-heritage.org.uk 📍 TN29 0NN).

🔔 Stay a while

🛏 Castaways, 101 Coast Drive, Lydd-on-Sea, TN29 9NW. 📞 01797 320017 www.castawaysdungeness.com

🧳 The Gallivant, New Lydd Road, Camber, TN31 7RB. 📞 01797 225057 www.thegallivant.co.uk

⛺ Herons Park Campsite, Dengemarsh Road, Lydd, TN29 9JH. 📞 07585 316316 www.heronspark.com

Listen up!

Before the days of sophisticated radar, the huge concrete sound mirrors built on Romney Marsh were an early way to detect signs of approaching enemy aircraft. Built between 1928 and 1935, different types of mirrors were developed and you can visit them by taking footpaths from Greatstone. To get up close with them, you'll need to go at a time when the RSPB are arranging access to its reserve (📞 01797 320588 www.rspb.org.uk 📍 TN29 9PN)

△▷ The old lighthouse worked well until obscured by the power station.

▷ Romney Marsh has a rich variety of plants, animals and maritime history.

SOUTH COAST

ngland's south coast is a stunning mix of jaw-dropping natural formations and busy cities bursting with top quality attractions. The journey on this part of the coast starts at the phenomenal Beachy Head, which graciously rises to a magnificent seaside peak and is one of the most famous cliffs in the country. To the west, Brighton is famous for its welcoming party atmosphere all year long. There's always something to do here, whether the weather entices you onto the famous beach or has you sheltering inside the famous pavilion.

Few cities can rival the wealth of museums that Portsmouth has to offer. A hoard of globally important attractions are awaiting you in the city, from a retired submarine to historic battleships armed with cannons and the remains of Henry VIII's *Mary Rose*. Seafaring history is also strong in neighbouring Southampton, where the *Titanic* set off for the United States in 1912. Much of the workforce on the doomed liner came from the city and you can discover more about the devastating blow the disaster brought to local families. Further west along the south coast brings

you to Sandbanks. You may not be able to live there, but it's a lovely place to enjoy a walk along the beach and gaze at some of the hottest properties in the country. Land prices on this stretch of English coast outstrip any other seaside settlement by a long way.

If you're looking for natural treasures around the coast of the UK, there's plenty to find on the south coast. Stunning coastal land formations abound on the shores of the Jurassic Coast, where you may also stumble upon dinosaur remains. This is one of the best places in the world to discover fossils and you'll see many families bashing rocks on the beach to see if a pre-historic creature lies within. Along the Jurassic Coast there are many awesome sights to behold, including the classic cove formation at Lulworth, the dramatic stack known as Old Harry and the stunning arch called Durdle Door. These are just part of the cache of goodies waiting to be explored on the south coast of England.

Old Harry's Rocks are just one of many jaw-dropping features carved out by the sea on the south coast.

Don't miss

- ✓ Heading up the i360 to get an unrivalled view of the south coast from Brighton
- ✓ A day seeing the world-class attractions in Portsmouth's Historic Dockyard
- ✓ Discovering the impact on the people of this coast caused by the sinking of the *Titanic*
- ✓ Spending time on the beach at Sandbanks, near some of the most expensive houses on the coastline
- ✓ Becoming a fossil hunter on the famous Jurassic Coast

53

BEACHY HEAD

BEACON OF THE SOUTH COAST

A natural star of the screen!

The incredible chalk backdrop of Beachy Head has been sought out by many film and TV directors over the decades. At 152 metres (500 feet) high, it's a stunning and unusual location that can make a massive impact on either the big or small screen. It's seen a secret agent parachute off the top in the opening moments of James Bond flick *The Living Daylights*, when the cliff doubled for a scene in Gibraltar. It was the launch pad for Chitty Chitty Bang Bang when it drove off the top and opened its wings to fly. Cate Blanchett stood on the edge in *Notes on a Scandal* and the huge chalk drop has appeared in many TV commercials. Take plenty of care on your visit to Beachy Head and keep well away from the edge because this is a notoriously dangerous natural feature. Rock falls are common and unfortunately many people have fallen to their death. While a large proportion of these are accidents, Beachy Head also has an unenviable reputation as a suicide hotspot. Expect to see signs offering help to those going through a bad patch. The Beachy Head Chaplaincy Team (www.bhct.org.uk) has search and rescue staff on hand to patrol the area looking for people at risk and to respond to emergency calls. The team deal with incidents on a regular basis.

△ The rising chalk cliff of Beachy Head is one of the stars of the south coast.

Getting here

Eastbourne is one of the principal locations on the south coast. Follow the A2270 to reach the town, and from there the A259 will take you towards Beachy Head. Travel east along the A259 coast road to reach Hastings. Both Eastbourne and Hastings are served by mainline rail services.

Beachy Head Lighthouse

Trinity House built the lighthouse on the shoreline in 1902 when the Belle Tout Lighthouse on the headland developed a reputation for being shrouded in mist. The tower is 43 metres (141 feet) tall but looks tiny next to the huge chalk cliffs. In a strange way, the lighthouse complements the cliff, emphasising the scale of it. Pictures of Beachy Head certainly benefit from having the red and white tower down at sea level.

△ Beachy Head Lighthouse standing before the huge cliffs.

Eastbourne's art scene

In a prominent position set back from the seafront and enjoying fabulous views of the South Downs, the Towner Art Gallery (☎ 01323 434670 www.townereastbourne.org.uk ♦ BN21 4JJ) has brought world-famous art exhibitions to Eastbourne. As well as being home to pieces from the renowned Towner Collection, the popular exhibition space has presented a varied programme of historic and contemporary art. If you're visiting with a young family, plan to visit at the weekend when art resources are put out along with learning packs to engage the budding young artists of the future.

△ **The Eastbourne Redoubt is a formidable seaside fortress.**

South coast fortress

If Napoleon had ever launched an invasion of southern England, the serving forces based at Eastbourne would have had something to say about it. The Eastbourne Redoubt (☏ 01323 410300 www.heritageeastbourne.co.uk ♦ BN22 7AQ) is a formidable fortress that stood ready to defend the nation from invading French soldiers and send them sailing back across the English Channel. It was one of a strong chain of fortresses built along the southern coast designed to deter Napoleon from choosing to launch an attack and keep the French at bay, should he have decided to chance his arm. The Eastbourne Redoubt is one of the best-preserved parts of this defensive line that is still surviving and today allows visitors to learn about the tensions it saw in the early 1800s. Soldiers were garrisoned here throughout the 19th century and once more during the Second World War, all these military eras being covered in the displays. Visit during the summer for atmospheric film screenings on this site overlooking the sea (www.eastbourneredoubt.co.uk).

The Battle of Hastings

A little further along the coast from Beachy Head, you can stand on the battle site where King Harold thrashed it out with William the Conqueror and the fate of England was determined (☏ 01424 775705 www.english-heritage.co.uk ♦ TN33 0AE). That day in 1066 had a lasting impact on our nation and you can learn all about it at the visitor centre through an introductory video and interactive displays. The battle site itself is now a peaceful place with wildflowers growing and birdsong breaking the silence. It's hard to imagine the carnage that took place so many years ago, on one day that altered the future of England.

54

BRIGHTON
YOUR DAY!

Prepare for take-off

Take a flight above the Brighton skyline to experience unrivalled views of the south coast. The British Airways i360 (☎ 03337 720360 www. britishairwaysi360.com ♀ BN1 2LN) stands 162 metres (532 feet) tall and its rotating glass viewing platform lifts off regularly to take passengers 137 metres (450 feet) above the ground. This means you'll be higher than those on British Airways' sister ride, the London Eye. Since opening in 2016, i360 has pulled thousands of tourists into the area and taken them to urban heights not experienced before in Brighton. The tower is an instantly recognizable addition to the skyline. You can book online, or just turn up to see if there's space on board. A journey to the top of the tower will take around 25 minutes.

△ Admire views of Brighton's seafront from the 162m-tall British Airways i360.

Have Pride in Brighton

For many years, Brighton has been Britain's unofficial LGBTQ capital and there is a strong, vibrant community here on the south coast. The best time to see the city celebrate diversity is to come down for the Pride celebrations (www. brighton-pride.org) in early August. Widely thought to be the biggest and best Pride festival in the country – and rivalling those elsewhere around the world – Brighton thrives when this party hits town. Expect huge names in pop, family areas, markets and some rousing costumes.

△ Brighton puts on one of the biggest Pride celebrations in the world.

A right royal venue

From the 1780s, Brighton became a favoured retreat of George, Prince of Wales. He lived in a small house overlooking the promenade, but in the early 19th century he set about transforming his home into something much grander. The result was the Royal Pavilion. The rooms, galleries and corridors were lavishly decorated and the skyline of the town changed forever. George became king in 1820 but owing to ill health only visited the Pavilion twice after it was finally completed. George's presence certainly had a positive impact on Brighton. Historical records show there were just 3,620 people living here in 1786 – a population boosted to 40,634 by 1831. The development of George's home created jobs for many nearby tradesmen and supported their families. The highly fashionable Regency era that swept into Brighton with the future King George IV has left an architectural legacy not only in the pavilion but also the elegant squares and housing of Kemp Town and Hove. Queen Victoria sold the pavilion to the town of Brighton in 1850 and removed many decorations to be used elsewhere as she thought it would likely be demolished; however, the people of Brighton used the pavilion to bolster the tourism industry that grew with the coming of the London to Brighton railway. Many events started to be held here, and towards the end of the century Queen Victoria returned many of the original possessions.

Brighton's piers

The contrast between the old and new Brighton is captured in the sight of the burned-out West Pier in the shadow of the i360. Built in 1866 and accommodating over 2 million visitors in 1919, the structure gradually started to collapse as the 20th century progressed. Access to the

▽ The elaborately designed Brighton Pavilion was the vision of King George IV.

△ Brighton Pier has seen many famous names perform and it continues to be a big draw.

pier head had long since stopped when the final fire destroyed the classic listed buildings there in 2003. But pier life is alive and well in Brighton thanks to the Palace Pier (☎ 01273 609361 www.brightonpier.co.uk ♦ BN2 1TW) – 525 metres (1,720 feet) long and dating back to 1899. Some huge names have performed here down the decades, including Stan Laurel and Charlie Chaplin. Today the emphasis is on family fun. Tread the planks to find a huge play area, some memorable rides, amusement arcades and a virtual reality gaming area.

Get ready to bike it

There are few ways as revitalising and refreshing to tour around a city than on two wheels. Fortunately, Brighton is well kitted out for

Stay a while

🛏 No. 27 Brighton Bed and Breakfast, 27 Upper Rock Gardens, Brighton, BN2 1QE. ☎ 01273 694951 www.brighton-bed-and-breakfast.co.uk

🧳 Brighton Harbour Hotel and Spa, King's Road, Brighton, BN1 1NA. ☎ 01273 323221 www.harbourhotels.co.uk/brighton

⛺ Housedean Farm Campsite, Brighton Road, Lewes, BN7 3JW. ☎ 07919 668816 www.housedean.co.uk

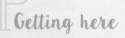

Getting here

Heading south, the A23, A24 and A27 all converge on the Brighton area. The trains coming into the town pull up centrally at the station on Terminus Road.

budding cyclists wanting to see the sights. Brighton Bike Tour (☎ 07914 786843 www. brightonbiketour.com ♦ BN2 9TQ) offers to take visitors on a range of routes, providing informative snippets along the way and – importantly – stopping off for a coffee and cake break at the Royal Pavilion. You'll see the main sights along with some others you may not have normally found, including a wildflower meadow, a secret garden and graffiti on back streets.

55

PORTSMOUTH
HARBOURING TREASURES

To the top of the tower!

Dominating the Portsmouth skyline since it was opened in 2005, the Emirates Spinnaker Tower is the perfect vantage point to appreciate the city's relationship with the sea (☎ 023 9285 7520 www.spinnakertower.co.uk ♀PO1 3TT). Standing on the 110-metre high (360-foot) Sky Deck with the wind blowing around you is an experience to remember. It's visible from 23 miles away and those at the top will be able to see all of Portsmouth, including a bird's-eye view of Portsmouth Historic Dockyard, Gunwharf Quays and the harbour. And if a trip up a tower isn't enough to get your sense of adventure flowing, there are some adrenaline-pumping experiences available. Fundraisers or those after a personal challenge can abseil down the 100-metre (330-foot) tower if they have the legs for it. Or go one stage further and leap from a platform 25 metres (82 feet) above sea level in an activity for the fearless known as 'The Drop'. Sounds like too much? Don't panic, you can also don a virtual reality headset to get the feeling of being out on the ribs of the tower without being outside.

Harbouring treasures

The hottest ticket to be bought in Portsmouth is the Full Navy Ticket at the Historic Dockyard (☎ 023 928 39766 www.historicdockyard.co.uk ♀PO1 3LJ). It's exceptional value and you'll need a couple of full days if you're going to make thorough use of it. The ticket gives you access to over a dozen attractions, covering centuries

SPINNAKER TOWER IN NUMBERS

- 💡 The spire is 27 metres (88 feet) tall and weighs 14 tonnes
- 💡 Contains 1,200 tonnes of steel
- 💡 Has had 2.5 million visitors to date
- 💡 There are 560 steps to the Sky Deck
- 💡 Weighs over 30,000 tonnes
- 💡 The lift to the top takes 30 seconds

△ The Spinnaker Tower dominates the skyline of Portsmouth

of naval history. There are many world-class moments across a range of sites. The Royal Navy's most famous warship, the *Victory*, is one of the top draws, well known for its role in the Battle of Trafalgar. Other highlights include the museum of the Royal Navy and the chance to explore a submarine. There's enough to keep you fully enthused in the Historic Dockyard alone and you'll soon realise more than one visit is needed to do justice fully to Portsmouth's attractions.

The *Mary Rose*

Standing in front of the Tudor warship is a humbling, jaw-dropping experience and a must for anyone who finds themselves in Portsmouth. Dating back to the time of King Henry VIII, the *Mary Rose* (☎ 023 9281 2931 www.maryrose.org ⦿ PO1 3PY) was one of several ships built to boost the seafaring power of English forces. The *Mary Rose* first set sail two years after Henry became king, in 1511, and was involved in several skirmishes with the French. In the summer of 1545, though, the fate of the *Mary Rose* was sealed as she was

⌂ Getting here

Portsmouth is one of the most accessible destinations on the south coast, with the A3(M) and M27 motorways leading here. If you're coming from the east, you'll need to take the A27. A train service can take you right into Portsmouth Harbour.

△ Visitors look down across the town's historic dockyard, the site of many museums and famous warships.

⌂ Stay a while

🛏 The Pier, 2 Bellevue Terrace, Southsea, PO5 3AT. ☎ 023 9282 3813 www.pier-hotel.com

🧳 Queen's Hotel, Clarence Parade, Osborne Road, Portsmouth, PO5 3LJ. ☎ 023 9282 2466 queenshotelportsmouth.com

⛺ Fishery Creek, 100 Fishery Lane, Hayling Island, PO11 9NR. ☎ 023 9246 2164 www.fisherycreekpark.co.uk

destroyed by a French ship, hundreds of men drowning as she sank. Immediate efforts were made to salvage her from the Solent, and a further attempt followed in the 19th century. But it was not until 1982 that a successful operation was carried out to recover the historic hulk from the seabed. Screened live on TV, the raising of the *Mary Rose* was a national event that grabbed the public's attention. Preserving the ship has cost millions and been time-consuming, but visitors today can enjoy a state-of-the-art interactive experience, which really brings home the incredible journey this Tudor legend has been on.

56

SOUTHAMPTON
CRUISING TO SUCCESS

Why visit?

★ Learn how the sinking of the *Titanic* had a devastating impact on Southampton

★ Study an incredible 1:25 scale model of the 'unsinkable' ship that departed from the city in 1912

★ Find out the connection between this region and iconic Second World War aircraft

Southampton

The largest city on the south coast, Southampton's relationship with the sea has shaped its economy and provided it with a plentiful supply of historical tales. Southampton is the port where the RMS *Titanic* set out on her maiden voyage and disastrously collided with the fateful iceberg. Southampton is the city where the Spitfire was first tested, and the earliest models were built at a factory in the city. Southampton was also one of the departure points for the ships on D-Day, a turning point in the Second World War that changed the fate of the nation. Although it may not have the tourist appeal that is enjoyed by nearby Portsmouth, there are plenty of reasons to make a date with Southampton on your coastal tour.

A titanic museum

Your insight into Southampton's oceanic connections should begin at SeaCity Museum on Havelock Road (☎ 023 8083 4536 www.seacitymuseum.co.uk ● SO14 7FY). The centrepiece exhibition explores the link with RMS *Titanic*, the world-famous vessel heralded as unsinkable that came to a tragic end on her maiden voyage to the United States. On 10 April 1912, the *Titanic* set off from Berth 44 in the White Star Dock and the rest, sadly, is history. Expect to be transported back in time to 1912 to see what Southampton was like at the point when the *Titanic* hit the headlines. Five years earlier, the White Star Line's transatlantic business transferred from Liverpool to Southampton,

🔔 Stay a while

🛏 Hamble Retreat, 86 Newtown Road, Warsash, Southampton, SO31 9GB.
☎ 01489 572315
www.hambleretreat.com

🧳 Southampton Harbour Hotel and Spa, 5 Maritime Walk, Southampton, SO14 3QT. ☎ 023 8110 3456
www.harbourhotels.co.uk/southampton

⛺ Sunnydale Farm Camp Site, Grange Road, Netley, Southampton, SO31 8GD. ☎ 023 8045 7462
www.sunnydalefarm.co.uk

▽ The SeaCity Museum houses a wealth of information about RMS *Titanic*.

△ St Mary's Stadium is a coastal home of Premier League football.

boosting the city's economy and turning it into the country's premier passenger port. At that time, there were 23 steamship companies operating from the city and it supported a huge range of secondary industries such as restaurants and hotels. The sights and sounds of Southampton's transportation heyday are explored in the museum, and the 1:25 scale model of the *Titanic* is a hypnotic exhibit you can spend an age studying. The sinking of the *Titanic* had a huge impact on many places, but nowhere was hit harder than Southampton. Over 500 families lost a member in the disaster, many of them being locally based crew working on board.

Reach for the skies

With the Solent region being at the centre of aviation research between 1910 and 1960, a visit to Southampton should include an investigation of this pioneering period and how it contributed to the two World Wars. During this golden age of development in the aviation industry, no fewer than 26 aircraft manufacturers were established in the region, working on everything from biplanes to space craft and everything in between. Perhaps the greatest plane to emerge from the Solent during this period was the Spitfire, which became a regular sight over the skies of southern England during the early 1940s. Helping to clinch a decisive victory in the all-important Battle of Britain, the Spitfire has forever earned a place in the hearts of the country's military and aviation enthusiasts. The Solent Sky exhibition (© 023 8063 5830 www.solentsky.org ♀ SO14 3FR) has over 20 different aircraft that visitors can explore, including one of the prized Spitfires that started life in Hampshire. It's a great place to look at how the Solent reached for the skies.

St Mary's

Few football grounds have a location as near to the coast as Southampton's. The stands are literally on the edge of the River Itchen at the point where it prepares to empty its load into the Solent (♀ SO14 5FP). Indeed, the main stand in the stadium is called the Itchen Stand. Visit www.southamptonfc.com for information on how to get tickets.

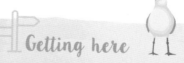

Getting here

Most people will be heading south to the city, which means you should follow the M3 as far as it goes. If you come from the east or west, take the M27. The city also has good rail connections with the rest of the country.

57

SANDBANKS
WONDERFUL BEACHES, NATURALLY

Why visit?

★ Spend the day playing and having a BBQ on what many consider to be the best beach in the UK

★ Take the ferry across to Studland for more glorious beaches and a National Trust café

★ Pitch up for a night under the stars at the eco campsite on Brownsea Island

The country's best beach?

The beach at Sandbanks has earned the reputation of being one of Britain's finest. With refreshing walks and outstanding views, people return to here time and time again to reinvigorate their soul. The sandy stretch here has scooped a Blue Flag award for over 30 consecutive years – more times than any other resort in the country.

Dog owners can make use of a designated walking area on the beach's western end, while cyclists will find the promenade provides a joyful route. Why not come fully prepared to spend the day here and make use of the barbecue area? Take care to read the advice on beach barbecues and beach parties before you set up on this beach, which is ideal for a celebration.

▽ Enjoy stunning sunsets on this gloripus section of the southern coast.

△ Some of the most expensive homes in the country are found at Sandbanks.

Spend the night in a tree

Take a boat from Poole Harbour to enjoy a few hours on Brownsea Island (☎ 01202 707744 ♥ BH13 7EE), a well-known wildlife haven and a great place for family fun. The small wooded island just a stone's throw from Sandbanks is owned and managed by the National Trust, so there are plenty of activities going on in the summer months. But for the ultimate adventure here you should come to spend a night in the eco camp. You can bring your own tent if you wish, but who could resist the chance to hire a pre-pitched tree tent or hammock. Booking ahead is essential, and it's heaven on a warm night. Find out more at www.nationaltrust.org.uk/features/brownsea-island-eco-camping.

Studland beaches

Every 20 minutes, the car ferry leaves Sandbanks and crosses the short stretch of water to the Shell Bay terminal, saving car drivers a 40km (25-mile) diversion around Poole. The ferry is called Bramble Bush Bay and can hold 48 vehicles, opening up opportunities for those visiting Sandbanks to flex their muscles a little. The voyage costs very little and it's worth having an explore around Studland. Another group of idyllic beaches await your exploration here, whether you're wanting to stretch your legs, have a paddle or attempt something a bit more energetic like a game of beach volleyball. South Beach and Middle beach are popular among locals and tourists alike and offer stunning views out to Old Harry Rocks. There's a National Trust café and shop on Knoll Beach, and nearby a 1km (1/2 mile) stretch of the beach has been approved for naturism. Signs warn those not wanting to get involved that there may be naked folk on this stretch of the beach. There are, though, plenty of other places to have fun here if stripping off is not your thing.

Getting here

Head west away from Bournemouth on the A338, following local signs for Sandbanks. The ferry terminal is at the end of Banks Road. Nearby railway stations are at Bournemouth and Parkstone.

△ Coastal defences are in place around Sandbanks to protect the valuable housing.

The guys who save lives

A rare chance to find out more about the people who are on hand 24/7 to help seafarers in distress is offered at the RNLI College Discovery Tour (◉ BH15 1HZ). The 90-minute sessions are led by one of the volunteers and show what kind of training is carried out by those who do such heroic work. A highlight is getting to see the Sea Survival centre, where much of the key training takes place in a wave tank and lifeboat simulator. Another hour-long tour takes you to see where the famous orange all-weather boats are built and repaired. We're so used to seeing lifeboat stations around our coast and the boats that are so valued on our waters, but this tour takes you to the heart of

the operation. Tours operate every day except Sunday and can be booked by calling 0300 300 7654 or emailing tours@rnli.org.uk.

Jetski!

Getting out on the sea is a great way to spend time at the coast and there are many ways to do it around Poole and Sandbanks. Perhaps the most invigorating and challenging is to hit the waves with Jetski Safaris (◉ 01202 706784 www.jetskisafaris.co.uk ◉ BH14 8JR). Leave your cares on the shoreline and spend an hour on the water, twisting and turning at speed. Thrilling stuff!

Home to the Beautiful People

The sandy spit of Sandbanks has been labelled Britain's Palm Beach by some media, referring to the posh property here that's unaffordable to most of the population. The land value on this small coastal concentration of land is the fourth highest in the world and is host to several celebrities and wealthy business folk. Even empty plots of land sell for millions here. Walking around Sandbanks is the closest you'll get in the UK to a tour of a Hollywood or Beverly Hills type area.

Stay a while

🛏 Grovefield Manor, 18 Pinewood Road, Poole, BH13 6JS. ◉ 01202 766798 www.grovefieldmanor.co.uk

🧳 Haven Hotel, Banks Road, Poole, BH13 7QL. ◉ 0800 484 0048 www.fjbhotels.co.uk/haven-hotel

⛺ Cleavel Point Camp Site, Wareham, BH20 5JN. ◉ 01929 480570 www.burnbake.com

58

THE JURASSIC COAST
BECOME A FOSSIL HUNTER!

Why visit?

★ Search for fossils in rocks strewn on the beach on a fascinating guide with an expert

★ Take a walk on the stunning pebbles of Chesil Beach, the largest example of a tombolo in the UK

★ See a series of brilliant natural features, include coves, arches and stack

△ Fossil hunters scout the Charmouth Beach looking for evidence of dinosaurs.

Charmouth Beach

Armed with a geological hammer, goggles and a sense of adventure, heading out on to Charmouth Beach can be an inspiring way to spend an afternoon. This is the premier location in Britain to search for fossils and your chances of coming away with an ammonite or belemnite are fairly high. The best thing to do is examine the beach at low tide to see what the sea has brought ashore. Famous around the world for what the ancient rocks have revealed, storms have occasionally exposed larger skeletons of Ichthyosaurus and Plesiosaurus. Equipment can be hired in local shops but keep away from the cliffs and on no account look for fossils in them – they are part of the Jurassic Coast World Heritage Site and there is also a constant risk of collapse. If it's destined not to be your day as a fossil hunter after scouring the beach, there are plenty of local finds on display in the visitor centre and a few pounds will buy you a decent example to take home in the many fossil shops of Charmouth and Lyme Regis.

Fossil-hunting tours

For a better idea of how to search for those creatures from millions of years ago, book to go on a fossil walk with a local expert (☎ 01297 560772 www.charmouth.org ♥ DT6 6LL). Starting with a 25-minute talk in the visitor centre, there's then plenty of time to search on the beach with the guide. Advance booking is recommended.

△ The jaw-dropping Durdle Door is one of our most famous natural arches.

She sells sea shells...

The Jurassic Coast region became world famous as a fossil-finding site in the early 19th century owing to the discoveries of Mary Anning. Her work on this shoreline led to the discovery of the first identified Ichthyosaur skeleton, along with a plesiosaur and pterosaur. Mary Anning is now immortalised in the famous tongue-twister 'She sells sea shells on the sea shore'.

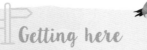

Getting here

The incredible landforms found along the Jurassic Coast make for an exciting and informative one- or two-day tour. All the key locations have ample parking and are accessible from either the A35, A3052 or B3157 at the points they pass close to the coast.

Lulworth Cove

Perhaps the finest example of a cove anywhere in the world, Lulworth is *the* place to see how different rock types resist coastal erosion at different rates. Once the waves created a gap in the limestone cliffs on the shore, it was much easier for the sea to carve out a circular cove in the softer clays that lay further inland. The sea then came up against a band of chalk, slowing progress of the erosion. The incredible shape of this huge cove attracts half a million visitors a year, with July and August being the really busy months. Although the cove is the main natural feature luring many here, there are some magnificent examples of folding cliffs nearby too. These sedimentary rocks were initially formed in horizontal layers but tectonic movement has pushed and twisted them into the mesmerising, impossible angles they now sit at.

Durdle Door

The most iconic view of this UNESCO protected stretch of British coast is a mesmerising arch on the Lulworth Estate (www.lulworth.com ⚲ BH20 5PU). Reached by a steep path from the clifftop car park, the moment Durdle Door comes into view is one that will take your breath away. It's such a stunning example of a natural arch that has been eroded by centuries of crashing waves that no photograph can do it justice. Visiting it is like stepping into a fairy tale. The name comes from the old English word 'thirl', which means to pierce or bore – something the sea has done over the course of time.

Old Harry and his wife

Park up at the National Trust car park at Studland (⚲ BH19 3AU) and walk past the Bankes Arms to pick up the path and discover the distinctive and famous chalk features at this eastern edge of the World Heritage Site. The stack off the headland was once attached to the coast, but the sea first eroded a cave, which then became an arch, and the stack was left standing alone after the collapse of the roof. Old Harry's Wife was another stack, but further erosion caused this to topple and become a stump. The process of erosion will no doubt continue here for thousands of years to come.

Chesil Beach

A stunning shingle formation and the largest tombolo in the UK, Chesil Beach needs to be seen to be believed (☎ 01305 206191 www.dorsetwildlifetrust.org.uk ⚲ DT4 9XE). Only by heading out for a walk on the 29km (18 mile) pebbly landform will you gain an understanding of how remarkable a place it is. Just 200 metres (650 feet) wide, its long, thin form looks

impressive from up on the cliffs. But for a real sense of what this windswept natural wonder is like, park up at the visitor centre and go for a trudge among the shingle.

🛎 Stay a while

🛏 The Beach Rooms, Hammonds Mead, Lower Sea Lane, Charmouth, DT6 6LR. ☎ 01297 560030 www.thebeachrooms.co.uk

🧳 Mariners Hotel, Silver Street, Lyme Regis, DT7 3HS. ☎ 01297 442753 www.hotellymeregis.co.uk

⛺ Wood Farm Caravan and Camping Park, Axminster Road, Charmouth, DT6 6BT. ☎ 01297 560697 www.woodfarm.co.uk

▽ Thousands of pebbles make up the Chesil Beach tombolo.

SOUTH-WEST

Generations of kids have made an annual pilgrimage to the south-west to enjoy the golden beaches of Cornwall and Devon. Our coastal adventures start in Dawlish Warren, where amusements sit next to nature and the power of the sea is very much in people's minds. This coast is where the Spanish Armada was spotted heading towards England. Head to Plymouth to stand on the spot where Sir Francis Drake was said to have been enjoying a game of bowls and discover about that period in our history. As we head into Cornwall, it's the future that's the biggest concern at the Eden Project, near St Austell. Discover different biomes and learn about environmental issues before topping off on a daring zip line.

The south-western tip of Cornwall is a special place, with stunning coastal views and plenty of fun to be had. Visit the Lizard peninsula to see the sunset or perhaps have a go at coasteering in an adventure you'll never forget. The National Trust's Kynance Cove is one of the most beautiful beach settings in the world. After spending a day playing in caves, what could be better than to take to the world-renowned Minack Theatre and enjoy a play in such a sublime setting. Land's End and Cape Cornwall offer cliff top coastal walks with an edge-of-the-planet feel, perfect for a day out getting some fresh air with a picnic. The busier north coast of Cornwall also offers a range of treats, starting at quaint St Ives with its maze of streets harbouring dozens

Don't miss

- ✓ Jumping off cliffs at the Lizard in a coasteering experience
- ✓ The hidden beaches and caves revealed at low tide at beautiful Kynance Cove
- ✓ Theatrical performances in a unique setting at the clifftop Minack
- ✓ An expert lesson at one of Cornwall's famous surf schools – followed by a pasty!
- ✓ Following in the steps of King Arthur at Tintagel in north Cornwall

of craft shops and art galleries. Bustling Newquay is a must-visit for people wanting a great night out, and it's also home to the Boardmasters festival. If food is more your thing, follow Rick Stein's footsteps to Padstow to sample seafood and other treats prepared in imaginative ways. Further up the coast, Bude's beaches are well known for surfing. For many, once they get the Cornwall bug there is nowhere else in the world they would rather go. If the sun shines on your time in the south-west, you can enjoy long days in incredible settings with plenty of fun in the water. Surf schools are big business here, and there are many with a good reputation to get you started on the waves. You'll be surprised to see how an hour or two of pro tuition can improve your moves and get you standing on your board. Take time to examine the folklore of this region as well, from the smuggling pirates making use of cave networks to the legend of Merlin the Magician and King Arthur at Tintagel. Interesting times abound in north Devon, too, as you spend days exploring the fascinating past of Clovelly and the literary significance of the Tarka Trail. And why not have a go at creating your own piece of sand art at Weston Super Mare after being inspired by the annual sand sculpting event.

Whichever day out you are on, remember that creams teas in this part of the world are obligatory! And after you adventures, there's always a bottle of local cider on hand to wash down your experience. Of course, when in our most south-westerly county, make sure you stick to my Cornish mantra – a pasty a day keeps the doldrums away.

Home to palm trees, rare plants and some of Britain's best summer weather, the south-west remains one of the most popular holiday hot spots.

59

DAWLISH WARREN

AMUSEMENT BY NATURE

Why visit?

★ Stroll along the natural sandy spit, which is constantly changing under the sea's pressure

★ Combine nature with fairground rides at the holiday town of Dawlish

★ Take a trip to the palm-tree-strewn town of Torquay, in the English Riviera

Dawlish Warren – resort and nature reserve

Sitting on a sandy spit sticking out into the Exe Estuary, Dawlish Warren Nature Reserve (☎ 01626 863980 www.dawlishwarren.info ♥ TQ12 4XX) is an important location for flora and fauna – and holidaymakers escaping the rat race. The beautiful dunes that reach out into the river mouth are a roosting site for wading birds and one of only two sites in the UK where sand crocus grow. Positioned next to this is a popular holiday park with associated amusements and fairground rides. Managing this environment, under daily pressure from the sea, is a major challenge for planners. A programme of replacing revetments, repairing groynes and adding dredged sand to the spit is underway and will last for years.

The walk to the end of the spit, where you get a lovely view of Exmouth across the water, is well worth doing. You'll see the management methods up close as this Humans vs Sea battle rages on. Check the tide times before you visit because some parts of the beach are impassable when the sea is high and there's a risk of being stranded for hours.

△ There are plenty of facilities for tourist enjoying the natural wonders at Dawlish Warren.

△ You don't have to walk far from the train station to be in isolated beauty.

Dawlish Warren is a changing landscape and even with a substantial management scheme it is still difficult to predict exactly how it will look in the coming decades. Eventually, the sea is likely to breach the sand dunes and form a tidal inlet called Greenland Lake in the middle of the warren. Habitats and species living around this inlet will change significantly. A recently built flood defence close to the visitor centre will stop water in Greenland Lake flooding nearby Dawlish Warren village, but there's no way to halt all the sea's power in this increasingly fragile environment.

Stormy weather

Dawlish hit the news headlines during the winter storms of 2014 when the railway line – sited tantalising close to the sea – collapsed. Closure of the line caused major disruption in the south-west, with rail services unable to serve parts of Devon and Cornwall. Services reopened after weeks of hard work and a £35 million bill.

Getting here

Most approach Torquay from the east, taking the A38 and then following the A380 into Torbay. Dawlish Warren is found to the north of Dawlish, just off the A379. Both Torquay and Dawlish Warren are on the national rail network.

Torquay

Head west along the coast from Dawlish and you'll arrive at the heart of the English Riviera. The region earned the nickname because of its mild climate and penchant for palm trees. In the heart of Torbay, tourism is now Torquay's mainstay and there is plenty for families to do on holiday. A nearby zoo, theatre and prehistoric cave all battle for the holidaymaker's cash. There are plenty of places to stay in Torquay, and most are thankfully much better organised than Fawlty Towers, the calamitous hotel from the classic TV series based in the town.

△ See the world in miniature at Babbacombe's model village.

Babbacombe's model village

Dropping in to see a model village is a seaside tradition for many families and there are few finer than that found in Torquay. Babbacombe Model Village (☎ 01803 315315 www.model-village.co.uk ♥ TQ1 3LA) is regularly updated, has 55 years' experience under its belt and boasts over 400 tiny buildings. Make your way around beautifully arranged scenes that celebrate life in the country over the last six decades and are home to a population of 13,000 miniature figures. It's not a visit that should be rushed – allow at least two hours if you're going to study plenty of the humorous, inventive sections and complete the spotter sheet available at the entrances. Keep your eyes peeled for famous mini celebs at the mansion. Journey between the clifftop and the beach at Babbacombe on the Cliff Railway, which has been taking folk up and down the steep slope since 1926 (☎ 01803 328750 www.babbacombecliffrailway.co.uk ♥ TQ1 3LF).

An insight into pre-history

Some of the earliest modern human remains in Europe have been discovered in Torquay, in and around Kents Cavern (☎ 01803 215136 www.kents-cavern.co.uk ♥ TQ1 2JF). Hand axes and a collection of animal remains have helped to piece together a picture of what life was like here 40,000 years ago.

🔔 Stay a while

🛏 The 25 Boutique, 25 Avenue Road, Torquay, TQ2 5LB. ☎ 01803 297517 www.the25.uk

🏨 The Grand Hotel, Seafront, Torbay Road, Torquay, TQ2 6NT. ☎ 0800 005 2244 www.grandtorquay.co.uk

⛰ Treacle Valley Campsite, Orestone Lane, Daccombe, Newton Abbot, TQ12 4ST. ☎ 01803 328294 www.treaclevalley.co.uk

PLYMOUTH
A PORT WITH A BEATING HEART OF HISTORY

Bowls before battle

Born in nearby Tavistock, Sir Francis Drake considered Spanish forces a lifelong enemy. When he was part of a fleet transporting slaves to the New World, an attack by a Spanish squad left only two ships intact. The writing was on the wall for Drake. In the late 1570s, he set off on a secret mission for Elizabeth I with the aim of attacking Spanish interests in South America. His return in 1580 brought not only a cache of Spanish treasure but also the pride of being the first Englishman to circumnavigate the globe. But the legend of Sir Francis Drake centres on what may have happened at Plymouth Hoe in 1588. On 20 July, he was playing a game of bowls when news reached him of the approaching Spanish Armada as the Catholic Spaniards attempted to oust the Protestant queen. Instead of rushing off into battle, the story goes that Sir Francis Drake instead calmly said he wished to finish off his game. It may be that he knew the conditions weren't right for English ships to set sail at that moment, but the tale has become one of the best examples of an Englishman keeping his cool in tough circumstances. A statue marking the achievements of Drake stands on the Hoe, from where you can share his view out across Plymouth Sands.

▽ Prominent Plymouth Hoe, where Sir Francis Drake learned of the Spanish Armada.

△ Follow the path of the Pilgrim Fathers, who left these shores here.

Departure of the Pilgrims

There have been few journeys more famous and influential than that of the Pilgrim Fathers, who left these shores in 1620 to colonise North America. After a series of problems and failed attempts at making the crossing, just 102 people left Plymouth on 16 September on a three-masted ship called the *Mayflower*. They ran into trouble during their voyage when one of the masts broke in two. Turning back to England was an option, but a successful attempt to mend the ship meant they could continue on the incredibly difficult journey that claimed the lives of two people on board. The Pilgrims eventually sighted land on 9 November and dropped anchor just off Cape Cod two days later. Each year, Thanksgiving in the United States marks the first harvest collected by the Pilgrims and is

one of the country's biggest holidays. Plymouth's Mayflower Steps mark the place where this historic, influential journey began, and you'll be able to see a British flag flapping in the wind next to the Stars and Stripes. Offering great views of the Barbican and telling the story of those early religious travellers, the Mayflower Museum has interesting exhibits over three floors (☏ 01752 306330 www.mayflower400uk.org ♥ PL1 2LR).

A moving tower

The huge Smeaton's Tower on Plymouth Hoe began life out to sea on Eddystone Reef in 1759. Costing £40,000, all was well until the 1880s when there was concern at the rate the rock was being eroded by the sea. An ambitious project was started to move the lighthouse to Plymouth, with two-thirds of it being transported brick by brick to its current location. Standing 22 metres (72 feet) high, visitors can climb its stairs and enjoy the iconic view of south Devon (☏ 01752 304774 plymhearts.org ♥ PL1 2NZ).

△ The unmistakable stripes of Smeaton's Tower.

Award-winning chippy

Serving fish and chips to locals and tourists on the seafront since 1979, the Harbourside is always popular and has won several accolades in the National Fish and Chip Awards over the years (☏ 01752 224112 www.harboursidefishandchips.co.uk ♥ PL1 2LS).

△ The oldest UK gin distillery still in operation has been fuelling Plymouth since 1793.

Getting here

South-west of Exeter in the south of Devon, Plymouth is built around the junction of the A38 and A386. North of the town centre, Plymouth's train station is well connected on the Cross Country and GWR lines.

Just the tonic!

With such a seafaring tradition surrounding Plymouth, it's not surprising to learn there is a long history of gin production – and drinking – here. The Plymouth Distillery (☎ 01752 665292 www.plymouthdistillery.com ♥ PL1 2LQ) is the oldest in the country still in operation and has been satisfying gin lovers since 1793. The same recipe has been used ever since and the distillery's gin-tasting tours are a fascinating way to develop a taste for this local speciality. The building also has a remarkable history – dating back to the early 1400s, it is now protected as a national monument. It was here that the Pilgrim Fathers spent their last night in the country before walking down to the *Mayflower* and sailing over to North America.

Stay a while

🛏 Old Pier Guest House, 20 Radford Road, Plymouth, PL1 3BY. ☎ 01752 309797 old-pier-guest-house. bestplymouthhotels.co.uk

🧳 The Grosvenor, 7–11 Elliot Street, The Hoe, Plymouth, PL1 2PP. ☎ 01752 260411 www.grosvenor-plymouth.com

⛺ Smithaleigh Caravan and Camping Park, Plymouth, PL7 5AX. ☎ 01752 893194

ST AUSTELL BAY

BOATS, BIOMES AND BEER

Fowey

A quintessential Cornish fishing village, Fowey has a lot of things going for it. As well as offering charming craft shops, some great pasty hotspots and quality seafront pubs, Fowey looks the part. Leave your car at the top of the hill and walk down the steep, higgledy-piggledy streets, where rows of houses are built into the hillside and the skyline is a patchwork of roofs, all different sizes and on varying levels. What makes Fowey stand apart from some of its rivals is its relatively remote setting; this is not somewhere you pass on

a major road. You have to make the effort to visit the small town, at the mouth of the River Fowey. Across the water, you can see nearby Polruan and an important passenger ferry keeps the two places connected with regular trips during the day. Another ferry links Fowey with the more distant Mevagissey, allowing passengers to take in views of the Polperro Heritage Coast they pass on the way. Those staying on land may want to sample a pint or two in the historic pubs, where ale from the local St Austell Brewery and Fowey Brewery are available. Getting a Proper Job is highly recommended.

△ The tight streets of Fowey twist and turn down to a lovely harbour.

Getting here

On Cornwall's southern coast, St Austell is close to the junction of the A390 and the A391. The train station is close to the centre of the town and has a regular direct service to London Paddington.

A phoenix from a china clay pit

In the mid-1990s, the working china clay pit on the edge of St Austell was coming to the end of its time. Similar spaces in Cornwall sit abandoned, resembling a moonscape exploited for its resources. But Tim Smit – the man who oversaw the restoration of Cornwall's Lost Gardens of Heligan – had a vision for the huge space. He

△ The biomes of the Eden Project are a wonderful environment to learn about how plants are used.

wanted to create a place where people could get up close with the world's most important flora and plans were drawn up soon after the last clay workers had left the pit. The concept of the Eden Project (📞 01726 811911 www.eden project.com 📍 PL24 2SG) started to gather pace and funding was fully secured in 2000, with education about environmental issues being a major goal from the outset. In this regard, the Eden Project leads by example, even managing to make its own soil through an ambitious compost scheme. Two huge biomes are the main focus of visits, one featuring an extensive range of flora from Mediterranean climates and the other being much hotter and more humid to house tropical plants and trees. Allow more time to tour the Rainforest Biome, which delivers at times hard-hitting information about the way soya, coffee and rubber are produced. Look out for

announcements about the Eden Sessions early in the year to find out which artists are playing a summer gig near the biomes. Previous artists to sing in the former clay pit include Pulp and Björk. The series of early summer concerts is now a well-respected addition to the festival calendar.

🔔 **Stay a while**

🛏 Artist's House, 40 Vicarage Meadow, Fowey, PL23 1EA. 📞 01726 833680

🏨 Fowey Hall Hotel, Hanson Drive, Fowey, PL23 1ET. 📞 01726 833866 www.foweyhallhotel.co.uk

⛺ Chuan-Vista, Trenance Downs, St Austell, PL25 5RH. 📞 01726 75197

0–60mph over Eden

A blend of excitement and trepidation greets thrill seekers at the top of the Hangloose tower as they prepare to be launched on to England's longest and fastest zip wire (☏ 01726 812724 www.hanglooseadventure.com ♥ PL24 2SG). Cruising over 660 metres (2,165 feet) at a top speed of 95kph (60mph), the Skywire takes you on an adrenaline-filled 45-second ride over the Eden Project's biomes. You'll be kitted out and shown an information video before taking a short drive to the launch tower and getting into position 100 metres (330 feet) above the ground. The astonishing view stretches right out to St Austell Bay in the distance, while the tourists in the Eden Project make their way to attractions beneath you. Your harness will allow you to be suspended horizontally from the zip wire, meaning the flight will be a Superman-style

experience. Nerves quickly subside once you're in the air and you can get on with enjoying the all-too-fast rush of excitement. When you're inside the Eden Project, the whirring of the zip wire is a familiar sound that triggers most people to glance up and see the two people pelting across the sky. It's something special being one of those flying adventure seekers and seeing the inquisitive heads gaze up in your direction. When the brake stops you at the other side, it's time to review the video footage you can capture by having your phone strapped to your helmet. And maybe you'll now have got the bug and fancy taking the plunge once more. A second journey down the zip wire can be made going backwards if you have the stomach for it! If the zip wire doesn't satisfy your thirst for thrills, there's also a drop swing called Gravity and a 10-metre (33-foot) freefall drop on the same site.

△ Are you brave enough to whizz over the Eden Project on a zip line?

62

THE LIZARD
ADVENTURES AT ENGLAND'S MOST SOUTHERLY POINT

⭐ Take the plunge and go coasteering off the jagged Cornish coast

⭐ Climb the stairs of the Lizard Lighthouse to see the workings of this iconic shipping beacon

⭐ Discover the point where Marconi made the first wireless transmission

Lizard

A charming settlement almost at the very end of the peninsula, Lizard village has a delightfully remote feel to it. Quite isolated in winter months and thronged with tourists in the summer holidays, the village pulls in visitors on their way to Lizard Point – England's most southerly location. It's reached from the village via a nice country path, or there is a National Trust car park a little closer to the edge. Posing for a photo on the cliff is a must, knowing everybody else on the mainland is further north. The dark green metamorphic rock in these parts is called serpentine and has been fashioned into jewellery, available in local shops. At lunchtime, make a visit to Ann's Pasties (☎ 01326 290889 www.annspasties.co.uk ♥ TR12 7PB) for some of the tastiest varieties of the Cornish snack available – all home-made and sold from a house.

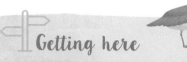

Getting here

From Helston on the A394, follow the A3083 all the way down the peninsula to Lizard village.

Adventure time

Opportunities to have an extreme sport adrenaline rush along the Cornish coast are plentiful. If sea kayaking, surfing or paddle boarding aren't enough, try your hand at coasteering with an experienced instructor. Lizard Adventure (☎ 07845 204040 www.lizardadventure.co.uk ♥ TR12 7NN) offers regular coasteering trips from Lizard village, providing the chance for the ultimate coastal escapade. After getting into a wetsuit and driving to the cliff edge, a steep path takes you down to the point where you will take the plunge – quite literally. Jumping off the rocks into the sea from a height of up to 10 metres (33 feet) requires nerves of steel and is not for the faint-hearted. Your group will negotiate about half a kilometre (1/3 mile) of rocky coastline. There'll be scrambling over rocks, tackling waves, dealing with currents, passing through cracks and diving into the ocean. Being in the sea and swimming your way beyond caves rarely seen by humans is an incredibly rewarding experience. Many find the three-hour voyage leaves them wanting more time in the water.

△ Lizard Point in Cornwall is the most southerly point in England.

△ Taking the plunge on a coasteering adventure is an invigorating experience.

Marconi's wireless history

At the turn of the 20th century, Italian inventor Guglielmo Marconi used the clifftops at Lizard as a base to carry out pioneering experiments. The first wireless transmissions were made from a hut overlooking the sea. A wireless telegraph station established at nearby Poldhu was the first to send a transmission to North America. The Lizard Wireless Station (TR12 7AP) has been restored to how it was in Marconi's time by the National Trust and can be visited by following the clifftop path.

 Fish and chips

For a seaside treat in Lizard, head for Smugglers chippy in the centre of the village (01326 290763 TR12 7NH).

Lizard's beacon

The iconic Lizard Lighthouse (01326 290202 www.trinityhouse.co.uk TR12 7NT) was built in 1751 and has helped ships avoid the treacherous rocks along the Cornish coast ever since. A light still shines from here across the sea and the foghorn sounds when visibility is poor. Pay a visit to the Heritage Centre and enjoy a tour of the lighthouse to learn about how the light has been updated over the years and eventually automated. You can even stay in one of the lighthouse keeper's cottages, which are now holiday homes run by Trinity House.

△ The Lizard peninsula is a popular place to take to the seas for the day.

Kynance Cove

One of the most idyllic beaches in the country, Kynance Cove should be visited at low tide to make the most of all it has to offer. When the sea recedes, the pebble-strewn beach near the small café lengthens to allow access to stunning rocks. A passage also opens to a secret beach around the corner, where the sea laps on to two shores and reveals caves with multiple entrances. Owned by the National Trust, this is one of their Cornish jewels and is rightly promoted as a near-tropical escape. A recent car park extension has been added to cope with the demand. During the busiest periods, Kynance Cove can become the victim of its own success and struggle to cope with the huge numbers of visitors. But catch this southerly cove at a quiet time and it will stay in your heart for ever. This is not a location ideal for surfers and body-boarders because of limited beach space and rip tides. But families seeking magical caves, stunning views and places to search in rock pools will not be disappointed.

▽ Stunning Kynance Cove is reached by walking down a steep track from a cliff-top car park.

△ A secret world opens up at Kynance Cove every low tide.

🛎 Stay a while

🛏 Chyheira, Ruan Minor, Helston, TR12 7LQ. 🕿 01326 290343
www.chyheira.co.uk

🧳 The Top House Inn, The Lizard, Helston TR12 7NQ. 🕿 01326 290974
www.thetophouselizard.co.uk

⛺ Henry's Campsite, The Lizard, Helston, TR12 7NX. 🕿 01326 290596
www.henryscampsite.co.uk

63

PORTHCURNO
A REAL CLIFFHANGER!

The Minack – an unforgettable theatrical experience

The clifftop setting of the Minack Theatre (☎ 01736 810181 www.minack.com ● TR19 6JU) is one of the world's most dramatic places to watch a play. Sitting on granite seats carved with the titles of previous works performed here, audiences have enjoyed coastal productions with a stunning Atlantic backdrop since 1932. Although the weather plays a large role in deciding how memorable the evening's performance will be, few theatrical experiences are better than this. Just imagine a good script on a warm summer night, with boats sailing across the horizon and waves crashing on to rocks beneath the stage. The famous theatre was the vision of Rowena Cade, who lived in Minack House and decided the cliffs below her garden would the ideal place to stage *The Tempest* when a local theatre group were looking for a venue. Working with her gardener, boulders and earth were moved to create seating and stage areas. Little by little, changes have been made to create a modern venue that uses the latest technology in a natural setting. Theatre-goers drive through narrow country lanes to reach the clifftop car park, bringing picnics and blankets to make a special night under the stars. The summer season of shows is always wide-ranging, featuring drama, comedy, Shakespeare and musicals. Theatre groups travel from all over the country for the chance to perform in such a unique setting. Book tickets well in advance and turn up early to get the best seats.

▽ Book tickets for the Minack Theatre and then pray the weather is good!

From Porthcurno to the rest of the world...

Spending a day at Porthcurno's beach is such an attractive proposition that there is often pressure on the local car parks. Arrive early to get the best access to the sandy stretch, which holds a secret beneath its sloping shores. It's from this southerly outpost that telegram messages were sent and received around the world via cables laid for thousands of miles along the ocean floor. The four corners of the British Empire could communicate with each other quickly and efficiently once the ambitious Victorian network of cables was in

Getting here

Penzance and the Minack Theatre are reached by taking the A30 towards the south-western tip of Cornwall. The train station at Penzance signals the end of the Cornish rail network and is well connected to London and cities further north.

△ The memorable walk across to St Michael's Mount at low tide.

place. All the communication routes came ashore at Porthcurno, from where information was relayed to London via a series of overland wires. The story of the 19th-century developments in messaging is told at the delightful Porthcurno Telegraph Museum (☎ 01736 810966 www.telegraphmuseum.org ● TR19 6JX).

Penzance

Famous for singing pirates and palm trees, Penzance is a relative metropolis of High Street shops and supermarkets for people living in the far reaches of the south-west. Bookshops, galleries and quirky outlets give the streets of Penzance an alternative and relaxed feel, ideal for an afternoon of browsing. Head down to the harbour to see a collection of fabulous boats and enjoy one of the sea-life safaris or fishing trips that leave every day. Film connoisseurs should head to the Savoy (☎ 01736 363330 www.penzance.merlincinemas.co.uk ● TR18 2SN) to enjoy a screening in England's longest-running cinema.

A journey through English history

Visible from practically everywhere in Mount's Bay, the distinctive tidal island of St Michael's Mount (☎ 01736 710265 www.stmichaelsmount.co.uk ● TR17 0HS) rises from the sea and provides a dramatic setting for one of the country's most famous castles.

Steeped in history, this prominent and iconic building has been home to the St Aubyn family since the 17th century and has served as a priory, fort and family home. Highlights include stained-glass windows gathered from churches around Europe that date back to 1500, along with a 15th-century granite cross in the priory. Tidal times dictate how you reach this popular National Trust property. At low tide, a brief walk along a cobbled causeway brings you to an information point, café and small harbour at the foot of the mount. When the sea creeps over the walkway, a boat service ferries tourists to and from the mainland.

Stay a while

🛏 Chy-an-Mor, 15 Regent Terrace, Penzance, TR18 4DW. ☎ 01736 363441
www.chyanmor.co.uk

🏨 Hotel Penzance, Britons Hill, Penzance, TR18 3AE. ☎ 01736 363117
www.hotelpenzance.com

⛺ Noongallas Campsite, Gulval, Penzance, TR20 8YR. ☎ 01736 366698
www.noongallas.com

64

CAPE CORNWALL
BEANS ON COAST!

Why visit?

★ Stand on the edge of the land at Cape Cornwall and gaze out across the Atlantic

★ Develop your skills on the waves at a surf school in Sennen

★ Walk past shipwrecks and tin mines along the Cornish coastal path

Cape Cornwall

Jutting into the Atlantic Ocean, the iconic headland at Cape Cornwall is visible from miles away. There's a well-established path leading visitors up the gentle slope to enjoy the far-reaching, 360° view at the summit. In the late 1980s, the future of this much-loved western cape was put in doubt as it was offered for sale. Conservationists feared large development would follow and the nature of the cape would be changed for ever, but a rescue package came from a most unlikely source – or sauce. Baked-

bean giant Heinz bought Cape Cornwall in 1987 and handed it over to the National Trust as a gift for the nation. It secured the future of what is an important site for both wildlife and Cornwall's rich industrial heritage. Between 1836 and 1883, a tin mine operated here. Employing 45 local men, four women and five boys at its height, the mine contributed enormously to the local economy. The chimney at the top of the hill was built in the middle of the 19th century to serve the tin mine's boiler and although demolition discussions took

△ Cape Cornwall'a chimney is a distinguishing feature of this land that juts out into the Atlantic.

△ The boats here are used for fishing and getting away from it all.

place when the mine closed, it was left to stand as a daytime beacon to warn shipping about the treacherous Brisons Rocks nearby. Cape Cornwall is a tranquil place to while away a few hours. Local artists come here to paint the ever-changing weather and sea conditions, while the handful of small boats are evidence that it's still used as a base for fishing. Most people arriving here are looking to enjoy the views and a brisk walk, perhaps finishing it off with some of the Cornish ice cream on sale in the car park.

Looking back

On Cape Cornwall Road, you cannot miss the huge home built at the turn of the 20th century by local mine investor Captain Francis Oats. Porthledden House (⚲ TR19 7NL) later became a hotel popular with golfers playing on the nearby course – in the 1930s, a pioneering landing strip was developed for wealthy golfers arriving at the remote links by air. During the Second World War, the house was home to a girls' school for evacuees and has recently undergone a decade-long restoration project.

Surf's up!

Cornwall is a Mecca for surf worshippers from all over the country. Persistently good waves battering the Atlantic coast and some of our warmest summer weather attracts thousands to the golden coast. Drive to the south-west on any weekend when the forecast is half decent and you'll see holidaymakers with boards on their cars and a smile on their face. For many locals, heading to the beach with a board is a way of life rather than an activity on their jollies. Sennen

🛎 Stay a while

🛏 Old Success Inn, Cove Hill, Sennen Cove, TR19 7DG, ☎ 01736 871232 www.oldsuccess.co.uk

🧳 The Land's End Hotel, Land's End, Sennen, TR19 7AA. ☎ 01736 871844 www.landsendhotel.co.uk

⛺ Sennen Cove Camping and Caravanning Club site, Higher Tregiffian Farm, Sennen, TR19 6JB. ☎ 01736 871588 www.campingandcaravanningclub.co.uk

Cove is one of the must-surf beaches in a county famed for glorious waves. Sennen Surfing Centre (☎ 01736 871227 www.sennensurfingcentre.co.uk ● TR19 7BT) offers a range of lessons for surfers at all levels. Whether you're after a private family tutorial or a small group with other beginners, the two-hour coaching sessions are fun and aim to get everybody taking part standing up on the board. There's also a range of merchandise sporting the surf school logo at the nearby shop. After enjoying a lesson and riding the waves for the first time, getting a hoodie to prove you did it is a proud moment!

△ A ruined church greets walkers as they make their way up to Cape Cornwall.

Getting here

Although Land's End just to the south is England's official western tip, it was once thought Cape Cornwall held this claim to fame. Head for St Just at the end of the A3071 and then go down Cape Cornwall Road until the land runs out!

Fish and chips and beer

Fresh fish and other local produce is served at the Kings Arms in St Just, a quaint pub with a traditional feel (☎ 01736 788545 www.staustellbrewery.co.uk/pub/st-just/kings-arms ● TR19 7HF).

Further along the coast

Head south to Sennen Cove, one of the most famous long, sandy stretches of beach in Cornwall – and you can pick up great fish and chips at 190 Degrees West (☎ 01736 872723 www.190degreeswest.co.uk ● TR19 7AX).

Stretch your legs

Cape Cornwall is blessed with world-class coastal footpaths heading both north and south. Choose either route and you're sure to enjoy a memorable stroll. If you head towards Geevor in the north you'll be heading through a World Heritage Site where abandoned tin mines dot the horizon and every view evokes memories of *Poldark*. Heading the other way takes you over the hills to Sennen and then to Land's End, with the coastal path passing the 2003 wreck of the German cargo ship RMS *Mülheim*.

Hidden treasure

Walk to the far side of the headland and you'll come across a Coastwatch station, perched on the cliffs with windows offering far-reaching views out to sea. Formerly part of the Coastguard network, this white building is now manned by volunteers who log the shipping traffic through satellite tracking and their own observations. Visitors are welcome to pop in for a chat and take a look through powerful binoculars to see some of the vessels sailing by.

65

ST IVES
A HAVEN FOR FOODIES AND ARTISTS

Why visit?

★ Pick out some artwork or treat yourself to a cake on the narrow streets filled with galleries and eateries

★ Channel your inner Surfer Dude and take an hour's beginner lesson with world-class instructors on the beach

★ Learn about the area's tin-mining past in several attractions based in the UNESCO World Heritage Site

Coastal art

With a long tradition of attracting artists and inspiring works of art, St Ives is a hotbed of galleries and exhibitions. Wandering along the narrow streets, it's impossible not to come across shops selling local art in a wide range of styles. From pottery to jewellery, paintings to sketches, there is something to appeal to all art lovers and suit most wallets. Since the early 1990s, St Ives has also been home to an outpost of the iconic Tate (☎ 01736 796226 www.tate.org.uk/visit/tate-st-ives ♥ TR26 1TG), which sits on the site of a former gas works and now attracts over 200,000 visitors a year. The recently expanded Tate St Ives exhibits work produced by artists with a link to the Cornish town. The Barbara Hepworth Museum and Sculpture Garden (☎ 01736 796226 www.tate.org.uk ♥ TR26 1AD) is also worth a visit. Managed by the Tate, the museum preserves the work of the local sculptor in the home she lived in.

Award-winning food

For a town of its size, St Ives boasts an enviably huge number of renowned eateries. Whether you're yearning for traditional fish and chips from the latest local catch, gourmet burgers, romantic dining or a delicious ice cream, there are mouthwatering treats everywhere you look. Start your day by tackling a Cornish breakfast at The Digey Food Room (☎ 01736 799600 www.digeyfoodroom.co.uk ♥ TR26 1HR) in what was once the UK's first surf shop. A traditional inn steeped in tradition is the Sloop on The Wharf, popular with artists, fishermen and tourists alike (☎ 01736 796584 www.sloop-inn.co.uk ♥ TR26 1LP).

△ The artistic and craft capital of south-west England.

Raiders from above!

Of all the locations to enjoy fish and chips by the seaside, St Ives is the place to keep a firm hold of your prize portion. Dive-bombing, fearless seagulls will think nothing of swooping in on your grub and they'll be off with it before you know anything about it. Chips, whole fish and precious pasties are all fair game as far as the seabirds are concerned. So, heed the warnings around town, consider where you will eat and keep your food covered up. Don't even think about feeding them.

Getting here

Follow the A30 south-west into Cornwall to reach St Ives Bay. The town's train station is conveniently located within walking distance of the harbour.

World-class heritage

Travelling along the rich coastal landscape to the west of St Ives takes you back in time to the days when tin and copper mining were the mainstay of the local economy. Remains of the mines can be seen dotted along the coast in often dramatic and picturesque locations. No wonder that this area was designated a World Heritage Site in 2006. There are many places to stop and enjoy the landscape, and at Geevor Mine you can explore the history of Cornish mining (℡ 01736 788662 www.geevor.com ♀ TR19 7EW). During the 19th century, Cornish miners were renowned as being among the most skilled in the world. With job insecurity rife in the local mines, Cornish men were happy to be recruited around the world. Areas of Mexico enjoy Cornish pasties to this day as a result of their influence.

Ride the waves

Whether you're a beginner or a pro, Porthmeor Beach is the place to be if you want to hone those surfing skills. Beach boys and girls wanting to ride the waves for the first time will find expert tuition at St Ives Surf School (℡ 01736 793938 www.stivessurfschool.co.uk ♀ TR26 1JZ), located right on the front and always a hive of activity. Lessons run throughout the week and even those lacking the hearty confidence of a die-hard surfer tend to be standing on the board before long. Tutors at this St Ives institution are of the highest calibre; every season there are world-class, award-winning surfers on their roll.

△ Surf's up at the school on St Ives' beach.

Stay a while

🛏 Green Apple Bed and Breakfast, St Ives Road, St Ives, TR26 2SX. ℡ 01736 600020 www.greenapplecornwall.co.uk

🏨 Carbis Bay Hotel, Carbis Bay, St Ives, TR26 2NP. ℡ 01736 795311 www.carbisbayhotel.co.uk

⛺ Hellesveor Holidays, Hellesveor Farm, St Ives, TR26 3AD. ℡ 01736 795738 www.hellesveorholidays.co.uk

NEWQUAY
DAYS OF SURF AND PARTIES

66

Why visit?

★ Rock up in the summer to see Newquay putting on the great Boardmasters Festival

★ Party the night away at Cornwall's coastal club capital

★ Take advantage of indoor attractions if your trip is blighted by wet weather

Summer of dreams?

Newquay's coastline has all the beauty, sandy fun and surfing opportunity that you'd expect in Cornwall. But the town also has something missing from many destinations in the south-west – the buzz of a party. Consequently, Newquay divides opinion. Many would say this popular place is in the top ten when it comes to UK holiday hotspots. Others would vote with their feet and stay away. But whatever your view, there's much about Newquay's unique reputation that is worth exploring.

Getting here

Follow the A30 into Cornwall and leave for Newquay along the A392. Newquay's train station is conveniently located near Great Western Beach.

△ Fistral Beach is one of the most popular surfing spots in Cornwall.

Bands and boards

Newquay's premier summer event was established back in 1981 – way before festivals became an essential date on the calendars of the cool. Since then, Boardmasters (www.boardmasters.com) has grown in size and reputation to become one of the most popular and hotly anticipated festivals of the summer. It's now attended by 150,000 people over five days, splitting the action between two venues. On Fistral Beach, international surfing competitions take place with the world's most polished stars showing off their rad moves. In Watergate Bay, some of the hottest names in rock and pop are on the billboard, performing against a backdrop of crashing waves. Book early to get the cheapest tickets.

△ Equipment is ready to be hired out for water-based adventures on sunny days.

201

Club capital

Among young folk celebrating their exams, students enjoying long summers and those after a good time, Newquay has become the UK's answer to Ibiza. The range of pubs and clubs is enough to sustain even the hardiest party animal and it's not uncommon for the streets to be packed on balmy summer nights with merry groups in fancy dress and friends on a hen party. Expect to see women in princess dresses, men dressed as superheroes and people consuming a lot of alcohol late into the night, before getting up and doing it all again the day after. Security guards and police are out in force on busy nights, checking ID and maintaining order. The streets in the morning can show the fallout from the night before.

▽ Sunset on Fistral Beach, where surfers of all abilities boost their skills.

Fistral Beach – surfers' paradise

When it comes to the hottest places to surf in Britain, Fistral Beach is always going to be right up with the best of them. The name means 'cove of the foul water' in Cornish, which gives a clue as to how wild the waves can get on this stretch of the Atlantic Coast. At around 750 metres (820 yards) long, this straight and sandy beach faces west out to the ocean; the next land you'd reach heading out from here would be in North America. And that's a key clue as to why this is the home for such great surfing, with the wind being able to whip up the waves over an unbroken sea. Not surprising, then, that major international competitions are held here and it's the home to the British Surfing Association's HQ. If you want to try your hand at riding the waves, there are several surf schools set up along the beach that run regular lessons, including the Newquay Surf School (☎ 07772 251778 www.surfingschool.co.uk ♥ TR8 4AA).

△ Lifeboats and lifeguards patrol Newquay's beaches to make sure everybody stays safe.

Seafood speciality

Fans of seafood are in for a treat all year round in Newquay, which is a great place to tuck in to fish and chips or try local crab in cosy pubs near the harbour. For those really wanting to get stuck into the local delicacies, make sure you time your visit to coincide with the annual Newquay Fish Festival (www.newquayfishfestival.co.uk). Taking place every September, it pulls in well-known chefs who make the most of the sea's produce and highlights the marine treats that are offered at the many eateries in the town.

Wet weather plan

Many of the activities people would like to do in Cornwall involve being outside, usually on the beach. But the weather doesn't always allow our holiday dreams to come true. When it comes down to having rainy day cards up your sleeve, there are few places that can beat Newquay. If you have a couple of hours to spare, head to the Cornwall Aviation Heritage Centre (☏ 01637 861962 www.cornwallaviationhc.co.uk ♀ TR8 4GP) for some exciting exhibits and the chance to sit in the cockpits of famous planes. For a swashbuckling adventure with your kids, set sail to Pirate's Quest (☏ 01637 873379 www.piratesquest.co.uk ♀ TR7 1RA) and come face to face with smugglers and mermaids!

Stay a while

🛏 Tregarthen Guest House, 1 Arundel Way, Newquay, TR7 3BB. ☏ 01637 873554 www.tregarthen.co.uk

🏨 The Headland Hotel and Spa, Fistral Beach, Headland Road, Newquay, TR7 1EW. ☏ 01637 872211 www.headlandhotel.co.uk

⛺ Hendra Holiday Park, Hendra Terrace, Newquay, TR8 4NY. ☏ 01637 875778 www.hendra-holidays.com

67

PADSTOW
CORNWALL'S FOODIE HEAVEN

Why visit?

★ Hire bikes and cycle into Padstow along disused railway lines on the Camel Trail

★ Bring your appetite with you and enjoy the town's excellent culinary reputation

★ Spot some of the backdrops used in the much-loved *Poldark* TV series

△ Padstow harbour, surrounded by some of the best foodie options in Cornwall.

Michelin-star attraction

You'll be hard pressed to find another town along the entire coast of the UK that has a foodie reputation to match Padstow's. When TV chef Rick Stein moved to the seaside destination in the early 1970s, he started a long and influential link with Padstow. Stein now has a restaurant, bistro, café and chip shop in Padstow, all sporting his name and prompting some to nickname the town Padstein. Other top chefs have moved in to bolster the reputation for excellent cuisine, providing a wonderful opportunity for culinary tourists to indulge in seafood specialities. The pinnacle of the town's foodie calendar comes in December when the annual Padstow Christmas

 ### Fish and chips

With a strong reputation for good seafood, there's a wealth of opportunity to grab fish and chips in and around Padstow – whether you prefer eating them inside or out. Many people will be attracted to Rick Stein's Fish and Chips, which is one of many eateries the TV chef owns in Padstow (☎ 01841 532700 www.rickstein.com/eat-with-us/steins-fish-chips ♦ PL28 8BL). Other options include Padstow's Chip Ahoy on Old School Lane (☎ 01841 534753 ♦ PL28 8BS). Further along the coast, check out the hearty portions at The Blue Fish Bar in Mawgan Porth (☎ 01637 860554 www.bluefishbar.co.uk ♦ TR8 4RA).

Festival takes place. Rick Stein and fellow chefs Paul Ainsworth and Nathan Outlaw are joined by over 60 other well-known cooks in a four-day celebration of food that features taster sessions and live demonstrations. It's a well-established Christmas gathering; expect to see the great and the good from the British food industry, with plenty of Michelin Star winners on hand to pass on tips. December may be chilly, but in Padstow there's plenty going on to spice up the winter nights (www.padstowchristmasfestival.co.uk).

The Camel Trail – on your bike!

A far nicer alternative to driving a car into Padstow is pedalling into town on a bicycle. The Camel Trail is a scenic route that beats the traffic, much of it hugging the tidal River Camel before arriving right in the middle of town. It's a very popular trail and is largely on the level because it follows the route of old railway lines, a feature that helps it attract over 400,000 users each year. The trail runs from Wenfordbridge, passing Bodmin and Wadebridge along its 29km (18-mile) route. Camel Trail Cycle Hire offer rentals for full or part days (01208 814104 www.cameltrailcyclehire.co.uk PL27 7AL).

Getting here

Just west of Wadebridge, the A389 leaves the A39 and winds into Padstow on Cornwall's north coast. Head for Wadebridge, Bodmin or Wenford Bridge to pick up the Camel Trail.

Stay a while

- Treverbyn House, Station Road, Padstow, PL28 8DA. 01841 532855 www.treverbynhouse.com

- Coswarth House, 12 Dennis Road, Padstow, PL28 8DD. 07907 626084 www.coswarthhouse.com

- Dennis Cove Campsite, Dennis Lane, Padstow, PL28 8DR. 01841 532349 www.denniscovecampsite.co.uk

The 'Obby 'Oss Festival

One of the country's most popular folk traditions takes place in Padstow every May Day. Kicking off with singing at a local pub on the night before May, the following day sees the area around the maypole lavishly decorated and two processions featuring hobby horses. Taking the role of the 'Obby 'Osses, male dancers prance around the town depicting a decades-old tale.

Poldark link

Fans of the hit TV series will recognise Tregirls beach, Levlizzick and the Camel Estuary, all of which have been used as a backdrop to some of *Poldark*'s coastal scenes.

Take a hike

Padstow is on the route of the South West Coast Path, which allows time to enjoy the area as it winds along both sides of the River Camel. The Saints' Way sets off from here on Cornwall's north coast, crossing the county before finishing at Fowey in the south. If you don't fancy such a big excursion, pick up the path from the town centre to the war memorial at the top of the hill for an epic view of Padstow and the beach beyond.

68

TINTAGEL
A PLACE OF LEGENDS

Why visit?

★ Discover the legend of King Arthur in the English Heritage visitor centre and explore the ruined castle

★ Travel over a newly built bridge linking the castle to the mainland for the first time since the 15th century

★ Walk down on to the beach and explore Merlin's Cave where the sorcerer is said to have lived

△ Step back in time and learn of legends by taking a stroll up to Tintagel Knight.

🛎 Stay a while

🛏 Bosayne, Atlantic Road, Tintagel, PL34 0DE. ☎ 01840 770514 www.bosayne.co.uk

🏨 Atlantic View Hotel, Treknow, Tintagel, PL34 0EJ. ☎ 01840 770221 www.atlanticviewhoteltintagel.co.uk

⛺ The Headland Caravan and Camping Park, Atlantic Road, Tintagel PL34 0DE. ☎ 01840 770239 www.headlandcaravanpark.co.uk

Excalibur, knights and the Round Table...

Wrapped up in the legend of King Arthur, Tintagel has a smattering of souvenir shops in the centre of the village. But the principal reasons to visit are found away from the centre, down a steep path towards the sea. Tintagel Castle is one of English Heritage's highest profile properties (☎ 0370 333 1181 www.english-heritage.org.uk/visit/places/tintagel-castle 📍 PL34 0HE). You can see just how popular it is in the summer months by the number of children wielding wooden swords and wearing imitation chain mail bought in the well-stocked shop.

At the bottom of the path, English Heritage's display covers everything you need to know about the castle's history and the legends surrounding it. A wide selection of books about King Arthur is also available. A steep pathway winds up to the ruined castle, which stands in a phenomenal clifftop location. In 2019, an ambitious project saw a bridge connect the castle's island with the mainland, just as the two would have been linked before a land bridge collapsed around the 15th century. This cuts out the need to climb 148 steps between the two halves of the site, though a steep hike back up to the village is needed when your visit is complete. If this is too much, a 4x4 vehicle is on hand to give you a lift for a small fee. Immerse yourself in tales of kings, magic and dragons at this superb historical site.

First Class House

With a famously wavy roof and a history dating back 600 years, the former farm building that eventually became the Post Office for the village is now looked after by the National Trust (☎ 01840 770024 www.nationaltrust.org.uk/tintagel-old-post-office ● PL34 0DB). There are six rooms to discover inside, and a cottage garden at the rear that provides the perfect antidote to busy streets full of pasty-seeking tourists.

A cave full of magic

Steps lead down to the small beach at Tintagel, and while the sandy expanse is nice enough, it's the cave that is the main attraction here. The huge entrance to Merlin's Cave lures you in for an explore during low tide, but fills with water at high tide so it's important to time your visit carefully. Once inside, allow time for your eyes to adjust as it's only then that you can fully appreciate the scale of this magnificent feature, said to be where the ancient magician lived. This natural cave, formed by erosion as the sea's waves battered the rock over centuries, is over 100 metres (330 feet) long and has a smaller exit at the other side of the island Tintagel Castle sits upon. On busy summer days, the passageway of the cave will be busy with people from all over the world, negotiating the slippery rocks and crystal-clear pools while wondering in the back of their mind whether Merlin actually existed, what kind of character he might have been and what sort of enchantment may have taken place in this most awesome of sea caves.

Trebarwith

Just 3km (2 miles) along the Cornish coast from Tintagel, you'll find a lovely beach at the end of a long country lane. Trebarwith Strand is one you'll need to check the tide times for because

△ A new bridge links the castle island with the mainland once more.

△ Boscastle's Museum of Witchcraft and Magic.

The Boscastle flood

The town is remembered by many for the devastating flood in the summer of 2004, which tore away buildings, destroyed a bridge, swept dozens of cars into the harbour and saw 91 people rescued. Exceptionally high rainfall landing on already saturated ground caused three local rivers to overflow, with a high tide adding to the problem. Several RAF helicopters were used in the operation to get people to safety urgently. Although damage to property and possessions was extensive, there were thankfully no fatalities. A plaque in the town centre recalls the event.

Getting here

Tintagel and Boscastle are both found on the B3263 in north Cornwall, which links with the A39.

the sand is entirely covered up when the tide is high. Thankfully, finding out tidal times in the Google Age has never been easier and you'll be able to maximise your sandcastle-building time. Trebarwith is a great place to sit and watch sunsets in the evening as the beach points directly to the west, and there's a café to keep you fed and watered in the holiday season.

Witchcraft and magic

Shrouded in tales of enchantment for centuries, it's perhaps unsurprising to find a museum dedicated to magic on this stretch of the north Cornwall coast. You'll find a fascinating range of items and regularly changing exhibitions at Boscastle's Museum of Witchcraft and Magic, which is near the harbour and has welcomed visitors since 1960 (☎ 01840 250111 www.museumofwitchcraftandmagic.co.uk ◉ PL35 0HD). Laid out over two floors, the museum contains 25 permanent displays and features over 3,000 objects – making it the world's oldest and largest witchcraft collection. Events and talks are also organised between April and October.

△ Pop into the local bakery for a pasty.

69

BEAUTIFUL
BUDE!

Why visit?

⭐ Make a day of it and hire a colourful beach hut as a base for your time at the beach

⭐ Enjoy a fabulous selection of beaches along this Cornish coast to suit all tastes

⭐ Bathe in Bude's outdoor sea pool, an ever-popular lido built in 1930

△ Hire one of Bude's lovely beach huts to make the most of your day.

Hit the hut

There are few activities more quintessentially English than hiring a colourful beach hut at the seaside and setting up for a day on the coast. The huts available on the north Cornwall coast vary in size and can be hired out by the day, offering protection from the weather, a place to leave your stuff and fast access to the beach. Although there's no electricity or water supply in the huts at Bude, coin-operated showers are available nearby.

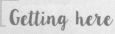 Getting here

After crossing over the Cornish border from Devon, look out for the turn-off to Bude from the A39.

Life's beachy

Families head to Bude to get away from it all and enjoy the silky-soft sand on the Cornish coast. They have plenty of beached-based options to choose from along this tasty stretch of seaside, ideal for bucket-and-spade fun-seekers. Summerleaze Beach is the best-loved and most popular in Bude, home to a small harbour, wonderful surfing conditions and the ever-popular outdoor sea pool. Sandymouth Bay is a National Trust beach a short drive to the north, where a generous expanse of sand is exposed at low tide and there's always room to play as it's quieter than those in the town. At Northcott Mouth, the rocky environment gives way to wonderful sandy areas when the sea goes out. Watch out for the spectacular geological folds in the cliffs and the remains of a shipwreck in the

△ Even when the tide is out, you can take a dip in Bude Sea Pool.

Stay a while

🛏 The Bude Haven Guest House, 7 Flexbury Avenue, Bude, EX23 8NS. ☎ 01288 352305 www.thebudehaven.com

🧳 Elements Hotel, Marine Drive, Bude, EX23 0LZ. ☎ 01288 352386 www.elements-life.co.uk

⛺ Cerenety Eco Campsite, Lynstone Lane, Bude, EX23 0LR. ☎ 07380 940849 www.cerenetycampsite.co.uk

sand. If surf is not your thing, don't go to Millook Haven Beach, but this one's for you if you like quieter retreats with a pebble-strewn shore that's popular for spotting seals and dolphins. If wild beauty is more your style, head to Blackrock Beach but check the tide times before you set off – this one gets cut off at high tide.

 ## Fish and chips

If you're staying in the Bude area for a week, just how many times is it acceptable to have fish and chips? Whatever the answer for your nearest and dearest, you'll find a big enough selection of eateries to suit your appetite. Among the best are The Barge, which is on the water, as its names suggests, at The Lower Wharf, Bude Canal (☎ 01288 356786 www.thebargebude.co.uk ♥ EX23 8LG). Also check out The Mermaid on Princes Street (☎ 01288 355056 ♥ EX23 8AT) and, out of town, Gillets Chippy in The Square at Kilkhampton (☎ 01288 321674 ♥ EX23 9QQ).

The tunnel of love

What started out as a tongue-in-cheek joke on the Internet has cooked up a stir by becoming the hottest tourist attraction in Bude – according to TripAdvisor reviews, at least. The Bude Tunnel is a simple covered walkway next to a Sainsbury's on Crooklets Road but has become the star of the town thanks to a Facebook campaign and hundreds of ironic reviews. At Christmas it gets decked out in lights and there's often tourists posing inside to have their photograph taken. It might just look like a shelter leading nowhere, but this is one of the oddest tourist attractions on the UK coast.

70

CLOVELLY
WHERE DELIVERIES ARRIVE BY SLEDGE

Why visit?

★ Meander along cobbled streets of a unique village untouched by the changes of time

★ Order a delicious cream tea – and then decide whether to put jam or cream on top

★ Get up close with one of the largest sculptures in the UK

The magical world of Clovelly

For some it's the cobbled streets, for others it's the higgledy-piggledy buildings, the donkeys or the quiet harbour. The historic village of Clovelly has many charming features that wow visitors negotiating the steep, uneven roads winding down to the shore. The entire village is privately owned and there's an access charge to pay on entry (☎ 01237 431781 www.clovelly. co.uk ♥ EX39 5TA) before you wander by the homes and shops, all the way down to the Red Lion Hotel at the bottom of the hill. Photo opportunities abound at every twist and turn. Your journey down the famous slope needs to be a slow and steady one to take in the dozens of listed buildings you pass, and also to get a

feeling for what life must be like for the people who live in this tourist attraction. Deliveries of wood and coal are left outside front doors, but there is no access for delivery vehicles into the cobbled maze of village streets. Instead, sledges full of goods are pulled up and down the stony passages to ensure residents are stocked up. You'll see the sledges outside some homes, and possibly hear them in action on their rounds. For quaint views, a feeling like you've gone back in time and a diverse range of craft shops, Clovelly is hard to beat. The village owes a great debt to the generations of donkeys who laboured up and down the steep slopes, carrying building materials, coal and post before taking the rubbish back out. When tourism began to

△ The famous donkeys of Clovelly have carried many goods up and down the hill.

increase in importance at Clovelly, the donkeys changed their role slightly and were used to pull luggage to and from hotels. Today the donkeys have an easier life, being looked after in the stables, giving children rides into the woods and posing for photos in the street.

 Fish and chips

If you're in the area and feel peckish, some of the best portions of fish and chips are served up at Mr Chips on The Quay at Bideford (☎ 01237 472709 ♦ EX39 2HW). Sylvesters on Meeting Street in Appledore is also a favourite place for locals to tuck in (☎ 01237 423548 ♦ EX39 1RJ).

Westwood Ho!

This seaside town has plenty more going for it than being the only place in the country to feature an exclamation mark. The stretch of sand along this glorious section of north Devon's coast is a magnet for families wanting to play and relax within an easy walk of all the facilities you could need. Move a little further along the Blue Flag beach, away from the bright lights of Westward Ho! towards the River Taw estuary, and you'll find yourself in a playground for adrenaline-hungry extreme-sport lovers. The increasingly popular Sandymere Beach is a haven for kite surfers. You'll be able to sit and watch them twist, turn and fly into the air in the strong winds regularly bombarding this coastline. Also a great spot for surfers and wind surfers, you can learn the ropes in lessons designed for all abilities. There are also courses for land-based kite sports and a kite-flying 'Power Hour' delivered by 514Elemental (☎ 07565 621446 www.514elemental.com).

△ Steep cobbled steeps and a heap of nostalgia are to be found in Clovelly.

Stay a while

🛏 Lew Barn, Bradworthy, Holsworthy, EX22 7SQ. ☎ 01409 241964
www.lewbarn.co.uk

🧳 The Red Lion Hotel, The Quay, Clovelly, EX39 5TF. ☎ 01237 431237
www.clovelly.co.uk

⛺ Adventure Camping, Abbotsham Road, Bideford, EX39 5AP. ☎ 01237 880028
www.adventure-camping.co.uk

Cream tea heaven!

Setting time aside for a cream tea is an essential part of the afternoon in the south-west. Fierce debate rages between those in Devon and Cornwall over the correct way to apply jam and cream on to the scone. The traditional Devonian method would see cream spread on both halves of the scone, topped off with jam. But in Cornwall, the jam goes on first and the cream tops off the tasty treat, traditionally served with a pot of tea. If you have divided loyalties or aren't sure which method would be best, feel free to try a different approach on each half of your scone. The best cream teas come with a warm scone fresh from the oven; you then cut it open yourself before adding the butter, jam and cream. Westward Ho! is home to one of the best places in the country to get a cream tea. Tea on the Green on Golf Links Road (☎ 01237 429406 www.teaonthegreen.net ⦿ EX39 1LH) has a superb reputation and, with vintage decor and a movie-themed menu, is a fun place to watch the world go by while enjoying a giant scone – or two!

Getting here

Clovelly and Westward Ho! are both located on the northern coast of Devon, well signposted from the main A39 road.

A journey to see *Verity*

Moving up the coast from Westward Ho! provides the chance to see a superb piece of art that stands proudly on the north Devon coast. Towering above Ilfracombe harbour, the 20-metre (66-foot) statue, called *Verity*, has divided opinion. Love it or hate it, the Damien Hirst creation has been pulling in the tourists since it was unveiled in 2012. Many people have made the journey to Ilfracombe solely to see the sword-wielding pregnant woman, holding the scales of justice and law books. *Verity* used to be the tallest statue in the country, pipping the Angel of the North by 25cm (10 inches). Now it stands just below the Kelpies in the pecking order, though it continues to be an important economic boost to the town. Looking up at *Verity* from different angles reveals contrasting interpretations. From one side you can see the outer body of the pregnant woman, while the opposite side shows her internal anatomy and the foetus. It's a wonderful addition to the harbour, where it is due to stand for 20 years.

△ **Windy conditions at Westward Ho! are ideal for lovers of extreme sports.**

71

THE TARKA TRAIL
A JOURNEY ALONG THE RIVER TAW

Why visit?

★ The walking and cycling route by the River Taw around Barnstaple is perfect for exploring the little villages along the coast

★ Read the famous tale of *Tarka the Otter* in the environment it was set in

★ Cycle to Instow and rest for a well-deserved drink while watching the boats on the estuary

On the trail of the otter

At 290km (180 miles) long, the Tarka Trail (www.tarkatrail.org.uk) is a fabulous recreational resource in north Devon. It takes walkers and cyclists on a figure-of-eight route that hugs the coast and then works its way down to Dartmoor. While some hardy folk will attempt to complete the whole route, most will dip into smaller sections and enjoy a sample of life along the rivers Torridge and Taw. The first part of the Tarka Trail was opened up in 1987, with other sections of the lengthy route being added on in the 1990s. Much of the route follows old railway lines that were bought from British Rail when the lines were scrapped. Cycling along the former Ilfracombe Branch Line, Bideford Extension Railway and the North Devon Railway is largely on the level, so you don't have to be of a Tour de France standard to enjoy the day out. Hire your ride from Tarka Bikes at Barnstaple train station (☎ 01271 324202 www.tarkabikes.co.uk ♥ EX31 2AU).

Getting here

Barnstaple is on the A39, which runs through north Devon. The train station is on the western side of the River Taw, on Station Road.

Fish and chips

Barnstaple is a good place to find your coastal fish and chips fix. Good options include The Pelican on Oakland Park (☎ 01271 345605 www.pelicanfishandchips.co.uk ♥ EX31 2BZ) or Woodys between the theatre and cinema on Boutport Street (☎ 01271 321242 ♥ EX31 1SX).

△ The Tarka Trail sticks to the edge of tidal rivers in north Devon.

△ Popular with walkers and cyclists, the Tarka Trail is a very accessible route.

Tarka the Otter

Henry Williamson's much-loved novel about the life and death of an otter in north Devon was first published in 1927 and has never been out of print. The award-winning book is packed with detailed descriptions of the local landscape around the Rivers Taw and Torridge – the 'Two Rivers' country where the otter spends his life. The ups and downs of Tarka the Otter's life was made into a 1979 film, narrated by Peter Ustinov and considered one of the best family flicks of all time.

Instow

The confluence of the two rivers featuring in *Tarka the Otter* is a great place to take some time and watch the world go by. Several bars and restaurants at Instow have views looking out on the water, where boats pass back and forth along the estuary. The Waterside Gallery on Marine Parade is another favourite place to pass the time as you check out the work of many different local artists.

Barnstaple

An exploration of the Tarka Trail is best tackled from outside the biggest town in north Devon. It's better to park up in Braunton or Instow and then investigate the trail as it passes through Barnstaple on its way along the tidal River Taw. The town, home to over 24,000 people, is a good place to pick up supplies you might need or ingredients for a picnic. The trail passes very close to a large supermarket and several other High Street chains.

🛎 Stay a while

🛏 The Spinney Country Guest House, Shirwell, Barnstaple, EX31 4JR. ☎ 01271 850282 www.thespinneyshirwell.co.uk

🏨 The Imperial Hotel, Taw Vale Parade, Barnstaple, EX32 8NB. ☎ 01271 345861 www.brend-imperial.co.uk

⛺ Whitemoor Farm Campsite, Bishops Tawton, EX32 0HY. ☎ 07860 180022 www.whitemoorcamping.co.uk

72

WESTON-SUPER-MARE

SAND OF HOPE AND GLORY

Why visit?

★ See world-famous sculptors working the sand into amazing works of art

★ Enjoy a day of traditional seaside fun, with rides and amusements on the grand pier

★ Time your visit to coincide with one of the many festivals the town delivers so well

Go Weston!

The long sandy beach at Weston-super-Mare on the north Somerset coast is a popular place to enjoy a stroll or relax on sunny days. Sand is also at the heart of one of the most innovative sculpture exhibitions you'll see on our shores. Over time, the prospects of Weston-super-Mare have matched those of many other UK seaside resorts. The coming of the railways opened up the town to Victorian tourists and led to a period of growth that lasted until the second half of the 20th century, when foreign travel put an end to the dominance of domestic tourism. Regeneration is underway, with new attractions and fruitful ideas giving Weston-super-Mare a fresh appeal.

The Grand Pier

An iconic landmark on the Somerset coast, the Grand Pier at Weston-super-Mare is ever popular with tourists and locals alike (☎ 01934 620238 www.grandpier.co.uk ♦ BS23 1AL). Opened in 1904, it was originally planned to be a docking point for boats coming across the Severn Estuary from Cardiff, but the route proved too dangerous. Like many piers around our coast, the wooden structure has been ravaged by devastating fires. It's needed a total rebuild on two occasions, firstly in 1930 and then following a blaze in 2008. The dense crowds that flocked here to see the newly rebuilt pier open in 2010 reflect just what it means for a coastal town to have a pier jutting out into the sea. True to its roots, the new pier is wooden and features plenty of family fun, including dodgems and a helter-skelter.

△ The newly rebuilt pier is a focal point for the town's tourism.

GRAND PIER IN NUMBERS

💡 A length of 366m (1,200 feet)

💡 65m wide (213-foot) pavilion

💡 13m wide (43-foot) walkway

💡 Supported by 600 iron piles

💡 100,000 people attended the reopening weekend in 2010

💡 The pier's second rebuild cost £39m

△ Weston-Super-Mare is famous for the stunning sand sculptures.

 Getting here

Leave the M5 at junction 21, taking the A370 towards the coast. Weston-super-Mare has a train station in the middle of the town.

Sculptures in the Sand

No doubt you've tried building a sand castle at some point in your life. You may even be one of those ambitious folk on the beach who attempts to build cars, boats and mermaids out of the sand for your kids to play with. Whatever your shoreline crafting abilities, you're sure to be left in awe and enthused to do better after a visit to the Sand Sculpture Festival at Weston-super-Mare (📞 01934 644176 www.westonsandsculpture.co.uk 📍 BS23 1BE). What started with just one sand sculpture a year has grown into an internationally renowned festival featuring a wide range of hugely impressive artworks. Sculptors specialising in the medium of sand come from all over the world to take part in the festival at what is now known as the sand sculpting capital of the UK. The pieces of sand art really are something to behold, with incredible detail of faces and animals. Each one is regularly dampened to stop them drying out. More than half a million people arrive in Weston-super-Mare every year to visit the festival and photograph some of the most ambitious and short-lasting artworks in the world.

 Fish and chips

Weston-super-Mare is well known for some fabulous fish and chip joints. Among the best are Papa's on Waterloo Street (📞 01934 626565 www.papasukltd.com 📍 BS23 1LN) and the Atlantic Fish Bar on Meadow Street (📞 01934 629667 www.atlanticfishbar.com 📍 BS23 1QL).

A town of many festivals

Aside from the summer-long sand sculpture festival, Weston-super-Mare prides itself on putting on a good show. One of the most popular is the midsummer Air Festival (www.westonairfestival.com), which sees a range of spectacular fly-pasts along the seafront. Earlier in the year, the seaside Literary Festival gives book lovers the chance to meet famous authors and buy books that will keep the winter weather at bay. Foodies will love the Eat Weston Festival (www.eatfestivals.org), a free-to-enter event showcasing the best of the region's food and drink. And all-round family fun is on offer at the end of season carnival in November, when an illuminated parade takes to the streets.

🔔 **Stay a while**

🛏 Albany Lodge, 9 Clevedon Road, Weston-super-Mare, BS23 1DA. 📞 01934 629936

🏨 Beachlands Hotel, 17 Uphill Road North, Weston-super-Mare, BS23 4NG. 📞 01934 621401 www.beachlandshotel.com

⛺ West End Farm Caravan and Camping Park, Locking, Weston-super-Mare, BS24 8RH. 📞 01934 822529 www.westendcaravan.com

WALES

With stunning beaches, incredible natural features and some of the coolest cities in Britain, a trip around coastal Wales is one to cherish. Cardiff, the capital city, has benefited from fantastic urban renewal of its waterfront and has become an exceptional cultural highlight. If you leave the bright lights behind you, though, it's not long before you're into some of the stunning coastal landscapes Wales is famous for.

The Gower Peninsula, close to Swansea, is a haven for walkers, wildlife spotters and those who like to learn more about historic shipwrecks. Further along the south coast of Wales there are isolated gems waiting to be discovered. Tucked away close to a missile firing range, you'll find the stunningly picturesque St Govan's Chapel in a seemingly impossible location. Charming craft shops and a stunning cathedral provide attractions that bely the size of tiny St Davids, which is also blessed with magnificent beaches within a short drive north and south. Heading up the west cost of Wales, there's a city leading a beautiful double life. Student life in the university town of Aberystwyth dominates in the close season, but gives way to family jollies during the summer months. This is the main resort on the central Wales coast and boasts some great facilities and walking routes. The colourful, architecturally splendid Portmeirion is a delight to wander around and you can stay the night in one of the stunning, unique buildings. Nearby, a heritage railway steams into the Snowdonian mountains and the beaches of the Llŷn Peninsula offer remote, sandy solitude. Families have a such a wide range of destinations to choose from in Wales. On the north coast, the vibrant centre of Llandudno is one of the best. It has a great promenade and the usual collection of amusements on the pier. The jewel in the crown here is the Great Orme, a hill that rises up from the coastline and houses an ancient mine reached by a steep tramway.

Don't miss

✓ Enjoying the revitalised waterfront in Cardiff

✓ Discovering shipwrecks and taking stunning walks on the Gower Peninsula

✓ Climbing down the cliff to view the stunning St Govan's Chapel

✓ Making a pilgrimage to the city of St Davids

✓ Stunning architecture and cult TV history in Portmeirion

Some of the country's most astonishing coastal scenery is found in Wales.

73

CARDIFF
CAPITAL OF A PROUD NATION

Enter the dragon

Since becoming the capital of Wales as recently as 1955, Cardiff has survived some tough economic times to emerge as a vibrant and exciting cosmopolitan centre. From TV tours and musicals to exhibitions highlighting the rich Welsh history, Cardiff is one of the most engaging places on the country's coast.

Getting here

The M4 motorway passes to the north of Cardiff, providing easy access for cars. Cardiff Central railway station is located in the heart of city for those arriving by train.

A capital fortress

Hidden behind the walls of Cardiff Castle, you'll find 2,000 years of Welsh history ready to be explored. From days of the site serving as a Roman fort to the building of Cardiff's famous Norman keep and beyond to when the castle was a family home gifted to the city, there is so much to explore at this key heritage attraction (☏ 029 2087 8100 www.cardiffcastle.com ♦CF10 3RB). Start with a guided tour of the house to see the opulent rooms decorated by Lord Bute before heading to the Norman keep and the smaller buildings within. Recently discovered Roman remains are also on display, while the Second World War shelters give an insight into how local folk crammed into the refuge praying for protection from German bombers. If you pose for a picture on the grass in front of the keep, you'll be in good company. Many famous people, from royalty to actors and sports stars, have been photographed here, before one of the country's most iconic buildings.

▷ Cardiff Castle keep, home to hundreds of years of Welsh history.

△ The redevelopment of Mermaid Quay has provided visitors to Wales with a delightful place to walk, shop and eat by the waterfront.

Exterminate!

Ever since *Dr Who* regenerated into the form of Christopher Eccleston and the hit sci-fi series received a reboot, Cardiff has had close personal ties with Daleks, Cybermen and Weeping Angels. Many of the programmes have been shot in and around the city. The film locations have attracted thousands of visits from fans wanting to see where the action took place. For many years, the BBC welcomed tourists to The Dr Who Experience, a major exhibition featuring original sets and props from the show. Although this is no longer open, there are several opportunities for Whovians to get in touch with their inner Time Lord. Tours of key locations are available by bus or on foot, calling at Amy Pond's village, several iconic buildings and the American diner visited by Matt Smith's Doctor. Those who have relished the spin-off *Torchwood* series should make their way to the Ianto shrine on the boardwalk of Mermaid Quay. Thousands of photographs and messages have been left here over the years for the fictional character killed off in 2009. For more information about the tours, visit www. britmovietours.com.

Mermaid Quay – part of a thriving bay

The vibrant shops and eateries at Mermaid Quay formed part of a flagship redevelopment project designed to boost the Cardiff waterfront that had suffered so much from industrial decline. Shoppers, diners and wandering tourists gaze out to a gorgeously wide expanse of water from the front of the quay. Until the late 1990s, Cardiff Bay and its docks were still tidal, exposing large mudflats twice a day at low tide. The Cardiff Bay Barrage helped to convert aesthetically unappealing, derelict docklands into an attractive waterfront in one of the biggest civil engineering projects in Europe at the time. Although opposed

△ In these stones, horizons sings – so says the iconic quote emblazoned on the Wales Millennium Centre.

by environmentalists and some locals, the project has brought economic life back into the Cardiff Bay area.

A Centre for the New Millennium

A cultural hub playing host to theatre, opera, ballet and dance, the Wales Millennium Centre (☏ 029 2063 6464 www.wmc.org.uk ⚲ CF10 5AL) became a major attraction as soon as it was opened in 2004. Adding a new dimension to the skyline of the capital city and helping to transform the Cardiff Bay area, the Millennium Centre is a striking building that is now one of the most recognisable in Wales. The exterior, containing 4,500 tonnes of steel and 2,000 tonnes of Welsh slate, features the bilingual inscription of words from the former National Poet Gwyneth Lewis: 'In these stones, horizons sing.' The building boasts Welsh craftsmanship and materials at every turn, making the centre's guided tours well worth booking on to. You'll find a wide range of artistic performances in

the centre's calendar, with bars and restaurants on hand to enhance the experience. It's a good idea to make a beeline here straight away because the city's visitor centre is found inside and the knowledgeable staff can help you make the most of your trip.

🛎 **Stay a while**

🛏 Number One Hundred, 100 Newport Road, Cardiff, CF24 1DG.
☏ 029 2010 5590
www.icardiff.co.uk/number-one-hundred

🏨 Clayton Hotel, St Mary Street, Cardiff, CF10 1GD. ☏ 029 2066 8866
www.claytonhotelcardiff.com

⛺ Cardiff Caravan and Camping Park, Pontcanna Fields, Fields Park Rd, Cardiff, CF11 9XR. ☏ 029 2039 8362
www.cardiffcaravanpark.co.uk

74

RHOSSILI
OUR FINEST GOWER

Why visit?

★ Get up close to a Victorian shipwreck that's still exposed at low tides

★ Step out on a thrilling walk to Worms Head and look for seals on the tidal island

★ Taste local products containing seaweed and splash out on other seafood specialities

Jutting out into the Bristol Channel, the Gower Peninsula is a holiday haven for outdoor enthusiasts craving miles of golden beaches, clifftop walks and some of the best surf in Wales. Packed with inspiring landscapes and fascinating wildlife, it's no surprise that this stretch of coast was chosen in 1956 as the UK's first Area of Outstanding Natural Beauty. Sitting at Gower's tip, Rhossili is a popular

Getting here

From Swansea, the A4118 takes visitors to the tip of the Gower Peninsula.

village with good tourist facilities and some fascinating history to explore.

△ The beautiful coastline of the Gower Peninsula, with Worm Head island wriggling out to sea in the distance.

Rhossili Bay – home of Victorian shipwrecks

A violent storm on an autumn morning in 1887 played havoc with a Norwegian ship loaded with timber and led to one of the most famous shipwrecks in Wales. The wooden remains of the *Helvetia* are one of the most photographed landmarks in South Wales and attract visitors of every type when they are exposed by the receding tide. Strong winds meant the *Helvetia* was unable to make its way into Swansea harbour and ended up becoming stuck on the dangerous Helwick Sands. The swelling sea carried the boat into Rhossili Bay, when the order was given for the crew to abandon ship. The wreck was discovered in the morning, surrounded by its expensive cargo. Much of the boat was sold off, but not all of it could be salvaged before it started to settle in the Gower sands. Battered and worn by every high tide, the wreck of the *Helvetia* has been worn down over the decades and it's not known how many future generations will still be able to

△ The aging wreck of the *Helvetica* is a fascinating sight at low tide.

△ Three Cliffs Bay is another wonderful place to spend time on the Gower Peninsula.

appreciate the distinctive Victorian shipwreck. A particularly dangerous stretch of coastline, the Gower Peninsula has experienced many shipwrecks over the decades. Evidence of another 19th-century incident can be found at the foot of Rhossili's cliffs. It was in February 1884 when the *Samuel*, carrying 500 tons of coal, ran ashore on rocks near Worms Head. The ship was broken up soon after the incident and then sold off. But the anchor remained in place and can still be seen on the exposed rocks at low tide, embedded into the landscape. The coal on board that tragic day was sold to local farmers at a cheap price, and in turn they sold it to folk in the nearby village. This heavily discounted source of fuel is said to have heated local homes for years after the event.

Three Cliffs Bay

Magically picturesque and named after the triplet of triangular crags punching the sky close to the sea, Three Cliffs Bay is one of the Gower's most prized treasures. It's an idyllic place to while away summer hours. There's a wide expanse of sandy beach for families to lounge on, sand dunes to explore and the dramatic ruins of Pennard Castle visible on the distant hillside. The natural rock arch within the cliffs adds to the impressive landscape and across the sea the north Devon coast lies on the horizon. Pennard Pill is the stream that flows into Three Cliffs Bay; it's a serene-looking river channel but houses dangerous currents, so bathing in it is

hosts a Cockles and Celts festival to celebrate the local food and music. Most of the rocky shorelines around the Gower Peninsula are strewn with the purple-black seaweed used to make another of Wales's breakfast staples. Much of the country's laver bread is now produced using seaweed from elsewhere, but some small local producers continue to operate in the Gower area. Laver bread breakfast cake, laver bread and cockle pâté and laver bread with mashed potato are just some of the innovative methods seaweed is incorporated into the local diet. Don't leave without sampling the region's seafood.

Worms Head

This tidal island is the high point of a great walk from Rhossili, across rock pools and up a hill rising from the sea to offer a tremendous vantage point. Many seabirds can be seen along the way, and you should look out for seals that come playfully close to the rocky coastline. The natural causeway to Worms Head is only accessible at certain times of the day, so it's important to coincide your visit with low tide. A lookout on the clifftop displays a notice advising when it's safe to cross.

△ The gnarled remains of the *Helvetica*.

not encouraged. Access to the isolated bay is by foot only and it's the best part of 1.6km (1 mile) from the National Trust car park at Southgate (♥ SA3 2DH).

Fruits of the beach

The Gower is famous for its use of seafood. Cockles are collected at low tide in the villages around Crofty by families who have worked in the industry for generations. Swansea market sells them and they're used locally in a number of dishes, including a traditional Welsh breakfast with bacon and eggs. During October, Swansea

Stay a while

🛏 Blas Gŵyr, Plenty Farm, Llangennith, SA3 1HU. ☎ 01792 386472
www.blasgwyr.co.uk

🧳 New Gower Hotel, 11 Church Lane, Bishopston, SA3 3JT. ☎ 01792 234111
thenewgowerhotel.wales

⛰ Hillend Caravan and Camping Park, Hillend, Llangennith, Gower, SA3 1JD.
☎ 01792 386204
www.hillendcamping.com

75

SAINT GOVAN'S HEAD

PEACE AMONG THE MISSILES

Why visit?

★ Walk down to the uniquely idyllic chapel by the sea

★ See the Green Bridge of Wales, an awesome natural arch

★ Stretch your legs on a section of the Pembrokeshire Coastal Path

Saint Govan's Chapel

When you first start the walk down to this remarkably isolated chapel (◉ SA71 5DR), the building is nowhere to be seen. After a few steps, it suddenly appears in front of you and is a truly breathtaking sight. Seeing stunning photographs of the chapel perched on the cliff before you visit will whet your appetite for one of the most stunning views in the country but won't prepare you for being here in real life. Only by arriving in this remote corner of Wales and negotiating the steep ascent will you be able to fully appreciate the gloriously unlikely location of this tiny place of worship, overlooking the waves crashing below. The path down actually meanders inside the building, a tiny structure measuring roughly 6 metres by 4 metres (20 x 12 feet). Once out through the other side, the best views of Saint Govan's Chapel are to be enjoyed when you turn your back on the sea. Perched up on the cliff face, the seemingly impossible positioning of this stone-built chapel makes it one of the most picturesque in the world. There are various routes over the rocks; make use of the anti-slip devices added to some of them.

△ Saint Govan's Chapel is one of the most awe-inspiring places of worship on the coast.

△ Crashing waves on the rocks below the chapel add to the remote atmosphere of this special place.

Saint Govan's Chapel – the highlight of this remote part of South Wales – is reached by turning off the B4319 and pressing on down long, winding roads, beyond Saint Govan's Country Inn and Buckspool. Movement around these parts can be severely affected by Castlemartin Training Area, a huge Ministry of Defence zone covering 2,430ha (6,000 acres) and active for 44 weeks a year. It's worth checking ahead because sometimes access to the Pembrokeshire Coastal Path and Saint Govan's Chapel can be restricted by firing tanks and army training – call Pembrokeshire Tourist Information Centre on

🔔 *Stay a while*

🛏 St Govan's Country Inn, Bosherton, SA71 5DN. ☎ 01646 661311

🧳 Old Kings Arms Hotel, Main Street, Pembroke, SA71 4JS. ☎ 01646 683611 www.oldkingsarmshotel.co.uk

⛺ St Petrox Campsite, St Petrox, Stackpole, SA71 5EQ. ☎ 01646 622561 www.stpetroxcampingandcaravansite.co.uk

01437 776499 for more information. From the car park, there's a bit of a scramble down to the chapel and the rocks can be slippery, so a sturdy pair of shoes is essential (📍SA71 5DR).

The Green Bridge of Wales

A jaw-dropping natural arch carved out by the sea over thousands of years, the Green Bridge of Wales (📍SA71 5EB) is a well-known and much-loved landform. Nearby sea stacks add to the charm of this large and delicate feature. Severe storms and the constant battering by waves see more rock eroded every year, meaning this phenomenal arch is still very much in a state of flux.

A coastal walking challenge

From Cardigan in the north to Amroth Castle in the south, the 300km (186-mile) Pembrokeshire Coast Path is one of the most dramatic long-distance treks in the country. Edging around our only national park to be dominated by the sea, this path covers all kinds of coastal landscapes. Rugged clifftops, seaside towns, wide beaches and small fishing villages are all ports of call. Although some hardy souls tackle the full length of the path all in one go, most simply dip into it to complete a small section during an afternoon. Whichever section you choose to step out on to, it won't leave you disappointed. Check out the official website (nt.pcnpa.org.uk) when planning your journey. The whole route has now been placed on Google Street View, which allows you to see the views along every section of the path.

Tenby

Head east along the coast to experience the bright lights of South Pembrokeshire. The small walled seaside town of Tenby is a family favourite, blending beautiful countryside with wide expanses of sand. There's also plenty going on in the town itself, with bars and cafés aplenty. Wander around the town's 13th-century walls and through the historic gatehouse to streets thronging with life during the summer months, and head down to the beach, which stretches along the Welsh coastline for 4km (2½ miles). The harbour is a pleasant place to eat, drink and while away time. From here you can also get a ferry to the monastic Caldey Island, 1km (over half a mile) out to sea.

Getting here

Saint Govan's Head is on the south coast of Pembrokeshire, inside the national park. Directly south of Pembroke, the B4319 takes you close to the main attraction.

△ Waves on the southern Welsh coastline have carved out many impressive caves and arches.

ST DAVIDS
A PEMBROKESHIRE PILGRIMAGE

△ The huge cathedral at St Davids is remarkably well hidden in a dip near the centre of the city.

Small city, big impact

The smallest city in the UK, St Davids is home to fewer than 2,000 people but contains some of the nation's prettiest sights. The stone cross dominates the centre of St Davids, and this is a fine place to take some time out, sitting and watching life go by. Roads leading off Cross Square contain several independent shops specialising in clothes, crafts, jewellery and chocolate. By far the biggest pull to St Davids is the magnificent cathedral, reached by heading down the hill from the city's cross. With an unusual location in a dip below the city, the 35-metre (115-foot) tower is hidden from much

of the surrounding area by hills and at best just pokes above the skyline. The unusually low elevation of the cathedral enhances the approach to it – you're treated to a view from above that takes in the whole building. It's a rare chance to get this perspective on a major cathedral and really is a breathtaking angle. Work started on St Davids Cathedral (☏ 01437 720202 www.stdavidscathedral.org.uk ⌖ SA62 6RD) in 1181 and was hit by difficulties that included a collapsing tower and a 13th-century earthquake. Before the present cathedral, the site was home to a monastic community established by St David as early as the sixth century. The sacred site, including the ruins of the Bishop's Palace and the fabulously peaceful modern cathedral, is open for you to explore. It's a place where many find spiritual inspiration.

Whitesands

With a wide expanse of beach and a reputation for producing some sizeable waves, Whitesands has become known as one of the most sacred places in Wales for surfing. A short drive up the coast from St Davids, the beach benefits from the shelter provided by Ramsey Island but can still conjure up surf 3 metres (10 feet) high. Lifeguards patrol the beach during the summer months, when a warm day can see the crowds squeeze down the steep, narrow lane leading to the beachside car park. Expect delays and arrive early to get a prime spot. Out of season, you may well have the whole beach to yourself. A decent café and shop keep tourists stocked up during the

summer, meaning it's an ideal beach for a family to spend a whole day. But do check the tide times before you set off – at high tide the sea comes a long way in and leaves just a thin stretch of sand, which can become overrun at peak periods.

Porthgain

Once a busy commercial harbour exporting locally quarried stone, today Porthgain is a quiet, relaxing village with a great pub and a penchant for art. The sheltered harbour is popular for brave souls who enjoy swimming in the chilly sea as well as experienced kayakers who make use of the relatively calm waters. The landscape is phenomenal in this idyllic village. Artists inspired by their surroundings sell their wares in two galleries, which have a high standard of products. Where Porthgain really excels is inside the kitchen of its pub and café. The Sloop Inn (☎ 01348 831449 www.sloop.co.uk ♥ SA62

▽ The picturesque harbour at Porthgain, which has impressive eateries close by.

△ The pebble-strewn St Brides Bay is ideal for a windy walk.

🔔 **Stay a while**

🛏 The City Inn, New Street, St Davids, SA62 6SU. ☎ 01437 720829 www.cityinnstdavids.co.uk

🏨 Twr y Felin, Ffordd CaerFai, St Davids, SA62 6QT. ☎ 01437 725555 www.twryfelinhotel.com

⛺ St Davids Camping and Caravanning Club Site, Dwr Cwmwdig, St Davids, SA62 6DW. ☎ 01348 831376 www.campingandcaravanningclub.co.uk

Getting here

Reaching St Davids can be a bit of a trek, one reason why Pope Calixtus II declared that two pilgrimages to St Davids Cathedral is equal to one to Rome. To make your own special visit, journey west along the A487 from either Haverfordwest or Fishguard to reach the city.

5BN) has been around since 1743 – even before local quarrying was established – and is a traditionally quaint pub with fantastic outdoor seating if you can grab a space. The Shed Bistro (☎ 01348 831518 www.theshedporthgain.co.uk 📍 SA62 5BN) used to be a stopping place for engines heading to the brickworks, but is now a spot for tourists to pause with coffee and a snack.

More surf

If Whitesands is too busy or you want to sample a range of beaches, head for St Brides Bay. This long, windswept stretch of sand and pebbles is well known for producing quality waves.

Oggie, Oggie, Oggie!

Family holidays to Cornwall are renowned for featuring a pasty or three on the beach, but it's not something many people associate with Wales. It turns out that the origin of the humble pasty may actually be linked with St Davids. Some locals claim the earliest prototype of the pasty was served to folk at the cathedral as early as 1181. Shops and pubs in St Davids proudly celebrate the heritage of the 'oggie' and you'll be able to pick them up with a range of fillings.

ABERYSTWYTH
A PLACE TO STUDY AND PLAY

77

Why visit?

★ Indulge yourself in one of the town's many exciting festivals

★ Dive into the largest collection of books in Wales at the National Library

★ Walk on the town's beautiful coastal path and admire the war memorial that pays a fitting and creative tribute

A tale of two towns

Around 10,000 young people study at Aberystwyth University, giving the town a youthful feel during term time. Established in 1872, the university maintains a good reputation and its student population ensures there's a good range of eateries, bars and coffee shops. That said, coming here to study is a far quieter affair than heading off to a big city. Some students in their late teens arrive in shock at the lack of shopping malls and large cinemas, while others thrive from day one in the beautiful setting. During the summer, something of a transformation takes place as the undergraduates go home and families with buckets and spades rock up, making good use of the guest houses and amusement arcades. Your experience of Aberystwyth will, to some extent, depend on the time of year you arrive. But whenever you come, you'll find this Welsh coastline has a plentiful supply of warmth and hospitality.

△ The university in Aberystwyth plays a vital role in the local economy.

△ Artistic visions of local scenes squeeze behind local benches.

National Library

The largest collection of books and periodicals in Wales is held in Aberystwyth. Over 5 million books, 1 million maps, 60,000 pieces of art, and 950,000 photographs are stored at the National Library of Wales (☎ 01970 632800 www.library. wales ♦ SY23 3BU), which was established in 1907. The national Screen and Sound Archive is also held here. At the heart of the library is a desire to preserve and collect historically important items dealing with Welsh life and language. Guided tours are available and give a valuable insight into the building, the history of the library and the collection it houses.

Getting here

For a town of its size, Aberystwyth can be a difficult place to reach. Many prefer to arrive by the trains regularly rolling into the centrally located station. Those coming by car should aim for either the A487 running north to south along the coast, or the A44 running into Wales from Worcester.

hand. Italian sculptor Mario Rutelli was in town working on another war memorial and he took on the job, giving his design and time without a fee. His ambitious and prominent memorial cost twice the available budget but extra funds were raised and the bronze statues were installed in November 1922, with an official opening taking place the following September. The figure at the top of the memorial represents Victory, while Humanity can be seen at the bottom emerging from the war. It provides a focal point for the town's acts of remembrance and allows those paying their respects to gaze north and south along Aberystwyth's lovely coast.

 **Byrgyr King**

For a hearty burger with a distinctly Welsh flavour, head for Byrgyr on Marine Terrace, where only local meat is used to create a delicious menu (📞 01970 624253 📍 SY23 2AZ).

△ The Aberystwyth war memorial represents both victory and humanity.

A fitting tribute

Dominating the skyline on Aberystwyth's seafront is one of the finest war memorials in the UK. Remembering the 111 local men who lost their lives during the Great War, this huge memorial stands atop a prominent headland. It can be seen from most places along the town's coastal walkway, even from the far side of the pier. Discussions around how to establish a war memorial in Aberystwyth were underway as the war raged on in Europe, though it was not until 1919 that a decision was reached and a design was chosen. When the original sculptor died before the first stone had been cut, it left townsfolk in quite a quandary, but thankfully a solution was to

▽ Aberystwyth harbour wall, juts out to sea, framed by steep cliffs.

A festival town

Time your visit to coincide with one of the many fabulous festivals that Aberystwyth hosts so well. The biggest of the year is The Big Tribute (www.thebigtribute.co.uk), an outdoor music extravaganza at the end of August featuring some of the best tribute acts in the world. Previous headliners have been homages to Jimi Hendrix, UB40 and Crowded House. Classical concerts and opportunities to learn about music form part of the Aberystwyth MusicFest held in late July (www.musicfestaberystwyth.org). Anybody interested in pottery should make their way to the International Ceramics Festival in July (www.internationalceramicsfestival.org) and film fans with a bloodlust will love Abertoir – Aberystwyth's popular horror festival (www.abertoir.co.uk).

△ Different coloured houses dot the seafront at this festival-famous town.

Stay a while

🛏 Maes-Y-Môr, 25 Bath Street, Aberystwyth, SY23 2NN. ☎ 01970 639270 www.maesymor.co.uk

🛎 Premier Inn, 36–37 Marine Terrace, Aberystwyth, SY23 2BX. ☎ 0333 234 6529 www.premierinn.com

⛺ Aeron View Camping, Blaenpennal, Aberystwyth, SY23 4TW. ☎ 01974 251219 www.aeronviewcamping.co.uk

78

PORTMEIRION
TAKING NO PRISONERS

Why visit?

★ Be inspired by the jaw-dropping architecture of a uniquely stylish village

★ Explore scenes made famous in the cult TV drama *The Prisoner*

★ Take a steam train from the coast into the Snowdonia mountains

A village like no other

An afternoon spent wandering around the village of Portmeirion will likely inspire you to delve into history, think differently about design and gaze open-mouthed at this collection of coastal buildings like no other on the British coast. There's a bewildering combination of bright colours, elegantly designed cobbled lanes, beautiful gardens and a fascinating mixture of architectural styles. If Gaudí had been Welsh, he would have lived and worked here. There are few coastal destinations where the best views are to be

had looking inland, but this is one of them. As well as getting a ticket to explore the village and its range of shops, visitors can stay overnight; the buildings in the village are a collection of hotels and self-catering accommodation (☎ 01766 770000 www.portmeirion.wales ♥ LL48 6ER). Allow a couple of hours to fully appreciate this fantastic collection of Italianate architecture, originally developed as a project to show how buildings could enhance the natural surroundings. Welsh architect Clough Williams-Ellis bought the site in 1925 after a long search for a suitable

▽ The garden chess board is one of the highlights of the grounds at Portmeirion.

location and transformed it into a design haven. Building began in the mid-1920s, following the Arts and Crafts architectural style. After a pause during the Second World War, the development continued. This time it was inspired by the Italian Palladian movement. The vision of one man who worked on it for nearly 50 years, Portmeirion has been an inspiration to thousands.

Getting here

This picturesque stretch of Snowdonian coastline is reached by taking the A487 out of the national park or by following it south from Bangor.

△ A fine collection of buildings produces jaw-dropping reactions at Portmeirion.

Portmeirion – home for 'Number Six'

Known to millions of cult TV fans around the world as the village that held Patrick McGoohan captive in *The Prisoner*, bright and colourful Portmeirion provided the perfect setting for what turned out to be one of the most surreal and much-loved TV dramas ever made. Consisting of just 17 episodes, *The Prisoner* was first aired in 1967 and tells the tale of a British spy who is abducted and held in a coastal settlement while authorities try to figure out why he abruptly resigned. Various methods are used to try and extract information from McGoohan's 'Number Six' character, all taking place among the wonderful architecture of Portmeirion village. McGoohan's role in *The Prisoner* went way beyond being the main protagonist. He was the writer and director of some episodes, as well as being an executive producer. *The Prisoner* followed McGoohan's success as spy John Drake in *Danger Man* and developed a cult status in the decades after it was first screened. The programme, which finished in a confusingly open-ended

 Welsh chippy

For fresh fish and chips in Porthmadog, head to The Creel on the High Street (☎ 01766 513653 ⚲ LL49 9NW).

△ Sculptures make every turn an interesting one throughout Portmeirion.

△ A steam train chugs along the Cob towards Porthmadog.

manner, still pulls visitors to Portmeirion today. On a walk around the village, look out for the bust of McGoohan and an information plaque commemorating *The Prisoner*.

Porthmadog

Journey to Porthmadog from Portmeirion and you'll cross 'The Cob', a 1.6km-long (1-mile) causeway built in 1811 to reclaim land from the sea. Today, it's the route taken by the A497, the Ffestiniog Railway and a recently installed cycle path. When it opened, those travelling on this route across the Afon Glaslyn were asked to pay a one-shilling toll, a charge that became 5p and remained in place until 2003 when The Cob was bought by the Welsh Assembly. Heading over Britannia Bridge into Porthmadog, you'll soon find yourself in a busy town that's home to the popular Purple Moose Brewery and its shop selling ale and merchandise (☏ 01766 515571 www.purplemoose.co.uk ♥ LL49 9DB). Dominating the town's tourist trade are the two heritage railway routes that lead out of Porthmadog, one winding north through the mountains to Caernarfon and the other climbing into Snowdonia towards Blaenau Ffestiniog. Travelling on a steam train with the oldest railway company still in existence is a great way to enjoy the world-class scenery (☏ 01766 516024 www.festrail.co.uk ♥ LL49 9NF).

When to visit?

Immerse yourself in all things *The Prisoner* by attending the 'Portmeiricon' convention in April and celebrating the best of cult TV (www.sixofone.co).

Harlech

Fourteen and a half kilometres (9 miles) further down the coast, historic Harlech Castle (☏ 01766 780552 www.cadw.gov.wales/daysout/harlechcastle ♥ LL46 2YH) is perched on the top of a rocky hill keeping a watchful eye on the surrounding land and sea. Built by Edward I, this formidable fortress oozes history and played an important role in the Wars of the Roses. The siege that took place here inspired the rousing song 'Men of Harlech'. .

79

LLŶN PENINSULA
INTO HELL'S MOUTH

Why visit?

★ Surf away to your heart's content at windy Hell's Bay

★ Visit the former home of the one and only Prime Minister to come from Wales

★ Enjoy a stroll on picturesque beaches framed by mountains and enjoy lunch at a top coastal bar

Porthdinllaen – the bar on the beach

A real highlight of the stunning Llŷn Peninsula, Porthdinllaen is an old fishing village now owned by the National Trust. Car access is restricted and the best way to reach this thin finger of land pointing into the Irish Sea is to walk – the best routes are either across the nearby golf course or from the National Trust car park at Morfa Nefyn, both strolls taking about 20 minutes. It's a stunning bay, affording far-reaching views to the mountains of Yr Eifl and Snowdonia. The village itself only has around two dozen buildings, with the famous pub Ty Coch at the centre (☎ 01758 720498 www.tycoch.co.uk ♀ LL53 6DB). Enjoying a pint and a meal here is a therapeutic affair, with the waves crashing on the shore. No surprise, then, that Ty Coch has been voted one of the top ten beach bars in the world.

△ Seaside strolls and a much-loved coastal pub await at Mortha Nefyn.

The heart of Wales

Speaking Welsh is the norm on the Llŷn Peninsula and whether you're sitting in a café or walking down the street, you're sure to hear locals conversing in this beautiful Celtic language. According to the Census in 2011, the proportion of people speaking Welsh on the peninsula was among the highest in the country and there is a tremendous feeling of national pride all around. Plaid Cymru, 'The Party of Wales', was formed here in 1925 during the National Eisteddfod in the coastal town of Pwllheli and it remains a powerful force in Welsh politics.

Thirteen kilometres (8 miles) along the shoreline, Criccieth is the childhood home of the only Welshman to become Prime Minister – David Lloyd George. The house he lived in is now a museum housing a wide range of his personal objects (☎ 01766 522071 ♀ LL52 0SH).

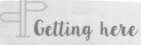

Getting here

Sticking out into the Irish Sea, the Llŷn Peninsula is in north-west Wales and accessed by the A499 and A497.

Supported by the sea

Over the centuries, many families have made a living from the waters around the Llŷn Peninsula. Today, tour boat operators and surf instructors are among those earning a crust from the Irish Sea. In days gone by, many settlements along this coast were supported by herring fishing. Shipbuilding was also alive and well in several of the small ports along this Welsh coastline, while traders from across the sea frequently sailed to and from Llŷn. Exports tended to be in the form of farming products such as butter, cheese and eggs. Imports included large amounts of salt, needed to preserve the meat and fish produced locally. Coal was imported to one of the beaches, providing power for local homes.

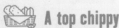

A top chippy

Feeling peckish? In Abersoch, aim for The Creel on Bodawen (☎ 01758 713577 ◉ LL53 7DS). It's a good local chippy with a fine reputation.

△ The charming coast at Criccieth.

HELL'S MOUTH FACTS

💡 Porth Neigwl was used as a bombing range in the run-up to the Second World War and air gunners used to shoot at moving targets, conveyed along a specially built narrow-gauge railway.

💡 The rare and endangered mason bee builds mud nests on sand dunes in Porth Neigwl. The area is now the focus of habitat management.

Porth Neigwl, or Hell's Mouth

A wide bay facing the south-west, Porth Neigwl takes the full force of gales that have built up over the Irish Sea and Atlantic Ocean. It's often a place you'll get blown about by strong winds, a trait that has made it extremely popular among the surfing fraternity. Long before extreme surfing moves were cool, though, this breezy bay brought terror to the lives of sailors who knew of its reputation as a widow-maker. Many wrecks at Porth Neigwl were fatal and earned the area an unpleasant English name – 'Hell's Mouth'. Biblical irony was in full supply when a 118-ton schooner called *Twelve Apostles* got into trouble at Hell's Mouth during 1898. No lives were lost on this occasion, thankfully, but the vessel had to be run aground and wrecked in order to save the crew.

Stay a while

🛏 Gwynle Boutique B&B, 12 Tanygrisiau Terrace, Criccieth, LL52 0DL. ◉ 01766 522529 www.gwynle.vpweb.co.uk

🏨 The Lion Hotel, Y Maes, Criccieth, LL52 0AA. ◉ 01766 522460 www.lionhotelcriccieth.co.uk

⛺ Nant-y-Big, Cilan, Abersoch, LL53 7DB. ◉ 01758 712686 www.nantybig.co.uk

80

LLANDUDNO

GREAT DAYS BENEATH GREAT ORME

Why visit?

★ Explore the summit of the Great Orme and investigate the world-renowned mines that were so important to the Bronze Age

★ Dive into the rabbit hole and follow Alice's adventures on a lengthy sculpture walk

★ Learn about the region's rich history in Conwy, at one of the most iconic castles in Wales

Great Orme

Llandudno is a coastal town on the up. After a wave of recent investment, it's a charming place to spend time, with a lot going on. Whatever time of year you come here, there's a quaint appeal to the town – be it the hustle and bustle of summer, the tinsel and turkey trips in late autumn or the quiet streets in the new year. Dominating the town, the prominent headland known as Great Orme is home to the best views and some cracking attractions. Getting to the top can be a slog if you walk, so consider taking the tramway (☎ 01492 577877 www.greatormetramway.co.uk ♥ LL30 2NB) or mile-long cable car (☎ 01492 877205 ♥ LL30 2LP), which make the trip far quicker and more exciting. The longest Cresta toboggan run in Wales is on the hill, giving thrill seekers a 750-metre (820-yard) ride to remember at the Llandudno Snowsports Centre (☎ 01492 874707 www.jnlllandudno.co.uk ♥ LL30 2QL). And if history is your thing, the Great Orme houses one of the world's most important Bronze Age sites (☎ 01492 870447 www.greatormemines.info ♥ LL30 2XG). Copper mined in passages here 4,000 years ago was blended with Cornish tin to make bronze and take a significant step forward in the development of tools and weapons.

△ The Great Orme Tramway provides one of the easiest ways to get to the top of the hill.

What's on?

A varied arts programme is always on offer at Venue Cymru, the principal theatre setting on this stretch of the coast. From festivals to comedy, musicals to drama, children's shows to classical concerts, the diverse range of performances is a real asset to Venue Cymru (℡ 01492 872000, www.venuecymru.co.uk, ⚲ LL30 1BB).

Alice in a Welsh Wonderland

Walking along the seafront at Llandudno, it's hard to miss the large oak sculpture depicting the unmistakable Mad Hatter from *Alice's Adventures in Wonderland*. Holding a teapot and gazing towards the Great Orme, he is part of a well-organised and inspirational town trail exploring links with Lewis Carroll's classic book. The real

girl influencing the famous tale was called Alice Liddell. As a child, she enjoyed several summer holidays here and recounted her adventures to the author – possibly providing ideas and locations for the story. It may be a tenuous link, but it's lots of fun. The many wooden sculptures around town include the Cheshire Cat and White Rabbit. They can be enjoyed with an audio guide and augmented reality experience available from the website www.alicetowntrails.co.uk, while a book costing £2.99 is on sale at the tourist information centre.

 Fish and chips

Llandudno and the surrounding coastal towns are awash with chippies, including many high-quality eateries. Here are three of the best. Fish Tram Chips is on Old Road near the tram station at the bottom of Great Orme, with space to eat inside or out (℡ 01492 872673 ⚲ LL30 2NB). Chish 'n' Fips (℡ 01492 872987 ⚲ LL30 1LQ) is out of the way on Victoria Street but well worth the search. And if you're in Conwy, check out The Archway on Bangor Road (℡ 01492 592458 ⚲ LL32 8NH).

🔔 **Stay a while**

🛏 The Sunnyside, 2–4 Llewelyn Avenue, Llandudno, LL30 2ER. ℡ 01492 877150 www.sunnysidellandudno.co.uk

🏨 The Winchmore Hotel, Central Promenade, Llandudno, LL30 1AR. ℡ 01492 877458 www.winchmorehotel.co.uk

⛺ Tan Y Bryn Farm Camp Site, Brynpydew Road, Llandudno, LL31 9JZ. ℡ 01492 549296 www.tanbrynfarm.com

△ The Mad Hatter in oak, part of the town's Alice in Wonderland trail.

△ Llandudno's Pier is full of North Wales' seaside fun, as well as providing a great perspective of the coastline.

Take a stroll

A walk along Llandudno Pier brings stunning views of Great Orme and the town's seafront. Standing over the Irish Sea can be spiritually invigorating or morally catastrophic, depending on the weather, but there's plenty to see and do here come rain or shine. You'll find several kiosks selling snacks, toys and jokes. There's also the usual smattering of amusements where you can play 2p games and enjoy the latest arcade adventures.

Further along the coast

A short drive or train journey across the River Conwy delivers the imposing sight of 13th-century Conwy Castle, built for Edward I (☏ 01492 592358 www.cadw.gov.wales/daysout/conwycastle ♥ LL32 8AY). It's a massive fortress and since 1986 has been part of the World Heritage Site that also covers Harlech and Caernarfon Castles. Conwy Castle was the most extravagant of Edward I's Welsh castles, with two fortified gateways, eight huge towers and a great hall. There is plenty to experience and it's an informative afternoon for the family. To the east, sandy stretches are to be discovered along Wales's north coast at Prestatyn and Rhyl. Water play areas, animal attractions and holiday parks ensure there are miles of fun to be had along the Irish Sea for young families wanting to make the most of the summer months.

Getting here

The North Wales Expressway provides easy access to this coastal gem, allowing day trippers to flock in from nearby Liverpool and Manchester. The A470 branches off the A55 at Llandudno Junction and heads straight into town. A regular rail service brings travellers to the centrally located station.

INDEX

abbeys 42, 44, 84, 106
Aberdeen 71–2
Aberystwyth 218, 233–5
abseiling 170
Ainsdale Beach 10
Albert Dock, Liverpool
    6, 7, 8
Alexandra Dock, Grimsby
    125
Allonby Beach 29
Alloway 36
Allt Smoo waterfall 56
Another Place (A. Gormley)
    4, 9
aquariums/sea life centres
    11, 111, 120
Arnside 4
artworks/artists 4, 6, 9, 15,
    42, 43, 49, 79, 84, 87,
    94, 102, 109, 134, 151,
    154, 156, 165, 197, 199,
    213, 215, 217, 231, 233,
    234, 242
Ayr 36–7
Ayrshire Coastal Path 37

Babbacombe Model Village
    184
Balnakeil 31, 56–7
Bamburgh 89–91
Banksy mural, Dover 154
Barnstaple 215
BBC Scotland tour 40
beach huts, Bude 209
Beachy Head 162, 164–6
Beadnell Beach 93
The Beatles 4, 6, 8
Bempton Cliffs 108,
    113–14
Ben Nevis 31, 46
bird watching 10, 15, 17,
    29, 59, 63, 69, 91, 108,
    113–14, 118, 128, 130,
    145, 226
Black Combe 23
Blackpool 1, 3, 4, 11–14
Blackrock Beach, Bude
    210

boat trips 8, 44, 50, 58, 63,
    66, 82, 91, 108, 114,
    131, 138, 146, 175,
    188, 195
boating lake, Scarborough
    111
Boscastle 208
Bow Fiddle Rock,
    Portknockie 67
bridges and viaducts 36, 48,
    50, 65, 75, 81–2, 120
Bridlington 108, 115
Brighton 3, 162, 167–9
British Airways i360,
    Brighton 167
Brownsea Island 175
Bude 181, 209–10
Burns, Robert 36–7, 71
Butlins 126–7

Caldey Island 229
Caledonian Canal 31, 47
Camel Trail cycle route 205
Campbeltown, Mull of
    Kintyre 42, 43
canoeing/kayaking 134,
    136, 138, 191
Cape Cornwall 180, 196–8
Cape Wrath 3, 31, 53–5
Cardiff 218, 220–2
castles 23, 42, 49, 51, 59,
    60, 68–9, 71, 84, 87, 93,
    110, 152, 195, 206, 220,
    225, 238, 243
cathedrals/churches/chapels
    17, 27, 36, 78, 87, 218,
    227, 230–1
Cavern Club, Liverpool 6
caves 56, 180, 191, 193,
    207
Charmouth Beach 177
Chesil Beach 179
Cinder Path cycle route 84,
    106–7
Clacton-on-Sea 141–3
Cleethorpes 3, 109, 123–5
Clovelly 181, 211–13

coast-to-coast canal
    network 79–80
Coast to Coast path 4,
    24, 26
coasteering 191
Cob causeway, Porthmadog
    238
Cook, Captain James 104
Coton in the Elms,
    Derbyshire 2–3
Couple (S. Henry) 94
craft village, Balnakeil 57
cranes, industrial 39, 139,
    140
Craster 84, 92–3
Creative Quarter,
    Folkestone 156
Criccieth, Llyn Peninsula
    239
Crofty 226
Cromarty 58, 63–5
Cromer 132
Crosby 4, 9–10
Cruden Bay 68–9
Cumbria Coastal Way 23
Cutty Sark 148
cycling 26, 29, 84, 106–7,
    128, 169, 205, 214

Dawlish Warren 180,
    182–4
'Dead Bod' graffiti, Hull
    109, 119–20
Deal 154
distilleries/alcohol industry
    25, 30, 44, 58, 62, 88,
    187, 188, 238
dolphins 63, 66–7, 210
donkeys, Clovelly 211–12
Dover 134–5, 152–4
Duncansby Head 61
Dundee 59, 73–5
Dungeness 135, 158–61
Dunkirk tunnels, Dover
    135
Durdle Door 163, 178
Dymchurch Wall 158

Eastbourne 165–6
Eastbourne Redoubt
    fortress 166
Eden Project, Cornwall
    180, 188–90
Emirates Spinnaker Tower,
    Portsmouth 170
erosion, coastal 108–9,
    114, 116–17, 132

fairgrounds and
    amusements 1, 11, 13,
    112, 126, 141, 142, 151,
    182, 216, 219, 243
Falkirk Kelpies statues (A.
    Scott) 59, 79, 213
Falkirk Wheel 59, 79, 80
Felixstowe 134, 139–40
festivals 18, 34, 71, 84, 99,
    102, 105, 125, 154, 167,
    181, 201, 205, 217, 226,
    235, 242
Filey 108, 115
First World War 110, 140,
    152, 234
Firth of Forth, swimming
    in the 58–9, 82
fishing industry 33, 52,
    67, 68, 92, 96, 119–20,
    125, 132
fishing, recreational 52, 195
Fistral Beach 201, 202
Flamborough Head 114
flooding 134, 138, 148,
    158, 183, 208
Folkestone 135, 155–7
food and drink
    East Coast 109, 111, 115,
        117, 121, 123, 124, 126,
        130, 132, 154
    East Scotland 58, 59, 62,
        67, 70, 71, 75, 77, 83
    North-East 84, 88, 90,
        91, 92, 93, 95, 96, 99,
        101, 103, 107
    North-West 6, 10, 14, 15,
        17, 19, 20, 23, 24, 25, 29
    South-East 134, 149, 154

South-West 181, 186, 188, 191, 192, 198, 199, 203, 204–5, 210, 212, 213
Wales 226, 232, 237, 239, 240, 242
West Scotland 30, 33, 44, 55, 57
Fort William 30–1, 46–7
Forth Bridges 81–2
fossil hunting 163, 177
Fowey 188

galleries 8, 49, 59, 84, 102, 119, 145, 165, 199, 215, 231
see also artworks/artists
Galloway 30, 32–4
Gibraltar Point Nature Reserve 128
Glasgow 30, 38–40
Glasgow Tower 38
Glenfinnan Viaduct 48
Glenlee 39
golf 29, 30, 35, 59, 76, 197
Gower Peninsula 218, 223–6
Grange-over-Sands 4, 18–19
Grangemouth, Falkirk 80
Great Orme 219, 241, 243
Great Yarmouth 138
Green Bridge of Wales 229
Greenwich 134, 147–8
Grimsby 125
Grip (A. Gormley) 42
guided tours/walks 4, 6, 19–20, 40, 64, 67, 76, 106, 114, 118, 154, 176, 177–8, 187, 220, 221, 233

Harlech 238
Heacham 133
The Helix, Falkirk 79
Helwick Sands 224
Heysham village 17
Historic Dockyard, Portsmouth 170–1
Hogmanay 58, 70, 82
Holderness 108, 116–18
Holy Island (Lindisfarne) 3, 84

Hornsea 116–17
horse racing 4, 18
horse riding 10
Howey, Captain Jack 159
Hull 109, 119–22
Humber Bridge 120
Humber Street, Hull 119, 122

Ilfracombe 213
Ingoldmells 126–7
Instow 215
Isle of Iona 44
Isle of Sky 50

John O'Groats 58, 60–3
Jurassic Coast 3, 163, 177–9

Kents Cavern 184
kite flying 9, 10, 154, 212
kite surfing 10, 29, 84, 101, 212
Kyle of Lochalsh 31, 49–50
Kynance Cove 180, 193

La'al Ratty (Little Railway) 21
Landguard Fort 140
Lands End 61, 180, 198
Leighton Moss nature reserve 17
Leith 83
Lennon, John 6
lifeboat stations 95, 100, 117, 176
lighthouses 31, 32, 41, 43, 53, 61, 99, 114, 117, 118, 129, 154, 160, 165, 186, 192
Lindisfarne (Holy Island) 84, 86–7
Liverpool 4, 6–7
Lizard Peninsula 180, 191–3
Lizard Point 191
Llandudno 219, 241–3
Llŷn Peninsula 219, 239–40
Logan Botanic Garden 33
London 134, 146–8
Lowestoft 134, 136–8
Lulworth Cove 163, 178

Madame Tussauds, Blackpool 11
Magical Mystery Tour, Liverpool 6
Mappleton 116–17
Marconi, Guglielmo 192
Margate 134, 143, 149–51
Marshside RSPB reserve 10
Martello towers 135, 141, 161
Mary Rose 162, 171
Mayflower 186
McCaig's Tower 45
McCartney, Paul and Linda 6, 30, 41–2
memorials see statues/monuments/memorials
Meridian Line 147–8
Merlin's Caves 207
Mermaid Quay, Cardiff 221–2
Mersey Ferries 8
Midland Hotel, Morecambe 16
Millennium Centre, Wales 222
Millennium Dome/O2 Arena 147
Miller, Hugh 64
Millook Haven Beach 210
Minack Theatre 180, 194–5
mini golf, Seahouses 90
model railways 149–50
model villages 184
mods and rockers, 1960s 143
monuments see statues/monuments/memorials
Morecambe Bay 2, 3, 4, 15–17, 19–20
Mounts Bay 195
Mull of Kintyre 30, 41–3
museums and heritage/visitors centres
East Coast 109, 121, 122, 125
East Scotland 68, 70–1, 72, 74–5, 78
North-East 87, 90, 100, 104
North-West 4, 7, 9, 10, 28
South Coast 162, 166, 170–1, 172–3, 177

South-East 135, 140, 145, 148, 149–50, 153, 156
South-West 186, 192, 195, 199, 200, 203, 208
Wales 222, 239
West Scotland 36, 38, 39, 43, 44, 52

Napoleonic Wars 110, 135, 141, 166
National Library of Wales, Aberystwyth 233
nature reserves 10, 17, 32, 84, 113, 128, 129, 131, 155, 161, 175, 182–3
Neptune's Staircase, Banavie 47
New Year celebrations 58, 70, 82
Newbiggin-by-the-Sea 84, 94–6
Newquay 181, 201–3
Nigg 64–5
Norfolk, North 131–3
North Bay, Scarborough 108, 111
North Coast 500 31, 51
North Sea Flood (1953) 138
North Sutor bird colonies 63
Northcott Mouth, Bude 209–10

O2 Arena/Millennium Dome 147
Oban 30, 44–5
Old Harry rock formation 163, 178–9
Old Leigh, Southend 145
Old Royal Navy College, Greenwich 148
Oulton Broad 138

Padstow 181, 204–5
Pavilion, Brighton 162, 168
Peasholm Park, Scarborough 111
Pembrokeshire Coastal Path 228, 229
Penzance 195
Peterhead, the 'Bloo Toon' 68–9

piers 10, 11, 13, 104, 123, 134, 141–2, 144–5, 168–9, 216, 243
Pilgrim Fathers 186, 187
Pleasure Beach, Blackpool 1, 11, 13
Plockton 31, 49
Plymouth 180, 185–7
Polperro Heritage Coast 188
Porth Neigwl/Hell's Mouth 240
Porthcurno Beach 194–5
Porthdinllaen 239
Porthgain 231
Porthmadog 238
Porthmeor Beach 200
Portknockie 67
Portmeirion 219, 236–7
Portsmouth 162, 170–1
Prestatyn 243
promenades 2, 15, 18, 94, 95, 111, 139, 142, 157, 174, 219
pubs 11, 23, 25, 69, 70, 92, 109, 123–4, 188, 198, 199, 203, 231–2, 239

Queensferry Crossing 82

railways 4, 9, 48, 124, 158, 159, 160, 219, 238
miniature 159, 160
model 149–50
Ramsgate 135
Ravenglass 4, 21–3
Ravenscar 84, 107
Redcar 100–1
Rhossili 223–6
Rhyl 243
RNLI (Royal National Lifeboat Institute) 90, 117, 118
College Discovery Tour 176
Robin Hood's Bay 24, 107
rock/shingle formations 61, 178–9, 229
Roman remains 21, 22–3, 220
Romney Marsh 158–60, 161
royalty, British 60, 77, 78, 83, 93, 110, 162, 166, 168, 171, 238, 243

Saddell Bay 42
Saint Cuthbert 87

St Andrews 59, 76–8
St Austell Bay 188–90
St Bees 4, 24–6
St Brides Bay 232
St Davids 218, 230–2
St Govan's Head 227–9
St Ives 180–1, 199–200
St Jus 198
St Mary's football ground 173
St Michael's Mount castle 195
Saltburn 103
Samphire Hoe, Folkestone 155
Sandbanks 163, 174–6
Sandwich 154
Sandymere Beach 212
Sandymouth Bay 209
Scarborough 108, 110–12
Science Centre, Glasgow 38
the Scores, Lowestoft 137
Scott, Sir Peter 129, 130
Seahouses 90–1
seal colonies 69, 84, 101, 107, 131, 210
Seal Sands 101
Second World War 45, 129, 135, 140, 142, 150, 152, 153, 156, 166, 197, 220
Sefton Coast 10
Sennen Cove 197–8
Shell Grotto, Margate 150–1
shipbuilding heritage 30, 39, 73
ships 39–40, 106, 121, 134, 138, 139–40, 148, 162, 186
shipwrecks 26, 37, 90, 198, 209–10, 218, 224–5, 240
Silecroft Beach 22
Silloth 4, 27–9
Silverdale village 17
Skegness 109, 126–8
Skye road bridge 50
Slains Castle, Cruden Bay 68–9
smokehouses 33, 75, 91, 92, 96
Smoo Cave, Balnakeil 56
Solent Sky exhibition, Southampton 173

South bay, Scarborough 110–11
South Queensferry 81–3
South West Coastal Path 205
Southampton 162, 172–3
Southend-on-Sea 134, 144–5
Spanish City, Whitley Bay 84, 97–9
Spey Bay 58, 66–7
Spitfires 150, 173
sports 4, 10, 18, 29, 35, 59, 76, 77, 78, 84, 173
see also water sports
Spurn Head 3, 117–18
Spurn Point 108–9, 116–17, 118
Stacks of Duncansby 61
Staffa volcanic island 44–5
Staithes 84, 102–4
Stanley Ghyll waterfall 21
statues/monuments/ memorials 4, 6, 15, 26, 36, 37, 42, 71, 79, 122, 234
steam trains 4, 21, 48, 107, 219, 238
Stein, Rick 181, 204, 205
Stevenson, Robert 32, 53
Stoker, Bram 68–9, 84, 105–6
Stonehaven 58, 70–2
Studland beaches 175
Summerleaze Beach 209
surfing 84, 93, 104, 181, 191, 197–8, 200, 202, 210, 212, 223, 231, 240

Tarka Trail 181, 214–15
Tate Gallery, Liverpool 8
Tay Bridges 75
Tenby 229
theatres 111, 137, 143, 180, 194–5, 222, 242
Thirle Door, Duncansby Head 61
Three Cliffs Bay 225–6
Thurso 62
tin and copper mines 196–7, 198, 200, 241
Tintagel 206–8
'Titan' crane, Glasgow 39
Titanic, RMS 162, 172–3
Torquay 183–4

Tower, Blackpool 1, 4, 11
Trebarwith Strand Beach 207–8
Troon 30, 35–7
Turner, J.M.W. 27, 151
Two Tree Island 145

Ullapool 31, 51–3

Verity (D. Hirst) 213
Victory, HMS 171
Vikings 71, 84, 87

Wainwright, Alfred 24
walking routes
East Coast 109, 117, 128, 129
North-West 4, 6, 23, 24, 29
South-East 134, 137, 161
South-West 180, 181, 198, 205, 214–16
Wales 218, 226, 229
West Scotland 31, 37
War of the Roses 89, 93, 238
the Wash 128–31
water sports 29, 84, 93, 104, 134, 136, 138, 181, 191, 197–8, 200, 202, 210, 212, 223, 231, 240
West India Docks 147
Weston Super Mare 181, 216–17
Westwood Ho! 212–13
Whitby 84, 104, 105–7
White Cliffs of Dover 134–5, 153
Whitehaven 25
Whitesands Beach 231
Whitley Bay 84, 97–9
Wigtown Bay 33–4
Wilberforce, William 122
wildlife spotting 45, 58, 59, 63, 66–7, 69, 84, 101, 107, 131, 145, 175, 195, 210, 218, 223
wind farms 100, 127
wind surfing 29, 93, 212
Worms Head 225

Zealand lifeboat 100
zip wires 190